WOMAN'S OWN COMPLETE STEP-BY-STEP COOKERY

WOMAN'S OWN COMPLETE STEP-BY-STEP COOKERY

CHANCELLOR
PRESS

First published in Great Britain in 1992 as four separate titles: *Woman's Own Soups, Starters & Snacks*, *Woman's Own Main Courses*, *Woman's Own Desserts* and *Woman's Own Cakes & Bakes*

This edition published in 1994
by Chancellor Press, an imprint of Reed Consumer Books Limited
Michelin House,
81 Fulham Road,
London SW3 6RB
and Auckland, Melbourne,
Singapore and Toronto

ISBN 1 85152 728 1

A CIP catalogue record for this book is available from the British library

Produced by Mandarin Offset
Printed in China

Contents

Soups, Starters & Snacks 8

Main Courses 82

Desserts 156

Cakes & Bakes 230

Introduction

Whether you are planning a special occasion meal for family or friends, a quick and easy snack or a midweek supper you're sure to find the perfect answer in this fabulous collection of recipes. Many old time favourites can be found as well as some new ones.

Try a real home-made Tomato Soup or go north of the border for a taste of the Highlands with Cullen Skink, a delicious and warming soup made from smoked haddock and potatoes.

We all love Roast Chicken but for a change, try Chicken & Leek Pie or Chicken Korma, a mild yet creamy curry. Every taste has been catered for, and as well as chicken there's a host of other delicious and succulent main meals for you to choose from, ranging from Cannelloni to Fish Casserole or Steak & Stout Pie.

'What's for pud?,' must be the cry echoed at many a meal time. Can you or your family resist a slice of Lemon Meringue Pie or Summer Pudding? I can't, neither can I say 'no' to a portion of Cheesecake, Sherry Trifle or Profiteroles with lashings of smooth rich and thoroughly wicked chocolate sauce.

When it comes to cakes and bakes, there's plenty of temptation. Choose Chocolate Brownies, an all-time American favourite, or switch to English traditionals like Eccles Cakes, Chelsea Buns or my family's favourite fruit cake, Cherry & Date Cake. Alternatively, try Chocolate Caraque Cake, the ultimate in chocolate cakes.

Each recipe is clearly illustrated with easy-to-follow step-by-step photographs, which demonstrate many of the techniques and skills used in the preparation of each dish. There are handy tips throughout, providing useful and interesting hints. All the recipes have been tried and tested in the *Woman's Own* Test Kitchen, so that you can cook each and every one with confidence knowing that they all work. So what more can I say than,

Happy Cooking and Bon Appetit!

Gina Steer

SOUPS, STARTERS & SNACKS

Looking for ideas for a starter or a snack? Try chilled Gazpacho Soup, a colourful and impressive starter for a dinner party or Winter Lentil Soup that'll keep the whole family warm and glowing. There's Pizza Margherita, Salad Niçoise or Chicken Satay – ideal for both formal or informal occasions, and delicious fish and shellfish recipes such as Bouillabaisse, Fishcakes or Dressed Crab. If you want a hearty and easy snack, how about Spanish Omelette or a Pasty and for vegetarians, there's Cheese Soufflé, Onion Tart and lots more.

WINTER LENTIL SOUP

Hearty and warming, this delicious soup contains all the ingredients needed to keep everyone warm and glowing during the cold winter months. Serve it with chunks of crusty brown bread.

Calories per portion: 257 **SERVES 6**

4 oz/100 g red lentils
2 small onions
2 bay leaves
1 medium carrot
4 oz/100 g swede
4 oz/100 g turnips
6 oz/175 g leeks
6 oz/175 g ripe tomatoes
3 oz/75 g streaky bacon
2 tbsp oil
6 oz/175 g ripe tomatoes
¾ pint/450 ml vegetable stock
1-2 tbsp tomato purée
grated rind and juice 1 small orange
salt and freshly ground black pepper
1 tbsp freshly chopped parsley

Wash the lentils thoroughly. Bring a pan of water to the boil then add the lentils. Peel the onions and chop one, then add to the pan with the bay leaves. Bring the pan to the boil, cover, reduce the heat then simmer for 30 mins or until the lentils are soft. Drain then discard the bay leaves. Meanwhile prepare the remaining vegetables. Peel the carrot, swede and turnip then cut into small dice. Wash and trim the leeks and slice. Make a small cross in the top of each tomato, place in a bowl, cover with boiling water, leave for 5 mins then drain. Peel the tomatoes discarding the core and seeds if preferred. Chop remaining onion.

Trim the bacon discarding the rind and cartilage, then cut or chop into small pieces. Heat the oil in a large pan then gently sauté the prepared onion and bacon for 5-8 mins or until they are softened.

Add the remaining vegetables except for the tomatoes and continue to sauté gently for a further 5 mins. Pour in the

HANDY TIP

If preferred, the soup can be passed through a food processor or liquidizer and blended until smooth. Add a little extra stock to help in the blending. Reheat.

stock and add the drained lentils.

Blend the tomato purée with 2 tbsp of water and stir into the pan together with the grated rind and juice of the orange. Bring the contents of the pan to the boil, cover the pan and reduce the heat and allow the soup to simmer gently for 25-30 mins or until the vegetables are soft. Stir in the chopped tomatoes with seasoning to taste and continue to cook for a further 10 mins. Adjust seasoning, sprinkle with the freshly chopped parsley then serve immediately with crusty bread.

1. Add the lentils to a pan of boiling water with 1 chopped onion and bay leaves

2. Peel the vegetables then slice the leeks and dice the turnip and carrots

3. Dice the swede and remaining onion. Cover the tomatoes with boiling water, leave for 2 mins, drain and peel

4. Heat the oil in a pan then gently sauté the chopped bacon and onion for 5-8 mins or until soft and transparent

5. Add the prepared vegetables then continue to sauté for a further 5 mins, stirring occasionally

6. Add the stock to the pan then the drained lentils. Blend the tomato purée with 2 tbsp of water and add to pan

MINESTRONE SOUP

It's everybody's favourite... minestrone, with its wonderful rich tomato flavour. Packed full of tasty vegetables and with a sprinkling of Parmesan cheese on top, it's a meal in itself – enough to satisfy the heartiest appetite.

Calories per portion: 208 — **SERVES 6**

1 onion
2 garlic cloves
1 leek
2 celery sticks
1 carrot
1 turnip
1 large potato
4 medium tomatoes
1 oz/25 g butter or margarine
2 tbsp olive oil
2 bay leaves
2 pints/1.2 litres vegetable stock
2 oz/50 g pasta twists
2 tbsp tomato purée
salt and freshly ground black pepper
3 oz/75 g green cabbage
3 slices back bacon
grated Parmesan cheese

Peel the onion, leaving the root on. Make cuts in both directions across the onion then cut down through the onion. Peel and crush the garlic cloves. Trim leek, wash thoroughly under cold water, cut into rings. Trim then wash or scrub celery, slice thinly. Peel carrot, turnip and potato, then dice.

Cut a small cross on the top of the tomatoes, place in bowl and cover with boiling water. Leave for 2 mins, drain then peel, cut into quarters and scoop out seeds. Chop flesh. Reserve all prepared vegetables.

Melt the fat with the oil in a large pan and fry the onion, garlic, leek, celery and bay leaves for 5 mins until softened. Add the stock, bring to the boil, reduce heat and simmer for 10 mins, then add the remaining diced root vegetables with the pasta twists. Continue to simmer for 10-15 mins or until almost cooked. Blend the tomato purée with 2 tbsp cold water, and stir into pan with seasoning to taste.

Wash cabbage thoroughly, drain and discard centre stalk, then shred. Remove the rind from the bacon, slice, then gently fry in a non-stick frying pan until lightly cooked. Add the chopped tomatoes, shredded cabbage and bacon to the soup and cook for a further 5-10 mins. Discard the bay leaves, adjust the seasoning and serve with grated Parmesan cheese and fresh brown bread.

If you wish to make the soup in advance, make as above but don't add cabbage and bacon. Cool quickly and store, covered, in fridge. Just before eating reheat then add cabbage. Fry bacon, stir in and serve.

HANDY TIP

Parmesan cheese has been made in Italy since before the time of the Romans. It is a cows' milk cheese and is used for grating when it is 2-4 years old. It is only made between the months of April and November. Fully mature Parmesan has a dark yellow, grainy texture and its rind is a dark brown. It has a sharp, fruity texture and is best if bought as a piece and grated just before use.

1. Peel onion and garlic, trim leek and cut into rings. Trim celery and slice

2. Make a cross in tomatoes, cover with boiling water, drain, peel and deseed

3. Melt fat with oil in a pan. Fry onion, garlic, leek and celery with bay leaves

4. Once the vegetables are softened, pour in the stock and bring to the boil

5. After simmering stock for 10 mins, add the remaining root vegetables

6. Fry the chopped bacon in a non-stick frying pan, until lightly cooked

CARROT SOUP

This is a super soup, made with fresh carrots and onion, flavoured with basil and fruity oranges, and topped with a swirl of cream. Serve it as a tasty starter or lunch-time snack – it's so easy to make when you follow this step-by-step recipe.

Calories per portion: 142 **SERVES 4**

1 large onion
1 lb/450 g carrots
2 tbsp olive oil
1½ pints/900 ml vegetable stock
few fresh basil sprigs
2 large oranges
salt and freshly ground black pepper
1 level tsp ground mace
1 level tbsp single cream

Peel and finely chop the onion. Peel and slice the carrots. Heat the olive oil in a large pan, then sauté the onion and carrots for 5 mins, or until the vegetables have softened slightly and the onion is transparent. Stir in the vegetable stock, together with one or two basil sprigs, which have been bruised slightly (reserve a couple of basil sprigs to garnish the soup).

Bring the soup to the boil, cover, then reduce for 30 mins or until the carrots are tender.

Meanwhile, prepare the orange zest for the garnish. Scrub and dry one orange, then, using a zester, pull firmly at an angle down the side of the orange so that the rind is removed in long thin strips without any of the bitter white pith beneath (this rind is always referred to as the zest).

Place the zest in a bowl and cover with boiling water. Leave to stand for at least 5 mins, before draining. Refresh in cold water. Leave to one side until required for garnishing soup.

Finely grate the rind from remaining orange and squeeze juice from both of the oranges. When carrots are cooked, remove pan from heat and discard the basil sprigs. Allow carrot mixture to cool, then place in a food processor or liquidizer. Blend to a smooth purée.

Rinse the pan and return soup to it, then stir in the grated orange rind (an easy way to remove the rind from the grater is to use a pastry brush). Season to taste with salt, freshly ground black pepper and mace.

Return the pan to the heat, then add the orange juice through a strainer. Cook gently, stirring occasionally, until piping hot. Pour soup into a warmed tureen, then swirl in the single cream.

HANDY TIP

During the summer, try serving this soup chilled as a delicious starter for a dinner party. Remember to add the cream and garnish after chilling.

Strain the prepared orange zest and use to garnish the soup, together with the remaining basil sprigs. For special occasions, serve with extra cream.

1. Heat the oil in a large pan, then sauté the chopped onion and sliced carrot for 5 mins or until softened slightly

2. Add the vegetable stock with one or two basil sprigs to the pan, then bring to the boil, cover and simmer

3. Scrub and dry one of the oranges, then, using a zester, carefully remove the rind in long thin strips

4. Discard basil sprigs, place the cooled carrot mixture in a food processor or liquidizer and blend to a smooth purée

5. Return soup to the rinsed pan and add the grated rind from the remaining orange together with seasoning

6. Return pan to the heat. Add orange juice through a strainer. Cook gently, stirring occasionally, until hot, then serve

CREAM OF TOMATO SOUP

Give everyone a delicious treat with this all-time favourite. Made from the finest of ingredients – plump tomtoes, onions and garlic, with a hint of fresh basil – it's really easy to prepare.

Calories per portion: 238 — **SERVES 4**

1½ lb/675 g ripe tomatoes, washed
2 garlic cloves
1 large onion
2 sticks celery
4 oz/100 g back bacon
2 tbsp vegetable oil
few basil sprigs
¾ pint/450 ml vegetable stock
salt and freshly ground black pepper
2-3 tbsp tomato purée
1 tbsp cornflour
¼ pint/150 ml single cream or low-fat fromage frais
extra basil sprigs to garnish

Make a small cross at the stalk end of each tomato. Place in a large bowl and cover with boiling water. Leave for 2 mins then drain, peel and discard the skins. Cut tomatoes into quarters, discard the core then, using a teaspoon, scoop out the seeds and discard.

Peel and crush the garlic. Peel and finely chop the onion. Wash and trim celery and chop finely. Discard any rind from bacon, then snip into pieces with kitchen scissors. Place garlic, onion, celery and bacon, in a large saucepan with oil and fry gently for 5 mins, or until onion is soft and transparent.

Add the prepared tomatoes and a few basil sprigs and cook gently for a further 5 mins. Pour in the stock and season with the salt and pepper. Bring to the boil, cover, then simmer gently for 15 mins, or until the tomatoes are pulpy and the vegetables are soft.

Allow to cool for 5 mins, then pass through a blender or food processor to form a purée. If a smoother soup is required, rub through a sieve and return to the rinsed pan.

Blend the tomato purée with 2 tbsp cold water and stir into the pan. Bring to just below boiling point. Blend the cornflour with 2-3 tbsp of cold water to form a smooth paste, and stir into the soup. Cook, stirring throughout with a wooden spoon, until the soup thickens slightly. Adjust the seasoning if necessary.

To serve, pour soup into a warm tureen and swirl in a little cream or fromage frais. Garnish the top with the rest of the basil sprigs. Serve remaining cream or fromage frais separately.

If preferred, allow the soup to cool slightly (for about 2 mins) then stir in all of the cream or fromage frais and serve immediately with chunks of fresh bread.

HANDY TIP

For a real indulgence, stir 2-3 tbsp of port into the soup before adding the cream. Served chilled, this makes a perfect starter for a buffet lunch.

1. Cover tomatoes with boiling water, leave for 2 mins, drain well, then skin

2. Cut peeled tomatoes into quarters, then scoop out seeds and discard

3. Crush garlic, peel and chop onion and wash, trim and chop celery finely; snip bacon into pieces and place in pan

4. Fry bacon, garlic, onion and celery in a large saucepan with oil for 5 mins, or until onion is soft and transparent

5. Add quartered tomatoes to the pan and cook gently for a further 5 mins, stir occasionally with a wooden spoon

6. Add a few basil sprigs to the pan, pour in the stock and bring to the boil. Cover then simmer gently for 15 mins

POTATO AND LEEK SOUP

What could be more warming on a cold, winter's day than a nourishing bowl of steaming hot potato and leek soup? Its creamy texture makes it ideal any time, – as a satisfying snack or delicious starter.

Calories per portion: 385 **SERVES 4**

1 lb/450 g potatoes
1 large onion
1 lb/450 g leeks
2 oz/50 g butter or margarine
2 bay leaves
1 pint/600 ml vegetable stock
salt and freshly ground black pepper
¼ pint/150 ml milk
¼ pint/150 ml single cream
½-1 tsp grated nutmeg

Peel the potatoes and dice into ½ in/1.25 cm cubes. Peel and chop the onion. Trim the leeks, discarding the root and very green part of the leek. (This part can be used for flavouring stocks and casseroles.) Slit the leeks down the centre from top to tail, then wash under plenty of cold running water to remove any dirt or grit. Drain well then slice into 1 in/2.5 cm rings.

Melt the butter or margarine in a large pan then sauté the diced potatoes and chopped onion with the bay leaves for 5 mins. Add the sliced leeks to the pan and continue to sauté for a further 3-4 mins.

Pour in the stock, then add salt and pepper to taste. Bring to the boil, then cover with a lid and simmer for 15 mins or until the potatoes are cooked.

Remove from the heat and reserve one third of the cooked vegetables. Discard the bay leaves. Pass the remainder of the vegetables and stock through a food processor or liquidizer and blend until smooth. If you do not have either of these in your kitchen, mash well with a potato masher then rub through a fine sieve.

Return purée to a clean pan and adjust seasoning to taste, then stir in the milk, cream and nutmeg to taste. Add the reserved cooked vegetables then reheat gently, stirring occasionally with a wooden spoon. Do not allow the soup to boil otherwise the cream may curdle and the pan may burn slightly, which will ruin the flavour of the soup.

1. Sauté potatoes and onion with bay leaves in butter or margarine for 5 mins

2. Add the sliced leeks to the pan and continue to cook for a further 3-4 mins

3. Pour in vegetable stock, add salt and pepper to taste, then bring to the boil

HANDY TIPS

Serve hot, garnished with a few blanched leek rings. When preparing leeks, reserve a few slices that are very pale green. Just before serving the soup, pour boiling water over them, leave for 2 mins, drain, then use as a garnish. Serve the soup with crusty wholemeal bread as a snack or with sliced brown bread as a starter. In the summer this soup is delicious if served chilled. It is then known as Vichyssoise. Make exactly as above except for the garnish and chill. Just before serving, stir, check seasoning then pour into a soup tureen or bowls.

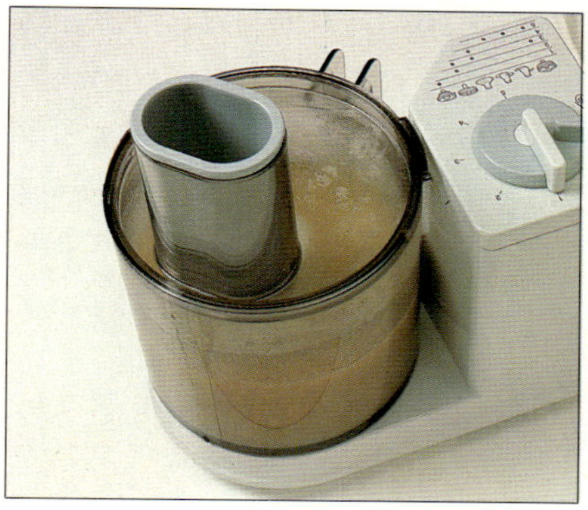

4. Blend two thirds of the cooked vegetables in food processor until smooth

5. After blending vegetables, leave processor on low and gradually add milk

6. Return soup to a clean pan, add the reserved vegetables and heat through

CULLEN SKINK

This Scottish fish and potato soup is hearty enough to be served with crusty bread as a main course. For a smoother version, just whizz the soup through a blender or food processor. It's a treat when there's a nip in the air.

Calories per portion: 266 — **SERVES 4**

1 finnan haddock, approx 12 oz/350 g
2 small onions
few sprigs of parsley
few black or white peppercorns
¾ pint/450 ml milk
1 lb/450 g potatoes
salt and freshly ground black pepper
1 oz/25 g butter
2 tbsp cornflour
freshly chopped parsley

Wash the finnan haddock, then pat dry using absorbent paper. Place on a board and with a very sharp knife, carefully remove the skin. You will find it easier if you hold the tail end firmly with one hand, then place the knife blade at a 45° angle between the skin and flesh. Make short strokes, slicing through between the skin and flesh. As you proceed up the fish, increase the angle of the knife, always remembering to grip the skin firmly. Reserve the fish skin for making stock.

Peel and slice one of the onions, then place the finnan haddock, onion, parsley sprigs (keep a couple back), and peppercorns in a frying pan. Make up ½ pint/300 ml of the milk to 1 pint/600 ml with water. Pour over the fish then bring to the boil. Reduce heat, then simmer gently for 10-15 mins or until the fish is cooked. Drain, reserving the fish and liquid but discarding the onion, parsley and peppercorns. Reserve any

bones from the fish, flake the flesh into medium-sized pieces, then cover and put to one side.

Meanwhile, place the reserved skin and bones into a pan with remaining onion, parsley sprigs, a few more peppercorns and remaining milk. Add ½ pint/300 ml of water, then bring to the boil and boil gently for 15 mins. Strain into a larger pan.

Peel the potatoes, slice into ¼ in/6 mm pieces then cook in boiling salted water for 10 mins or until tender. Drain. Add the cooked potatoes, the reserved liquid from cooking the fish, and the flakes of finnan haddock to the fish stock. Bring to a gentle boil, then season to taste. (Be careful with the amount of salt as finnan haddock can be quite salty.) Add the butter, then cook gently until piping hot.

Blend the cornflour to a smooth paste with 4 tbsp of water, stir into the soup and cook until thickened. Serve immediately sprinkled with freshly chopped parsley.

HANDY TIPS

Traditionally, the soup is thickened with potatoes. To do this, cook 1½ lb/675 g potatoes in total, and mash them. Add to the soup with flaked finnan haddock and cook as recipe, omitting cornflour. If finnan haddock is unobtainable, use undyed smoked haddock.

1. Wash and dry the finnan haddock, place on a board and remove skin

2. Place fish in a pan with one onion, parsley, peppercorns, milk and water

3. When fish is cooked, drain, place on a plate. Remove bones, flake fish

4. Place skin and bones in pan with remaining onion, parsley, peppercorns, milk and water

5. Strain the cooked fish stock through a fine sieve into a larger pan. Leave to one side while cooking potatoes

6. Add cooked potato to fish stock, with the reserved cooking liquid and fish. Bring to the boil then season to taste

Chicken Chowder

When it's cold outside, there's nothing more satisfying than coming home to a bowl of hot home-made soup. Full of succulent pieces of chicken, crisp sweetcorn and chunks of potato, this soup is easy to make and good for you.

Calories per portion: 441 | **Serves 6**

2½ lb/1.25 kg free-range chicken
3 medium onions
1 carrot
1 stick celery
few sprigs of parsley and thyme
3 bay leaves
2 fresh or frozen corn on the cob
2 oz/50 g butter or margarine
12 oz/350 g potatoes
2 oz/50 g plain white flour
salt and freshly ground black pepper
¼ pint/150 ml single cream or buttermilk

Remove any giblets from the chicken and discard fat from inside the cavity. Wash chicken under cold running water, then place in a large saucepan. Cover completely with water. Peel the onions, place one in the pan, chop the remaining two and reserve.

Peel the carrot and trim and scrub celery. Cut the celery in half then place the herbs on the inside of one piece, place the other half on top and tie together with string to form a bouquet garni. Add the carrot and bouquet garni to the pan, bring to the boil, cover, then simmer gently for 1 hr or until the chicken is cooked. Allow the chicken to cool for about 20 mins in the pan, then remove and leave until cool enough to handle. Strain and reserve the cooking liquid. When the chicken is cool, strip off and discard the skin. Remove the meat from the bones and cut into small pieces. Cover and reserve in the fridge.

If using fresh corn on the cob, remove husks and silky threads, wash, then cook in boiling water for 15 mins or until tender. Drain, and when cool enough to handle, carefully cut kernels away from the cobs. (If using frozen corn on the cob, cook in boiling water for 5 mins, leave to cool, then cut the kernels away.) Do not add salt to pan.

Melt fat in a large pan, peel then slice the potatoes, add to pan with the reserved chopped onion and cook for 5 mins or until onion is soft. Add the flour and continue cooking for 2 mins. Draw the pan off heat, then gradually stir in 2 pints/1.2 litres reserved cooking liquid, making up with water if necessary. Bring to the boil, stirring throughout, then add the chicken, sweetcorn and seasoning if necessary, and cook for a further 5 mins. Draw pan off heat, stir in the cream or buttermilk, reheat gently then serve.

Handy tip

Try adding one red and one green pepper, deseeded and chopped, for more flavour. Add to pan with the chopped chicken meat and seasoning.

1. Place the chicken in a large pan. Add the onion, carrot and bouquet garni

2. Strip off the chicken skin and discard. Remove meat and cut into pieces

3. Cook the corn until tender, drain. Cool, then carefully cut kernels from cob

4. Melt fat, then add the chopped onion and potato. Fry gently for 5 mins

5. Add flour to pan and continue to cook over a gentle heat for 2 mins

6. Add chicken pieces, then stir in sweetcorn kernels, and adjust seasoning

BOUILLABAISSE

Try a taste of true French cuisine with this delicious fish soup flavoured with herbs and spices. Served with chunks of crusty bread, it'll make a hearty and sustaining lunch or supper snack.

Calories per portion: 265 | **SERVES 6**

few saffron strands
2 lb/900 g mixed fish, cleaned, such as red mullet, monkfish or cod, depending on availability
8 oz/225 g fresh mussels
8 oz/225 g fresh clams
2 large onions, peeled
2 sticks celery
8 oz/225 g tomatoes
2 garlic cloves
2 tbsp olive or vegetable oil
2 bay leaves
1 orange
salt and freshly ground black pepper
few whole prawns
1 tbsp freshly chopped parsley

Place saffron in a small bowl, pour ¼ pint/150 ml boiling water over it and leave to infuse for 30 mins.

Clean fish by removing any scales with a round-bladed knife. Wash well under cold water. If using monkfish remove any skin, discard centre bone and cut into 2 in/5 cm cubes. Leave mullet whole. Skin cod if using, and cut into 2 in/5 cm cubes. Scrub mussels and clams, discarding any that are open, remove beards from mussels and leave in separate bowls of cold water.

Chop the onions, wash and trim celery, then chop finely. With a sharp knife, make a small cross in stalk end of tomatoes. Place in bowl, pour boiling water over them and leave for 2 mins. Remove and discard skins, then chop. Peel and crush garlic.

Heat oil in a large pan, add the onions and celery and gently fry for 5 mins until onions are soft but still transparent. Add bay leaves, garlic and tomatoes, stir lightly.

Using a julienne cutter, add julienne strips of orange rind to pan. Alternatively, finely grate orange rind and add to pan. Add seasoning. Fry for 5 mins.

Arrange the prepared fish, except for shellfish, in a thick layer over the vegetables in the pan. Strain the saffron liquid through a sieve, and then add to the pan with enough water to just cover the fish.

Bring to the boil, cook uncovered for 8 mins. Drain the shellfish, then add to the pan and continue cooking for a further 5-8 mins, or until the fish is cooked but still retains its shape. Add the whole prawns for last 2 mins of the cooking time. Discard any shellfish that have not opened. Sprinkle with chopped parsley and serve in a warmed soup tureen with brown bread.

HANDY TIP

Saffron is a natural colouring and is obtained from the stigmas of yellow crocuses. If saffron is unavailable use ¼-½ tsp turmeric dissolved completely in ¼ pint/150 ml hot water.

1. Remove scales from red mullet with round-bladed knife, starting from tail

2. Scrub mussels and clams, discard open ones. Remove beards from mussels

3. Chop onions and celery. Pour boiling water over tomatoes, discard skins

4. Heat oil in a large pan then fry onion and celery for 5 mins or until softened

5. Add tomatoes, garlic, bay leaves, orange rind, seasoning. Fry for 5 mins

6. Arrange fish in thick layer over vegetables. Strain saffron liquid, add to pan

CREAM OF CUCUMBER SOUP

This delicious, creamy soup with its light, delicate flavour highlights the very best of summer. Quick and easy to prepare, it's perfect served with Melba toast.

Calories per portion: 265 **SERVES 6**

1. Cut bread from the stale loaf into very thin slices, remove crusts and place on a baking sheet

2. To flavour the milk, infuse with one peeled onion and 2 fresh bay leaves. Bring to just below boiling point

3. Peel the cucumber, cut in half lengthways then scoop out the seeds and discard. Chop cucumber flesh

1 stale white loaf, uncut
1 pint/600 ml milk
2 onions
2 fresh bay leaves
1 large or 1½ medium-sized cucumbers
2 sticks celery
3 oz/75 g butter or margarine
1 lemon
1 pint/600 ml vegetable stock
2 oz/50 g plain flour
salt and freshly ground black pepper
1 tsp freshly grated nutmeg
¼ pint/150 ml single cream
a few sprigs tarragon

Set oven to Gas 1, 275°F, 140°C. Use the bread to make Melba toast: place loaf on bread-board and cut the thinnest slices you can. Remove crusts, then place slices on a baking sheet in the bottom of the oven for 1½ hrs to dry out.

Pour the milk into a small pan. Peel one of the onions and add to pan. Wash and dry bay leaves and add to pan. Bring milk to just below boiling point, remove from the heat. Cover and leave to infuse for 15 mins.

Peel the cucumbers very thinly, cut in half lengthways, then scoop out and discard seeds, using a teaspoon. Chop flesh.

Wash and trim celery and chop. Peel, then chop remaining onion.

Melt 1 oz/25 g of the butter or margarine in a large pan, then fry the chopped vegetables for 5 mins. Wash and dry the lemon, then grate the rind finely into the pan. Squeeze the lemon. Pour in the stock and lemon juice, bring to the boil, cover and simmer gently for 10-15 mins or until soft.

Meanwhile, melt the remaining butter or margarine in a small pan. Stir in the flour and cook, stirring, for 2 mins. Remove from the heat. Strain the infused milk, then gradually mix into the roux, beating well between each addition. Return pan to the heat and cook, stirring throughout, until the sauce is thick, smooth and glossy. Season with salt, pepper and the freshly grated nutmeg.

Pour the cooked cucumber and stock into a food processor. Add the sauce, then purée until smooth. If the soup is to be served hot, reheat gently, add cream and allow to come to just below boiling point.

If soup is to be served cold, cool quickly after puréeing by transferring to a clean bowl and standing bowl in a sink with enough cold water to come halfway up the sides of the bowl until cool. Stir in the cream, chill in the fridge, covered, for at least 2 hrs. Garnish with sprigs of tarragon and a few slices of cucumber. Serve with Melba toast.

HANDY TIP

When making Melba toast it is essential that you use bread that is 1-2 days old so that you can slice the loaf really thinly. The toast can be made with brown bread if preferred.

4. Melt the fat then after sweating the vegetables for 5 mins, grate the lemon rind finely into the pan

5. Pour in the vegetable stock and the lemon juice, bring to the boil, cover and simmer for 10-15 mins, or until soft

6. Place cooked cucumber and stock in to a food processor, add the sauce, purée until smooth, add cream

PEA AND HAM SOUP

Warm them up in winter with our delicious, nourishing soup. It's so full of flavour and will keep the healthiest appetite happy. Serve hot for lunch or supper with crusty chunks of freshly baked brown bread. The whole family will love it.

Calories per portion: 446 | **SERVES 4**

6 oz/175 g dried green lentils
few sprigs parsley
few sprigs rosemary
2 bay leaves
8 oz/225 g piece unsmoked bacon, such as collar
1 large onion
1 garlic clove
2 large carrots
8 oz/225 g leeks
2 oz/50 g butter or margarine
3 pints/1.7 litres vegetable stock
salt and freshly ground black pepper

Pick the lentils over discarding any stones or grit. Wash thoroughly under cold running water. Place in a large bowl then cover with water. Leave lentils to soak, preferably overnight. Drain and put to one side.

Place the herbs in a small square of muslin. Tie up to form a bouquet garni.

Trim bacon, discarding any fat, rind or gristle. Cut into small cubes, approx ½ in/1.25 cm. Peel and chop the onion. Peel and crush garlic. Peel carrots, trim, then cut into small dice. Trim leeks, wash well under cold running water. Slice thinly.

Heat fat in a large pan, add the bacon and vegetables. Fry gently, stirring occasionally for 5-8 mins or until vegetables have softened but are still transparent. Add the drained soaked lentils and mix well together. Place the prepared bouquet garni in the pan then pour in the stock. Bring to the boil, cover, then reduce heat and simmer gently for 1–1½ hrs or until lentils are soft and mushy and the soup is a thick consistency. Discard bouquet garni and add salt and pepper to taste. Serve piping hot with fresh brown bread.

HANDY TIPS

Many supermarkets and butchers sell the knuckle-end of a hock of bacon. This is a very economical cut of meat. If using one, wash well, place the whole knuckle in the pan with the lentils and stock and cook until tender. When the bacon knuckle is cooked and the lentils soft, remove knuckle, strip off the skin and rind, discard. Chop bacon into small pieces, return to the soup. Heat through thoroughly. Don't forget to soak your knuckle if it's a smoked one. Soak overnight, then discard liquid. Check salt content before adding any more.

For a tasty alternative, try Leek and Split Pea Soup. Cover 3 oz/75 g yellow split peas with boiling water, leave for 2 hrs, drain. Peel and chop 1 large onion, fry gently in 1 tbsp oil. Add split peas, 2 pints/1.2 litres vegetable stock with seasoning. Bring to boil, cover, then simmer for 1 hr. Trim, wash, then slice 1½ lb/675 g leeks, add to pan, continue to cook for 15-20 mins or until leeks are tender. Adjust seasoning, then serve.

1. Wash the lentils thoroughly then cover with water and leave to soak

2. Make a bouquet garni with the parsley and rosemary sprigs and bay leaves

3. Trim the bacon, discarding any fat, rind or gristle. Cut into small cubes

4. Fry the onion, garlic, carrot, leeks and bacon gently in the fat until softened

5. Add the soaked and drained lentils to the softened vegetables and mix well

6. Place the bouquet garni in the pan, add the stock and bring to the boil

Gazpacho

Sun-ripened tomatoes, crisp tangy peppers, cool fresh cucumber and a hint of garlic. These are the ingredients for a perfect Gazpacho. Serve it iced with plenty of croûtons. It's ideal as a starter for hot sunny days.

Calories per portion: 306 **Serves 4**

1½ lb/675 g ripe tomatoes
1 large Spanish onion
1 large garlic clove, peeled and crushed
½ cucumber, peeled
1 green pepper, deseeded
juice 1 lemon, strained
2-3 tbsp white wine vinegar
3-4 tbsp olive oil
½ pint/300 ml tomato juice
salt and freshly ground black pepper
½ red pepper, deseeded
3 slices white or brown bread
2 tbsp vegetable oil
ice cubes

Make a small cross on the top of each tomato. Place in a large bowl and pour over boiling water. Leave to stand for 2 minutes. Using a draining spoon, remove the tomatoes from the bowl, peel away the skins and discard. Cut the tomatoes into quarters, discard the seeds and cores.

Peel and chop the onion and place in food processor or liquidizer with the tomato quarters and garlic. Blend for 2-3 mins to make a purée.

Cut the cucumber in half lengthways and discard the seeds. Dice or chop finely and add 2 tbsp to the tomato purée. Reserve remainder for serving. Dice or finely chop the green pepper, add 2 tbsp to the tomato purée, reserving the remainder.

Add the lemon juice, vinegar, olive oil, tomato juice with salt and freshly ground black pepper to taste. Blend for 2-3 mins or until a smooth purée forms. Check seasoning, pour into soup tureen and chill for at least 2 hours.

Finely chop the red pepper and mix with the reserved green pepper.

Discard the crusts and cut the bread into ¼ in/6 mm cubes. Heat the vegetable oil in a frying pan. Fry bread cubes for 5-8 mins, stirring throughout until golden brown and crisp. Drain well on absorbent paper.

Just before serving add ice cubes to the Gazpacho and sprinkle the top with a little cucumber, pepper and croûtons. Serve remaining cucumber, peppers and croûtons separately with some hot crusty French bread.

Handy tip

Gazpacho can be made in advance and kept in the fridge. Stir before serving, add ice cubes, and garnish.

1. If tomato skin doesn't peel easily, return to hot water for another minute

2. Discard tomato core, and reserve seeds to flavour stews or casseroles

3. Chop onion finely – leaving the root on while doing so helps prevent tears

4. Cucumber skin and seeds can be bitter, so discard them and dice flesh

5. Blend the Gazpacho on a high speed to ensure that a smooth purée forms

6. Fry bread cubes quickly and drain well for really crisp, golden croûtons

TARAMASALATA

Smoked cod's roe, garlic, breadcrumbs and olive oil, flavoured with lemon, make this popular dish. Traditionally served in Greece as an appetizer with pitta bread.

Calories per portion: 526 — **SERVES 6**

FOR THE MELBA TOAST:
½ uncut large white loaf, preferably at least 2 days old
FOR THE TARAMASALATA:
12 oz/350 g smoked cod's roe
1 medium onion
3 oz/75 g fresh white breadcrumbs
2 garlic cloves
1 large lemon
8 fl oz/250 ml olive oil
rock salt
freshly ground black pepper
lemon slices and parsley to decorate

Preheat oven to Gas 1, 275°F, 140°C To make Melba toast, place the loaf on a bread-board, cut the thinnest slices you can. Trim and discard the crusts then place slices on a baking sheet on the bottom shelf of the oven and leave for 2 hrs to dry out. Check the bread occasionally to ensure it doesn't burn.

If you prefer, the bread can be dried out any time you are using your oven at a low temperature. Once cold, store in an airtight tin until required. It will keep in the tin for 2-3 weeks.

To make the Taramasalata, skin the cod's roe and break up into small pieces. Place in the bowl of a food processor and process for a few minutes until smooth.

Peel and finely chop the onion, add to the cod's roe together with breadcrumbs. Peel and crush the garlic cloves, add to the mixture then process again until smooth.

Finely grate the rind from the lemon and squeeze then strain the juice, add to the processor and process again until smooth. (It is important to only switch the processor on for short bursts, and to ensure that no mixture is caught underneath the blade, as the mixture at this stage is fairly stiff. If you just leave the processor running it could be too much for the motor.)

Gradually add the olive oil, drop by drop, to the mixture, scraping down the sides of the bowl if necessary. When all the oil has been added, gradually blend in approx 6 tbsp tepid boiled water to form a smooth dropping consistency. Add a little freshly milled rock salt and ground black pepper, check for taste. Turn into a serving bowl, cover and chill for at least 1 hr before serving. Decorate with lemon slices and parsley and serve with Melba toast.

HANDY TIP

You can also make Taramasalata by hand. Beat the cod's roe until smooth, then add the oil drop by drop. Add remaining ingredients when you've added half of the oil.

1. Cut very thin slices from the bread then trim and discard the crusts, place on the baking sheet

2. Skin the cod's roe, break up into small pieces, place in food processor, and process until smooth

3. Peel and finely chop the onion, then add to the cod's roe together with the breadcrumbs and garlic

4. Finely grate the lemon rind, add to the mixture together with the strained lemon juice

5. Add the olive oil, drop by drop, blending throughout until a smooth dropping consistency is achieved

6. Add freshly milled rock salt and ground black pepper to the Taramasalata then chill before serving

COQUILLES SAINT-JACQUES

Slices of scallops poached gently in white wine with succulent sliced button mushrooms and coated in a delicate white sauce make this spectacular dish.

Calories per portion: 255 | **SERVES 4**

4 prepared scallops in shells
¼ pint/150 ml dry white wine
1 onion, peeled and sliced
1 carrot, peeled and sliced
few parsley stalks
sprig of thyme
4 oz/100 g button mushrooms
1½ oz/40 g butter
1 oz/25 g plain flour
1 egg yolk, size 3
salt and freshly ground black pepper
extra 1 oz/25 g butter, optional
2 tbsp fresh breadcrumbs
2 tbsp melted butter
lemon and cucumber twists to garnish

Preheat oven to Gas 9, 475°F, 240°C, 15 mins before serving. Using a small sharp knife, remove the scallops from their shells then wash lightly and dry on absorbent paper. Clean and trim the scallops, if liked the skirt can be used in the stock.

Place the dry white wine with ¼ pint/150 ml of water in a frying pan with the peeled and sliced onion and carrot, parsley and thyme. Bring to the boil, simmer gently for 8 mins. Add the washed scallops and simmer for 4 mins. Remove the scallops, strain and reserve the cooking liquid. Cut the corals away from the scallop white meat and reserve. Cut the white meat into slices.

Wipe the mushrooms and slice thinly. Heat the butter then gently cook the mushrooms for 2 mins, drain, place in a small bowl. Add the sliced scallops and toss in the melted butter. Drain and reserve. Add the flour to the remaining fat in pan and cook for 2 mins. Remove from heat then gradually stir in the reserved cooking liquid. Return the pan to the heat and cook stirring throughout until the sauce thickens. Remove from the heat, cool slightly then beat in the egg yolk. Return to the heat and cook for a further 2 mins to cook the egg. Take care not to boil the sauce otherwise you may have small pieces of cooked egg in the sauce rather than a smooth sauce. Season to taste and if using, whisk in the further 1 oz/25 g butter.

If using scallop shells for serving, scrub well, plunge into boiling water for 2 mins, drain and dry well.

Place a little sauce in the base of each shell, top with the mushrooms, then the white meat and lastly the coral. Cover completely with the remaining sauce. Sprinkle the top with the breadcrumbs and pour a little melted butter over each. Cook in oven for 6-8 mins or until piping hot and golden brown on top. Serve garnished with cucumber and lemon twists.

HANDY TIP

When buying the scallops, ask the fishmonger for the concave scallop shells so you can use them as serving dishes.

1. Using a small sharp knife, remove the scallops from their shells, wash lightly and dry on absorbent paper

2. Clean and trim the scallops, if liked use the skirt in the stock. Place white wine, water and vegetables in pan

3. Gently poach the scallops in the white wine and water with the onion, carrot and herbs, simmer for 8 mins

4. Cut the corals away from the scallop white meat and reserve. Cut the white meat into slices

5. Scrub shells, plunge into boiling water, dry. Place a spoonful of prepared sauce in the base of each cleaned scallop shell

6. Arrange the sliced mushrooms, then the sliced white meat, then the coral, coat with sauce

Smoked Fish Pate

Deliciously light flakes of smoked haddock and mackerel, with a subtle tang of lime, make this pâté a luscious starter for any meal. Served with crispy Melba toast, it's sure to impress everyone.

Calories per portion: 685 | **Serves 4**

1 lb/450 g piece of undyed smoked haddock
½ pint/300 ml semi-skimmed milk
1 bay leaf
1 sprig each of dill, parsley and thyme
½ medium onion, peeled and studded with 4 cloves
12 oz/350 g smoked mackerel fillets
zested rind and juice of 1 lime
4 oz/100 g butter or margarine, softened
4 oz/100 g fromage frais
4 tbsp mixed peppercorns
FOR THE CUPS:
6 slices white bread
cherry tomatoes and parsley to garnish

Wash and dry the haddock then place in a frying pan with the milk, herbs and onion. Bring to the boil, then reduce heat and simmer gently for 10-15 mins or until cooked. Allow to cool in the cooking liquid, before draining and discarding liquid. Discard skin and any bones from the haddock, flake finely.

Discard the skin from the smoked mackerel and carefully scrape away any of the dark flesh on the skinned side. Flake mackerel and then mix with the haddock. Sprinkle with the lime rind and juice, cover lightly and leave for 30 mins for the flavours to develop.

Cream 2 oz/50 g of the fat until soft, stir in the fish and fromage frais. Mix well, spoon into four individual pâté or ramekin dishes. Smooth the tops, cover, chill in the fridge for 30 mins.

Melt remaining fat, pour over the pâté to completely cover tops. Lightly crush the peppercorns in a pestle and mortar, sprinkle on top of the fat. Chill the pâtés for a further 30 mins.

Meanwhile, make the Melba cups by toasting the bread on both sides until golden. Using a 4 in/10 cm round plain pastry cutter, cut out a circle from each slice. Holding toasted rounds flat, slide a knife between the toasted edges to split the bread. Return to the grill and toast untoasted side uppermost, until golden, and the edges have curled up. Serve warm with the pâté, garnished with cherry tomatoes and parsley.

HANDY TIP

If liked substitute the smoked haddock with cod and replace the mackerel with smoked trout.

1. Simmer the haddock in the milk with the onion and herbs for 10-15 mins

2. Drain fish then carefully remove skin from the haddock and discard. Flake fish

3. Skin mackerel and flake, mix with haddock, sprinkle with lime rind and juice

4. Spoon the prepared pâté into four individual dishes, pressing the mixture down with the back of a spoon

5. Cover pâtés with melted butter then lightly crush peppercorns and sprinkle over the top

6. Make Melba cups by splitting toasted rounds of bread then toasting again until edges curl

Chicken Satay

Super, spicy Chicken Satay is a delicious Far Eastern dish served with a delicate nutty sauce. You can cook it over charcoal or under the grill to make an impressive and unusual supper or first course. Your friends and family will love it.

Calories per portion: 384 **Serves 4**

1 shallot
1 in/2.5 cm piece root ginger
1-2 garlic cloves
1-2 fresh chillis
1 tsp chilli powder, optional
1½ tsp turmeric
2 tsp light soft brown sugar
2 tbsp white malt vinegar
1 tbsp lemon juice
2 tbsp vegetable oil
½ pint/300 ml coconut milk or semi-skimmed milk
4 oz/100 g roasted peanuts
1 lb/450 g chicken breasts, skinned
fresh chilli rings to garnish

Peel then roughly chop the shallot and the root ginger. Peel the garlic (the amount you use depends on how garlicky you like your food) and roughly chop. Deseed and chop the fresh chillis. Place the chopped ingredients in a mortar.

Add chilli powder, if using, and turmeric, then pound with pestle until thoroughly blended. (Alternatively, place spices in a food processor and blend together.)

Handy tip

If liked, thin strips of lean lamb, cut from the leg or shoulder, or beef (use rump steak), can be used instead of the chicken. The lamb will take 16-20 mins to cook. All types of satay can also be barbecued over charcoal.

Add sugar, then mix in vinegar, lemon juice, oil and milk.

Place the roasted peanuts in a food processor or coffee grinder and grind to a coarse or fine consistency, depending on whether you prefer a smooth or chunky sauce. Stir the peanuts into the marinade and mix thoroughly.

Place the prepared marinade in a saucepan, bring to the boil, then simmer very gently for 8-10 mins, stirring occasionally. Remove from heat and allow to cool.

Trim off and discard any fat from chicken, wash flesh and pat dry with kitchen paper. Using a sharp knife, cut into long, thin strips. Place chicken in a shallow dish and spoon half the cooled peanut marinade over. Cover, then chill in the fridge for at least 2 hrs, turning occasionally. Cover and chill the remaining marinade.

Cover 8 wooden kebab sticks with cold water and soak for 2 hrs (to prevent the kebab sticks from catching alight during cooking).

When ready to cook the satay, preheat grill to medium. Drain the chicken, reserving marinade, and thread on to the soaked kebab sticks. Place on grill pan and grill for 10-12 mins, or until cooked, turning frequently and brushing occasionally with marinade.

Place remaining marinade in a small pan, bring to the boil and cook for about 2 mins. Pour into a small bowl, garnish with fresh chilli rings and serve with the Chicken Satay.

1. Pound the chopped shallot, ginger, garlic, chillis and spices in a mortar

2. Place the peanuts in a food processor and process to required consistency

3. Trim fat from chicken breasts. Using a sharp knife, cut into long, thin strips

4. Place chicken in dish, spoon half the marinade over. Cover, then chill

5. Thread chicken on to soaked wooden kebab sticks. Reserve marinade

6. Place kebabs on grill pan and cook under preheated grill, turning frequently

Plaice Goujons

Thin strips of fish encased in egg and breadcrumbs, then fried until crisp and golden... this recipe is ideal when time is short. Add chips, a twist of lemon and a bowl of tartare sauce, and you'll serve up a mouthwatering treat.

Calories per portion: 537 | **Serves 4**

FOR THE TARTARE SAUCE:

1 egg yolk, size 3
½ level tsp dried mustard
½ level tsp salt
freshly ground black pepper
½ level tsp caster sugar
1-1½ tbsp white wine vinegar or lemon juice
¼ pint/150 ml olive oil
2 tbsp freshly chopped tarragon
1 tbsp freshly chopped parsley
1-2 gherkins, finely chopped
a few capers, finely chopped

FOR THE GOUJONS:

1 lb/450 g plaice fillets
1 oz/25 g flour
1 egg, size 3
4 oz/100 g breadcrumbs
oil for deep frying
tarragon sprig and twist of lemon to garnish

Place egg yolk in a bowl with the mustard, salt, pepper and sugar. Add 1 tsp vinegar or lemon juice, mix well. Gradually add oil, one drop at a time to begin with. Whisk constantly until smooth and thick. After adding half the oil, the remainder can be added in a thin steady stream, but whisk continuously while oil is being added.

If the mayonnaise becomes too thick, add a little more vinegar or lemon juice. Once all the oil has been used, stir in the remaining vinegar or lemon juice with the chopped herbs, gherkins and capers. Cover and leave to stand for 1 hr to allow flavours to blend and develop.

To make the goujons, place fish fillets on a board then, holding the skin at the tail end, remove skin with a sharp knife. Cut the fillets into 3 in x ½ in/7.5 cm x 1.25 cm strips. If necessary, trim the edges to give a neat shape. Place flour in a small bowl and season. Beat egg and place in a shallow bowl, place breadcrumbs in another bowl. Coat strips of plaice in seasoned flour, then dip in beaten egg and coat in breadcrumbs. If liked, coat again.

Heat oil in a deep fat fryer to 350°F, 180°C. Fry the fish in small batches for 3-5 minutes or until crisp and golden. Drain well on absorbent paper. Repeat until all the strips have been cooked. Garnish and serve with the tartare sauce and freshly fried chips.

HANDY TIP

If liked, cod or haddock can be used instead of plaice. Cook for 4-6 mins. Or try using thin strips of skinned and boned chicken breast. Cook for 4-6 mins.

1. Mix the egg yolk with mustard, seasoning, sugar and vinegar. Whisk in oil

2. When oil has been incorporated, stir in remaining vinegar, herbs and pickles

3. Place fillets on a board. Hold firmly with one hand, then skin with a sharp knife

4. Cut the fillets into 3 in x ½ in/7.5 cm x 1.25 cm strips and trim edges to neaten

5. Dip strips into seasoned flour, then beaten egg and finally in breadcrumbs

6. Heat oil to 350°F, 180°C. Fry goujons for 3-5 minutes or until crisp and golden

SWEET & SOUR PRAWNS

Tender succulent prawns, with a hint of ginger and garlic, coated in a light, crisp golden batter and served with a delicious tangy sweet and sour sauce and fried rice. This dish is quick and easy to cook.

Calories per portion: 379 | **SERVES 6**

2 tbsp light soy sauce
3 tbsp dry sherry
2 tbsp groundnut oil
1 in/2.5 cm piece root ginger
1-2 garlic cloves
3-4 spring onions
1 lb/450 g peeled prawns, thawed if frozen

FOR THE SAUCE:

½ small red pepper
½ small green pepper
1 carrot
¼ pint/150 ml fish stock
1 tbsp light soy sauce
2 tbsp white wine vinegar
1 tbsp clear honey
1 tbsp tomato purée
1-2 tsp cornflour

FOR THE BATTER:

5 tbsp cornflour
2 eggs, size 5, beaten
oil for deep fat frying

Mix the soy sauce, sherry and oil together in a medium-sized glass bowl. Peel and finely grate the root ginger, peel and crush the garlic. Trim the spring onions, wash well, dry, then chop finely. Add the ginger, garlic and spring onions to the bowl and mix well.

Dry the prawns thoroughly, add to the bowl and stir well. Cover and chill for at least 1 hr, turning occasionally.

To make the sauce, cut tops off the peppers, discard seeds and pith, then cut into thin strips. Peel carrot, slice thinly, cut into thin strips. Place in a small bowl, pour boiling water over, leave for 5 mins, then drain.

Mix the stock, soy sauce, vinegar, honey and tomato purée together in a small saucepan, bring to the boil, then simmer for 5 mins.

Mix the cornflour to a paste with 2 tsp of water, stir into the pan and cook until thickened. Add the drained pepper and carrot strips, stir well then leave on one side.

To make the batter, sift the cornflour into a mixing bowl, add the eggs and beat well until smooth.

Drain prawns then place small amounts in the batter and coat well. Heat the oil in a deep fat fryer to 350°F, 180°C. Drop small spoonfuls of the coated prawns into the batter and fry for 4-5 mins until golden brown. Drain on absorbent paper, and repeat with remaining prawns. Warm the sauce through, then pour a little over the cooked prawns. Serve remaining sauce with rice, to accompany prawns.

1. Mix the soy sauce, sherry and oil together. Add the ginger, garlic and onion

2. Drain prawns, place in marinade and leave, covered, for at least 1 hr

3. Deseed peppers, remove pith then cut into strips. Peel carrot and cut into strips

HANDY TIP

As a tasty alternative to the prawns, why not use small cubes of raw cod, or boned monkfish.

4. Mix the cornflour and eggs together to form a smooth batter. Beat well

5. After marinating, drain prawns, then place in prepared batter and coat well

6. Heat oil and fry the prawns for 4-5 mins or until golden brown. Drain well

FRIED CALAMARI

Follow this easy step-by-step guide and give your family a delicious taste of one of the most popular of all Mediterranean dishes. Served with slices of lemon as a starter or crusty bread and a salad for a main meal, it's a real fish favourite.

Calories per portion: 480 **SERVES 4**

2 lb/900 g squid
FOR THE BATTER:
4 oz/100 g plain flour
1 tsp baking powder
pinch of salt
1 egg, size 3
1 tbsp olive oil
oil for deep frying
TO GARNISH:
parsley sprigs
lemon slices

First prepare the squid by pulling the head and tentacles (arms) away from the body. Peel off and discard the thin mottled skin. Rinse the squid in cold water, draw back the rim of the body pouch and locate the top end of the quill-shaped pen. Grasp gently then pull the pen and any entrails free from the surrounding flesh, discard. Wash again. If tentacles are reasonably large, use these. Place the squid's head and viscera (which contains the ink sac) on a chopping board and cut tentacles away from just below the eye. Discard the head and viscera (a bony beak-like mouth, complete with teeth, that lies within the flesh connecting the base of the tentacles). Slice the tentacles and the body into rings. Wash and dry on kitchen paper.

To make the batter, sift the flour, baking powder and salt into a bowl. Make a well in the centre and add egg. Mix the oil with ¼ pint/150 ml water and add to the egg. Beat well, gradually incorporating the flour to make a smooth batter.

Heat oil in a deep fat fryer to 350°F, 180°C. (If you don't have a thermometer, the oil is ready when a small spoonful of the batter dropped into the oil sizzles and rises to the surface in 30 seconds.) Coat a few of the squid rings in batter (use a slotted spoon or your fingers, whichever you prefer), then place in the oil.

HANDY TIPS

The flesh of squid should be firm to the touch. Only the tentacles and fleshy body sac are eaten. The tentacles are usually chopped, then cooked. The body section can be sliced or stuffed – try a lemon and coriander stuffing.
In some Mediterranean recipes the ink is used – remove intact before cooking. If the squid has been previously frozen, the ink will have coagulated. To thaw, place the frozen granules of ink in a little hot water until liquid.

Cook rings in oil for 1-2 mins or until puffed up and golden. Drain on kitchen paper and keep warm while cooking remaining rings.

Serve the calamari hot, garnished with parsley sprigs and lemon slices.

1. Pull head and tentacles away from body. Carefully peel off skin, discard

2. Gently pull out the transparent quill and any remaining entrails

3. Place the head and viscera on board, cut tentacles away below eye

4. Discard head and viscera. Slice the tentacles and body into rings

5. Coat the squid rings, a few at a time, in the prepared batter

6. Cook rings in oil for 1-2 mins until puffed up and golden. Drain

Salad Nicoise

This salad originates from the Côte d'Azur and can be served as a starter or main meal. You can vary the ingredients slightly, but always use flaked tuna, French beans and black olives. It's a tasty change to traditional salads.

Calories per portion: 398 | **Serves 6**

8 oz/225 g new potatoes
8 oz/225 g French beans
2 garlic cloves
few sprigs of parsley
4-6 slices white bread
2 tbsp olive oil
1 oz/25 g butter or margarine
14 oz/400 g can tuna in brine
4 eggs, size 3
1 red pepper
8 oz/225 g firm ripe tomatoes
red and green oak-leaf lettuce
2 oz/50 g can anchovy fillets
few black olives, pitted
FOR THE DRESSING:
1-2 tsp caster sugar
1 tsp dry mustard powder
salt and freshly ground black pepper
1-2 garlic cloves
3 tbsp white wine vinegar
6 tbsp olive oil

Wash and scrub the potatoes. Cook in plenty of boiling salted water for 12-15 mins until cooked. Drain and leave to cool completely.

Wash French beans, trim off tops and tails, then cook in boiling salted water for 5-8 mins, or until cooked but still crunchy. Drain and leave until cold.

Peel garlic cloves, crush in a pestle and mortar or garlic press. Finely chop the parsley. Trim crusts from bread then cut into small cubes.

Heat oil and fat in frying pan and fry garlic gently for 2 mins. Add the bread cubes and parsley and continue to fry, turning the bread frequently, until golden brown. Drain on kitchen paper.

Drain tuna and flake into large chunks. Cook eggs in boiling water for 10 mins, plunge into cold water and leave until cold. Shell and quarter.

Deseed pepper, then wash thoroughly and cut into chunks. Wash and dry tomatoes, cut into quarters. Wash lettuce and dry with kitchen paper. Drain anchovy fillets, separate and roll into curls.

Place the lettuce leaves on a large serving platter, arrange all the prepared ingredients, except croûtons, attractively on top. Scatter the olives over.

To make the dressing, place the sugar, mustard, salt and pepper in a screw-top jar. Peel and crush the garlic, then add to jar with the vinegar and oil. Screw the lid on and shake vigorously.

Drizzle a little dressing over the prepared salad and serve the remainder separately. Serve the salad with the garlic croûtons and fresh crusty bread.

Handy tip

Make extra dressing then keep the remainder in a screw-top jar for up to 3 weeks in the fridge.

1. Wash French beans, trim tops and tails and cook in boiling salted water

2. Peel and crush garlic, finely chop the parsley and cut bread into cubes

3. Heat fat in frying pan, fry garlic for 2 mins, add bread cubes and parsley

4. *Make vinaigrette dressing in a screw-top jar, shake vigorously before use*

5. *Drain the tuna well, place on a plate, and gently flake into large chunks*

6. *Boil eggs, then plunge into cold water. Leave until cold, shell and quarter*

Fish Mousse

Encased in thin slices of smoked salmon, this delicious fish mousse is delicately flavoured with chives and served with a smooth nutty avocado sauce. It's the perfect start to a special dinner party or ideal for a light summer's lunch.

Calories per portion: 305 | **Serves 4**

- **6 oz/175 g white fish fillet, such as haddock or cod, skinned**
- **¼ pint/150 ml milk, or milk and water mixed together**
- **1 stick celery, trimmed**
- **2 slices onion**
- **1 small carrot, peeled**
- **1 bouquet garni**
- **6 oz/175 g smoked salmon, sliced very thinly**
- **2 tbsp freshly snipped chives**
- **¼ pint/150 ml fromage frais or low-fat natural yogurt, or single cream**
- **2 tsp gelatine**
- **salt and freshly ground black pepper**
- **1 egg white, size 3**
- **dill sprigs and lemon twists to garnish**

FOR THE SAUCE:

- **1 small ripe avocado**
- **1 tbsp lemon juice, strained**
- **3 fl oz/85 ml fromage frais or single cream**

Handy tip

In very hot weather use a little extra gelatine to ensure a good set.

Place the fish fillet in a frying pan with milk, or milk and water, celery, onion, carrot and bouquet garni. Simmer over a gentle heat for about 10 mins or until cooked. Drain, reserving fish. When cold, discard any bones and flake fish.

Meanwhile, line four ramekin dishes with slices of smoked salmon, reserving a little for the tops. Ensure the slices overlap slightly and that they come over the top a little. Cover and leave to one side.

Place the cold flaked fish in a food processor and blend until smooth. Place in a bowl and add the chives. Stir in fromage frais, yogurt or cream.

Dissolve gelatine in 1½ tbsp hot water, allow to cool slightly then stir into the mixture with salt and black pepper. Whisk egg white until stiff, fold into the mixture.

Spoon into prepared ramekins, fold salmon edges over then place reserved salmon on top to completely encase mousse. Leave in the fridge to set for at least 2 hrs.

To make the sauce, carefully peel the avocado and discard the stone. Place in a food processor with the strained lemon juice and blend until smooth. Add the fromage frais or single cream and then thoroughly blend again.

To serve, turn the fish mousses out on to individual plates. Spoon a little avocado sauce over and garnish with dill sprigs and lemon twists. Serve the remaining sauce separately. Serve the mousses with thin slices of brown bread and butter.

1. Line four individual ramekin dishes with thin slices of smoked salmon

2. Place the flaked cooked fish in a food processor and blend until smooth

3. Place the fish in a mixing bowl then add snipped and washed chives

4. Stir in the fromage frais, yogurt or cream, followed by dissolved gelatine

5. Spoon the mousse mixture into the 4 dishes lined with smoked salmon

6. Fold the edges of the salmon over, and place reserved slice on top

Lamb Kebabs

Serve up a taste of the Mediterranean with our delicious kebabs. Made from tender ground lamb, freshly chopped mint and coriander, with just a hint of lemon, they're simple to prepare and an ideal dish for a mid-week family treat.

Calories per portion: 358 | **Serves 4**

1 lb/450 g ground lean lamb
3 large spring onions
2 sprigs fresh coriander
2 sprigs fresh mint
4 oz/100 g fresh white or brown breadcrumbs
1 lemon, preferably unwaxed
salt and freshly ground black pepper
1 egg, size 3, beaten
1 tbsp sunflower oil
lemon wedges and radish roses to garnish

Handy tips

You can vary the flavour of the kebabs – try adding 2 peeled and crushed garlic cloves to the basic mixture. Replace the herbs with 1½ tsp ground coriander and 1½ tsp ground cumin, or 2 deseeded and chopped chillis and 1 tbsp chopped parsley.
You can also cook the minced lamb kebabs on a barbecue. Make as above. Once the coals have turned grey and are ready to be used, brush the kebabs lightly with oil, then cook over coals for 8-12 mins, turning as necessary.

Preheat the grill to a moderate heat 5-10 mins before cooking the kebabs.

Place the ground lamb in a large mixing bowl. Trim the root and most of the dark green top from the spring onions. Make a slit down one side and discard the outer layer of onion. Wash and dry well, then, using a pair of kitchen scissors, snip into very small pieces and add to the bowl.

Wash and dry the coriander and mint, chop finely, then add to the mixture together with the breadcrumbs. Finely grate the rind from the lemon into the bowl (use a dry pastry brush to remove the rind from the side of the grater). Stir the mixture well, then season to taste with salt and ground black pepper.

Add the egg, then mix together until all the ingredients are well distributed throughout and come together to form a ball in the centre of the bowl. Mould the mixture into small oval shapes, approx 2 in/5 cm in length (you may find it easier and less messy if you wet your hands before shaping the kebabs).

Thread the lamb on to four kebab skewers, taking care not to break up the meat, cover lightly, then chill for at least 1 hr.

Just before cooking, brush the lamb with the oil, then grill, turning frequently, for 10-15 mins, or until golden brown.

Garnish with lemon wedges and radish roses and serve on a bed of freshly cooked pasta, with a salad and warm strips of pitta bread.

1. Trim the spring onions, discard outer layer. Wash and chop the fresh herbs

2. Add onion, herbs and breadcrumbs to lamb. Grate lemon rind into bowl

3. Season, add beaten egg, then stir until mixture comes together to form a ball

4. Mould the mixture into oval shapes (wet hands slightly for easier moulding)

5. Thread lamb shapes on to kebab sticks, taking care not to break up meat

6. After chilling, place kebabs on rack lined with foil, brush with oil, then grill

MOULES A LA MARINIERE

Mussels really are delicious! They're so simple to prepare and quick to cook. And served with a creamy wine sauce, crusty bread and a glass of white wine, they make a starter that will impress friends and family.

Calories per portion: 570 | **SERVES 4**

4 lb/1.75 kg fresh mussels
1 tbsp salt
3 oz/75 g unsalted butter
3 shallots, peeled and chopped
1-2 garlic cloves, peeled and crushed
½ pint/300 ml dry white wine and ¼ pint/150 ml fish stock
½ oz/15 g freshly chopped parsley
2 sprigs fresh thyme
2 bay leaves
6 black peppercorns
1 oz/25 g plain flour
¼ pint/150 ml single cream
French bread to serve

Scrub mussels in plenty of cold water, scraping off any barnacles on the shells and removing dirt. Scrape beards off shells with a sharp knife. Discard any mussels that are open at this stage. Dissolve salt in water in a large bowl or sink, then leave mussels to soak for at least 30 mins to remove any sand or grit. (This stage is extremely important. If you don't soak the mussels, they will be gritty when you eat them.) Drain the mussels, discarding any that have now opened.

Melt 2 oz/50 g of the butter in a 4 pint/2.25 litre saucepan. Sauté the shallots and garlic for 3-5 mins, until soft and transparent but not browned. Add the wine and stock, half the parsley, the thyme, bay leaves and peppercorns. Cover and simmer for 10 mins. Strain, then add drained mussels a handful at a time to the liquid; bring to the boil. Cover with a close-fitting lid, cook over a constant heat for 3-5 mins, shaking the pan occasionally or until the mussels have opened. Now discard any which remain shut. Drain, reserving liquid.

Discard top half of shells, place mussels in tureen or serving dish, keep warm while finishing sauce.

Pour the liquid into a clean pan and boil rapidly until reduced by half.

Cream the remaining butter with the flour, then, using a balloon whisk, whisk small knobs of the butter and flour into the liquid. Cook, whisking throughout until the sauce is thick. Add remaining parsley with cream and season.

Pour over mussels and serve immediately with crusty bread and a glass of white wine.

HANDY TIP

Mussels are highly nutritious, rich in mineral salts, iron, vitamins A,B,C,D and protein, but they need to be bought and eaten the same day, as they quickly go bad.

1. Place mussels in plenty of salted water. Scrub to remove dirt

2. Using a small, sharp knife, scrape off barnacles and discard beards

3. Sauté the shallots and garlic, add wine, stock, bay leaves and remaining herbs

4. Add mussels to the liquid a few at a time. Cover with a close-fitting lid

5. Pull mussels apart, discarding top shells, and keep warm while making sauce

6. Whisk the butter-and-flour paste, in small knobs, into the boiling liquid

Dressed Crab

This impressive dish is ideal for a light summer's lunch, served with a selection of salads and a glass of chilled white wine, or as a starter for a dinner party. And just because it looks impressive don't think it's difficult to make.

Calories per portion: 254 | **Serves 4**

2 crabs, approx 1½ lb/675 g each, cooked
2 eggs, size 5
salt and freshly ground black pepper
1 oz/25 g fresh brown breadcrumbs
juice of 1 lemon
curly endive to garnish

Crabs are normally sold ready cooked but when buying, test the weight of them in relation to their size. Avoid any that feel light, as this may mean they have recently shed their shells and have little flesh.

Wash the crab well under cold running water before starting. This prevents any pieces of dirt getting into the flesh. When preparing the crab, place shell upside down on a work surface with the underside facing you. Then remove the claws from the body by twisting against the direction the large claws or pincers are facing, followed by the eight legs. Reserve.

To open the shell twist off the bony tail, then insert a sharp, rigid knife between the main shell and underside. Twist and pull them apart. From the underside piece, discard the dead men's fingers or gills (these are soft greyish and elongated). Then discard the stomach sac which is bag-like and slightly furry. The rest of the crab flesh is edible.

Cut the underside portion in half then using a skewer, prise out the white flesh from all the crevices. Place in a bowl. Then take the shell and scoop out the dark meat, keeping it separate from the white meat. If the crab has a lot of roe this can be mixed in with the dark meat.

Using a rolling pin gently crack open the large pincers, extract the meat with a skewer and flake finely. Put with rest of white meat.

Around the empty shell you'll notice a thin line running about ¼ in/6 mm from the edge. Using the handle of a wooden spoon or the tip of a rolling pin, carefully tap to remove the thin shell outside the groove. Wash the shell and oil lightly. Reserve.

Meanwhile, boil the eggs for 10 mins, plunge in to cold water, then leave until cold. Flake the white crab flesh and mix with salt and pepper to taste. Mix the brown breadcrumbs into the dark meat with 1-2 tbsp lemon juice.

Arrange the white flesh into each side of the cleaned shells with the dark meat in the centre. Remove shells from eggs, sieve yolk and finely chop white. Arrange in straight lines in between the dark and white meat.

Place on serving platter and garnish with endive. Carefully arrange the smaller claws around it and then decorate with lemon twists. Serve with thinly sliced brown bread and butter.

HANDY TIP

Keep the shells afterwards as they make attractive dishes for starters. Wash well after each use.

1. Place the crab, shell side down, flat on a board, then carefully twist off the claws or pincers, then the legs

2. Insert a sharp, strong knife between main shell and underside, twist then pull free

3. Discard dead men's fingers or gills (shown left on board) from underside of crab

4. Discard stomach sac, cut underside in half, using a skewer prise out flesh

5. Scoop out the dark meat from the shell and keep separate from the white

6. Crack the larger claws with a clean rolling pin and extract all the meat

CHEESE SOUFFLE

Does your heart sink when you think of making a soufflé? Follow this step-by-step guide and it will turn out perfect every time. It really is as light as a feather – and great for supper or as a starter for a dinner party.

Calories per portion: 401 | **SERVES 4**

2 oz/50 g butter or margarine
2 oz/50 g flour
7 fl oz/200 ml milk, warmed
4 eggs, size 3, separated
salt and freshly ground black pepper
4 oz/100 g mature Cheddar cheese, finely grated
1 tsp ready-made mustard, optional

Set oven to Gas 4, 350°F, 180°C, and place a baking sheet in the oven to heat through. (Putting the soufflé on to a hot baking sheet will help it to rise.) Lightly grease a 6 in/15 cm soufflé dish.

Melt the butter or margarine in a saucepan, stir in the flour and cook for 2 mins until the mixture forms a ball in the centre of the pan. Remove from the heat and gradually stir in the milk, beating well between each addition. Return the pan to the heat and cook for 3 mins, stirring throughout or until the mixture thickens.

Allow to cool slightly, add the egg yolks one at a time, beating well between each addition. Add seasoning, cheese and mustard, if using.

Whisk egg whites with a pinch of salt until stiff and standing in peaks, carefully fold into the cheese mixture. Pour the mixture into the soufflé dish and place in the oven on the hot baking sheet. Cook for 50-60 mins or until well risen and golden brown. Serve immediately.

HANDY TIP

Once you've tried and enjoyed a cheese soufflé, ring the changes by varying the ingredients. Keep the method the same, but omit the cheese and instead add to the cooked white sauce 4 oz/100 g cooked finely-flaked smoked cod or haddock from which you have discarded all the bones and skin, with 1 tbsp freshly chopped parsley. Or try replacing 2 oz/50 g of the cheese with 3 oz/75 g cooked and finely chopped mushrooms which have been thoroughly drained.

1. Melt butter in the pan, stir in flour and cook over a gentle heat

2. Gradually add the milk, beating well between each addition until thickened

3. Cool slightly, add egg yolks one at a time, then add cheese and seasoning

4. Whisk egg whites until stiff and standing in peaks – a pinch of salt helps

5. Fold egg whites into the cooled mixture a little at a time. Do not over mix

6. Spoon mixture into greased soufflé dish and lightly tap the dish to level top

CHICKEN GUMBO

Spice up your meal-times with this delicious Cajun dish, full of tender chicken, sausages and vegetables, and seasoned with chillis, Tabasco, paprika and ground peppers. Serve it with rice to soak up the sauce and treat the family to a tasty change.

Calories per portion: 735 | **SERVES 8**

- **2 x 2 lb/900 g corn-fed oven-ready chickens**
- **3½ tsp salt**
- **2 tsp paprika pepper**
- **2 tsp freshly ground black pepper**
- **1½ tsp freshly ground white pepper**
- **5 tbsp oil**
- **2 onions**
- **2 red peppers**
- **2-4 chillis (amount depends on how hot you like your food)**
- **3 sticks of celery**
- **8 oz/225 g okra**
- **2 tbsp flour or filé powder**
- **4 pints/2.25 litres chicken stock**
- **3 smoked pork sausages or Italian or Spanish sausages**
- **1 bunch of spring onions**
- **¼-½ tsp Tabasco sauce**
- **1 tbsp freshly chopped parsley**
- **8 oz/225 g long-grain rice, freshly cooked**

HANDY TIPS

Gumbos vary from area to area and there is no hard and fast rule – you can vary the ingredients according to personal taste and availability of produce.

Many gumbos contain okra, but you can still make it without them. Filé powder is a Cajun thickening agent.

Wash and dry the chickens, then, using a large sharp knife, cut each one into eight portions. Wash and dry again. Mix together salt and peppers, sprinkle half over the chicken portions. Reserve the remainder.

Heat 4 tbsp oil in a frying pan, sauté the chicken in batches until browned, then drain on kitchen paper. Peel and finely chop onions. Deseed the peppers and chillis, and chop finely. Trim, wash and chop the celery and okra.

Heat the remaining oil in a pan, then sauté half of the prepared vegetables for 10 mins, or until they are softened. Sprinkle in the flour or filé powder and cook gently for a further 15 mins, or until the mixture is golden brown. Reserve.

Place the stock and remaining prepared vegetables in a large saucepan, bring to the boil, then stir in remaining salt and peppers mixture. Cut sausages into chunks, then add to the saucepan with the browned chicken and simmer gently for 1½ hrs. Add the reserved vegetables and cook for a further 25 mins. Skim off any fat that rises to the surface. Trim, wash and chop the spring onions, then add to the saucepan with Tabasco sauce to taste. Cook for 10-15 mins.

Transfer the gumbo to a serving dish or tureen and sprinkle with chopped parsley. Divide freshly cooked rice equally between individual serving dishes and spoon the chicken gumbo over the top of each. Serve with freshly baked corn or crusty bread.

1. Wash and dry chickens, then, using a sharp knife, cut each into eight portions

2. Mix together salt and peppers, sprinkle half over chicken portions and sauté

3. Peel and chop onions. Chop peppers, chillis and prepared celery and okra

4. Place stock and half the vegetables in a pan, stir in reserved seasonings

5. Add the sausages and chicken to the pan, then simmer gently for 1½ hrs

6. Add reserved vegetables to pan, cook for a further 25 mins, then skim off fat

BEEFBURGERS

Give the kids a treat with these delicious home-made beefburgers. By preparing the beef yourself, you can guarantee they are lean – and, served with our chilli'n'tomato ketchup, they're great.

Calories per portion: 391 **SERVES 4**

FOR THE CHILLI'N'TOMATO KETCHUP:
1 small onion
1 garlic clove
8 oz/225 g ripe tomatoes
½ green pepper
1-2 red chillis
1 tbsp tomato purée
1 tbsp white wine vinegar
1 tsp ground cloves
1 tbsp clear honey
FOR THE BURGERS:
1 lb/450 g lean beef, such as topside
2 onions
1 egg, size 3, beaten
salt and freshly ground black pepper
2 tbsp oil
4 baps
few lettuce leaves

Preheat the grill 10 mins before grilling the burgers. To make the chilli'n'tomato ketchup, peel and finely chop the onion, then peel and crush the garlic clove. Peel the tomatoes, then deseed and chop roughly. Deseed and finely chop the green pepper.

Place chopped onion, garlic, tomatoes and pepper in a small pan. Deseed the chillis and chop finely. (When handling the chillis, take care not to touch your face – especially your eyes and mouth. Wash hands thoroughly after preparing the chillis.) Add the chillis, tomato purée, vinegar and cloves to the pan, then place over a gentle heat and stir in the honey. Bring to the boil, then reduce the heat, cover and leave to simmer gently for 40 mins, or until mixture forms the consistency of chutney.

Meanwhile, prepare the beefburgers. Trim beef, discarding any fat or gristle. Cut meat into thick strips, then dice into small pieces. Using two large sharp knives, and working the knives as though you are beating a drum, chop meat finely (alternatively, pass it through a mincer). Peel and chop one onion, place in a mixing bowl and add meat and beaten egg. Season to taste. Mix well, then, using your hands, shape into burgers (you may find it easier if your hands are slightly wet).

Lightly brush the burgers with a little oil, cook under a preheated grill for 3-4 mins, or until sealed. Turn burgers over, brush again with a little oil and grill for 3 mins. Continue to cook the burgers for 5-6 mins, or until cooked.

Peel and slice the remaining onion, fry gently in remaining oil for 5-8 mins. Drain. Split baps in half and toast lightly.

Sandwich lettuce, cooked burgers, onion and a little ketchup between the baps. Serve with remaining ketchup, chips, dill cucumbers and coleslaw.

HANDY TIP

Make burgers and cook as above, then top with one slice of drained pineapple and one slice of cheese, cook under preheated grill until golden brown.

1. Place onion, garlic, tomatoes and pepper in pan. Deseed and chop chillis

2. Place pan over a gentle heat, stir in honey. Reduce heat, cover and simmer

3. Trim beef, discarding any fat or gristle, cut the meat into thick strips and dice

4. Using two sharp knives, work them as though beating a drum, chop meat

5. Place the chopped onion and the prepared meat in a mixing bowl. Season

6. Using slightly wet hands, shape the minced beef into burgers before grilling

ONION TART

Deliciously crisp, light pastry, sweet-tasting onions and a rich creamy filling flavoured with Gruyère cheese, make this great French dish the ideal light lunch or supper for all the family. Serve it hot or cold with a fresh mixed salad and crusty bread.

Calories per portion: 328 — **SERVES 8**

FOR THE PASTRY:
8 oz/225 g plain white flour
pinch of salt
2 oz/50 g butter or margarine
2 oz/50 g white vegetable fat
FOR THE FILLING:
12 oz/350 g onions
1 bunch of spring onions
1 oz/25 g butter or margarine
3 eggs, size 3
¼ pint/150 ml single cream
salt and freshly ground black pepper
1 oz/25 g Gruyère cheese

Preheat the oven to Gas 6, 400°F, 200°C, 15 mins before baking the pastry. Sieve the flour and salt into a mixing bowl. Cut the fats into small cubes and add to the bowl. Using your fingertips, lightly rub the fats into the flour until the mixture resembles fine breadcrumbs. Mix to a firm but pliable dough with about 4 tbsp cold water. Turn out of bowl and knead lightly on a floured surface until the pastry is smooth and free of any cracks. Wrap in greaseproof paper and chill in the fridge for 30 mins.

Roll the chilled pastry out on a lightly floured surface and, using the rolling pin to help you lift it, line a 9 in/23 cm loose-bottomed flan or quiche tin. Roll the pin across top to remove any excess pastry. Place a sheet of tin foil over the pastry, then cover with baking beans and bake blind in the oven for 10 mins.

Remove paper and beans from the pastry case and continue to cook for a further 5 mins. Remove from oven, then reduce oven temperature to Gas 4, 350°F, 180°C.

Peel and thinly slice the onions. Trim, wash and chop the spring onions. Melt the fat in a frying pan, then gently sauté the onions for 8-10 mins, or until soft and transparent. Add the spring onions and continue to cook for a further 2 mins. Drain well, then arrange in the cooked pastry case.

Beat together the eggs, cream and seasoning, then pour over the onions. Finely grate the cheese and sprinkle over the top, then return the tart to the oven. Cook for 25-30 mins, or until the filling has set and the pastry is a golden brown.

Serve hot or cold with some extra grated cheese, crusty bread and a mixed salad.

HANDY TIP

As an alternative,try using 8 oz/225 g leeks instead of the spring onions, adding 4 oz/100 g streaky bacon, derinded and chopped, to the onions.

1. Chill the prepared pastry for 30 mins in the fridge. Roll out the pastry then, using the rolling pin to help lift it, line the tin

2. Roll the pin across the top to remove any excess pastry, then cover with tin foil and baking beans, bake blind

3. Peel and thinly slice the onions. Trim the spring onions, then wash and chop them

4. *Melt fat in frying pan then gently sauté onions and spring onions, drain well, then arrange in cooked pastry case*

5. *Beat together the eggs, cream and seasoning, then gently pour over the cooked onions*

6. *Finely grate the cheese, sprinkle over the top and cook until filling has set and the pastry is golden*

TORTELLONI

Treat them to a classic taste of Italy with this delicious pasta dish. Filled with spinach and cheese, then covered with a super, fresh tomato sauce, it's a main meal the whole family will love – and it's perfect for vegetarians, too.

Calories per portion: 948 | **SERVES 4**

FOR THE PASTA DOUGH:
1 lb/450 g strong plain flour
½ tsp salt
6 eggs, size 1
2-3 tbsp olive oil
FOR THE SPINACH FILLING:
1 garlic clove, peeled and crushed
12 oz/350 g fresh spinach, prepared, cooked and finely chopped
6 oz/175 g ricotta cheese
1½ oz/40 g Parmesan cheese, grated
2 eggs, size 5
salt and freshly ground black pepper
1 tsp grated nutmeg
FOR THE TOMATO SAUCE:
1 lb/450 g ripe tomatoes
2 tbsp olive oil
1 onion, peeled and chopped
1 garlic clove, peeled and crushed
2 sticks celery, trimmed and finely chopped
2 tbsp tomato purée
basil sprigs
¼ pint/150 ml white wine or vegetable stock
1 tbsp cornflour

To make the pasta dough, place the flour on a clean working surface, make a well in the centre and add the salt, eggs and olive oil. Gradually mix the flour into the eggs and oil until the mixture forms a stiff but pliable dough, then knead until smooth and elastic. This will take about 5-10 mins. Cover with a clean cloth and leave to relax for 1 hr. Meanwhile, mix together filling ingredients in a large bowl and leave covered until ready to use.

To make the sauce, peel the tomatoes then chop roughly. Heat the oil, then sauté onion, garlic and celery for 5 mins. Add chopped tomatoes and cook for a further 10 mins. Stir in the tomato purée, basil (reserving a few sprigs for garnishing), and wine or stock. Season. Cook for a further 10 mins. Pass through a blender until smooth, then return to the rinsed pan. Just before using, blend the cornflour with 2 tbsp water, stir into sauce. Heat until thickened. Keep warm.

To prepare the tortelli, thinly roll out the pasta dough and cut out 2½ in/6.5 cm circles. Place 1 tsp prepared spinach filling in the centre of each pasta circle. Dampen edges, then fold over to form a half-moon. Gently curve each piece into a ring and pinch ends together, ensuring shape remains curled. Lay the tortelli apart on a clean, lightly floured tea towel. Leave to dry for a few minutes.

Cook the pasta in boiling, salted water for 5 mins, or until cooked. Drain well. Mix into the prepared tomato sauce, then serve right away with a side salad, garnished with reserved basil.

HANDY TIP

Add 1 tsp of olive oil to the water when cooking the tortelli to prevent them sticking together.

1. Mix together all the filling ingredients, then leave covered until ready to use

2. Carefully cut out 2½ in/6.5 cm circles from the thinly rolled-out pasta dough

3. Place 1 tsp prepared spinach filling in the centre of each pasta circle

4. Dampen edges of pasta, then fold to form a half-moon shape. Pinch edges

5. Gently curve each pasta piece into a ring until the two ends are touching

6. Pinch the ends firmly together, then leave to dry on a clean tea towel

Kedgeree

Moist, succulent chunks of salmon and smoked haddock, gently poached in white wine and herbs, then mixed with rice and lightly sautéed onion. Kedgeree is a delicious dish, ideal for an informal supper, brunch, or as a starter.

Calories per portion: 382 | **Serves 6**

2 eggs, size 3
6 oz/175 g long-grain rice
1 salmon tail, approx 1 lb/450 g in weight
few parsley stalks
2-3 bay leaves
2 onions, peeled
¼ pint/150 ml white wine or fish stock
8 oz/225 g undyed smoked haddock
4 oz/100 g butter
1-2 tsp curry powder, or to taste
salt and freshly ground black pepper
sprigs of fresh coriander or parsley to garnish

Allow the eggs to stand at room temperature for 30 mins. Bring a pan of water to the boil, then gently place the eggs into the water. Bring back to the boil, then cook eggs gently for 10 mins. Remove from the heat, drain, then place under cold running water. Leave in cold water until required.

Cook the rice in a saucepan of fast boiling salted water for 12-15 mins, or until just cooked. Drain and rinse under cold water. Reserve.

Descale the salmon and wash thoroughly. Place in a frying pan with the parsley stalks and bay leaves. Slice one onion, add to pan, pour in the white wine or stock and ½ pint/300 ml water. Bring to the boil, cover, then simmer gently for 10 mins, or until the fish is cooked. Remove from the pan and drain, reserving cooking liquid.

Wash smoked haddock, place in clean frying pan with more parsley stalks, bay leaves and the reserved liquid. Cook as before for 10 mins. Drain. When the salmon and haddock are cool enough to handle, discard the skin and bones and flake the flesh into large chunks.

Melt the butter in a clean pan. Peel and finely chop remaining onion, then cook in the melted butter for 5 mins. Add curry powder and cook for 2 mins. Add reserved rice and chunks of fish.

Heat through, stirring until piping hot. Shell the hard-boiled eggs and slice thinly. Add to the kedgeree, with salt and pepper to taste. Stir well, then pile kedgeree on to a warmed serving dish and garnish with sprigs of fresh coriander or parsley. Serve hot.

Handy tips

You can vary the fish according to your budget and, if you prefer, you can use just one type of fish. Remember that fish doesn't keep for very long, so if necessary, freeze it straight after buying it (as long as it hasn't been frozen before) and thaw just before using. Never keep cooked fish – it should always be used on the day it's cooked.

1. Cook rice in boiling salted water, drain, rinse under cold water. Reserve

2. Poach salmon in wine and water with parsley, bay leaves and onion for 10 mins

3. Fry the chopped onion in melted butter for 5 mins. Stir in curry powder

4. Remove the salmon skin, remove flesh from bones, flake into large chunks

5. Add the flaked, cooked, smoked haddock to rice and mix thoroughly

6. Mix in salmon, add salt and freshly ground pepper. Heat thoroughly

Spanish Omelette

This version has got to be the most famous of all omelettes... using mainly potato and onion, it's so tasty and filling. Serve it tapas style in small squares for a super family snack, or make a meal of it with salad and crusty bread.

Calories per portion: 172 **Serves 6**

1 lb/450 g potatoes
2 red peppers
1 green pepper
1 large Spanish onion
2-3 garlic cloves
12 oz/350 g ripe tomatoes
2-3 tbsp olive oil
8 eggs, size 3
salt and freshly ground black pepper
1 tbsp freshly chopped oregano

Peel the potatoes then cook them in boiling salted water until tender. Drain well and reserve.

Wash and dry the peppers, trim the tops, discard seeds and the membrane inside. Slice thinly, place in boiling water for 3 mins, drain and reserve. Peel the onion, slice thinly. Peel and then crush the garlic cloves.

Make a small cross on the stalk end of each tomato, place in a small bowl, cover with boiling water, leave for 2 mins, drain then skin. Cut each tomato into quarters, discard the core and seeds, then chop and reserve.

Heat olive oil in a large, heavy-based frying pan. Add the sliced onion and crushed garlic, then fry gently, stirring frequently until the onions are soft and transparent and just beginning to turn golden.

Dice the cooled potatoes into

¼ in/6 mm cubes. Add to the frying pan with the reserved, blanched peppers, and continue to cook for a further 2 mins. Stir in the chopped, skinned tomatoes.

Beat the eggs with 2 tbsp cold water and salt and pepper. Pour into the pan, then cook for 3-4 mins over a moderately high heat. This will allow the egg to set lightly on the bottom.

Using a spatula gently push the set egg from round the outside edge of the frying pan to the centre. Lower the heat slightly then continue to cook, gently pushing the egg to the centre until it is completely set. As you are gently stirring, make sure that you keep the vegetables evenly distributed throughout the omelette.

Once the omelette is set, place under a preheated grill to lightly brown the top and to ensure that the omelette is completely set in the centre.

Serve cut into wedges sprinkled with the oregano.

1. Wash and dry the peppers, trim the tops, discard insides and slice thinly. Place in boiling water for 3 mins

2. Heat olive oil in a large heavy-based frying pan, add sliced onion and crushed garlic and fry gently

3. Add the cubed potatoes and sliced peppers to the frying pan and cook for a further 2 mins

4. Beat eggs with 2 tbsp water and seasoning. Add to pan and cook for 3-4 mins

5. Lower the heat and push the egg to the centre until it is completely set

6. Once omelette is set, place under a preheated grill to lightly brown top

HANDY TIPS

While cooking, take care that the heat is not too fierce, otherwise the bottom of the omelette may burn slightly. If liked, Spanish sausage, salchica or chorizo can be diced and added to the omelette, along with the potatoes and peppers. Marjoram may be substituted for the oregano.

Pasties

Originating in Cornwall, these pasties make a delicious and nutritious snack. Made from tender pieces of meat, potato, carrot and onion, they're encased in a light pastry. Serve hot or cold to satisfy the biggest of appetites.

Calories per portion: 778 **Serves 8**

FOR THE PASTRY:
1½ lb/675 g plain white flour
½ tsp salt
6 oz/175 g butter or half-fat polyunsaturated margarine
6 oz/175 g white vegetable fat
FOR THE FILLING:
2 sticks celery
6 oz/175 g potatoes
3 oz/75 g carrots
3 oz/75 g turnip or swede
1 oz/25 g butter or margarine
2 tbsp oil
12 oz/350 g braising steak
salt and freshly ground black pepper
4 fl oz/120 ml beef or vegetable stock
1-2 tsp mixed herbs, optional
1 egg, size 3, beaten

Preheat oven to Gas 6, 400°F, 200°C. Sift flour and salt into mixing bowl then rub in butter or margarine and vegetable fat until mixture resembles fine breadcrumbs. Mix to a soft and pliable dough, with 8 tbsp cold water. Turn the dough out on to a lightly floured surface and knead gently until smooth. Wrap and chill for 30 mins.

Meanwhile, wash the celery and chop into ¼ in/6 mm dice. Peel the potatoes, carrots and turnip or swede. Cut into ¼ in/6 mm dice.

Melt the fat with 1 tbsp oil in a frying pan, and cook the diced vegetables gently for 5-8 mins or until softened but not browned. Drain and reserve.

Trim the steak, discarding any fat or gristle and cut into ½ in/1.25 cm pieces.

Heat remaining oil and fry the meat, stirring occasionally until browned all over. Continue to cook gently for 10 mins. Place the meat in a mixing bowl with vegetables, season to taste.

Moisten with the stock then mix in the herbs if using. Cover the filling and allow to cool completely.

Roll out the pastry on a lightly floured surface and cut into eight 7 in/18 cm circles. Dampen the edges with cold water and place 2 tbsp of the prepared filling in the centre of each circle. Fold over in a half moon shape and pinch edges firmly together. Using the thumb and finger, roll the edge over to give a rope effect.

Place on a lightly greased baking tray and brush with the beaten egg. Bake in the oven for 15 mins then brush again with the egg. Reduce the oven temperature to Gas 4, 350°F, 180°C, and continue to cook for a further 20-25 mins or until golden brown. Serve hot or cold with a selection of vegetables or a salad. These pasties will freeze very well.

HANDY TIP

The rope effect is traditional and comes from olden days when Cornish miners would take their pasties down the mines. In those days the pasties were larger, with a savoury filling at one end and a sweet filling at the other. The miners held the pasty by the rope of pastry to eat and then discarded the rope after eating the pasty. This meant they didn't have to come above ground to wash their hands before eating.

1. Cut vegetables into ¼ in/6 mm dice, then fry in oil and butter for 5-8 mins

2. Cut the steak into ½ in/1.25 cm pieces and fry in the oil until browned

3. Roll pastry out on a lightly floured surface, cut out eight 7 in/18 cm circles

4. Dampen edges of circles and place 2 tbsp of prepared filling in the centre

5. Pinch edges together. Using forefinger and thumb, roll edge for rope effect

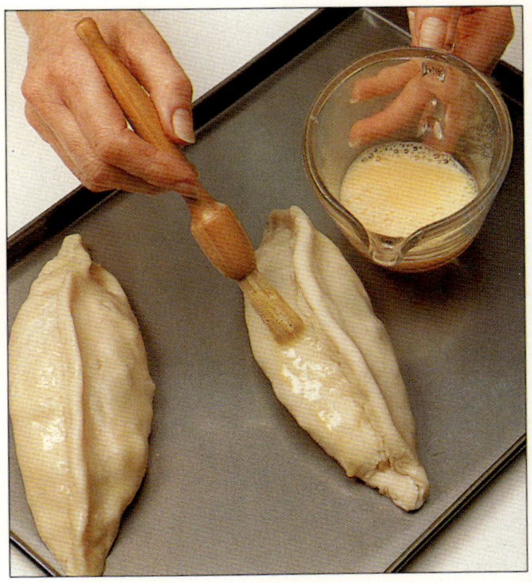

6. Brush pasties with egg. Bake, brushing with egg halfway through cooking

FISHCAKES

Succulent flakes of fish mixed with creamy mashed potatoes and subtly flavoured with lemon and coriander. Served with mixed vegetables, they make a delicious and nourishing supper dish that the whole family will enjoy.

Calories per portion: 249 **MAKES 8**

1½ lb/675 g fresh fish fillets, such as undyed smoked haddock, cod or whiting
½ pint/300 ml semi-skimmed milk
2 bay leaves
1 medium lemon
1½ lb/675 g potatoes
1 oz/25 g butter or margarine
salt and freshly ground black pepper
1 tsp anchovy essence
1 tbsp freshly chopped coriander or parsley
2 eggs, size 3
4 oz/100 g fresh white breadcrumbs
oil for shallow frying
TO GARNISH:
lemon slices
fresh coriander sprigs

Wash fish, place in a large frying pan with the milk and bay leaves.

Using a zester or grater, remove rind from the lemon and add to pan. Poach the fish gently for 10 mins, or until cooked. Drain, reserving 2-3 tbsp of the poaching liquid. Allow the fish to cool, then discard skin and bones. Flake flesh.

Meanwhile, peel potatoes, cut into chunks, then cook in boiling salted water for 15 mins, or until soft. Drain, then mash with the fat and enough reserved poaching liquid to form a smooth mash. Season with salt and pepper to taste.

Add the flaked fish to the potato, then the anchovy essence and chopped coriander or parsley. Mix well, cover and chill until cold.

Shape into eight 3 in/7.5 cm wide x 1½ in/4 cm deep fishcakes. It may be easier to dust your hands and the work surface lightly with a little flour to prevent the mixture sticking to your hands or the work surface. Place mixture on a baking sheet and cover, then chill until firm.

Beat the eggs, place in a bowl or shallow dish. Dip the fishcakes first in the egg, then in the breadcrumbs. Ensure fishcakes are completely coated.

Heat the oil in a large frying pan to a depth of about 1 in/2.5cm. Carefully cook the fishcakes, a few at a time, for 4-5 minutes on both sides, or until golden brown, crisp and well cooked. Drain on absorbent kitchen paper.

Garnish the fishcakes with lemon twists and sprigs of fresh coriander. Serve piping hot with mixed vegetables.

HANDY TIP

Eat the fishcakes the day they're made. Otherwise, freeze them, interleaved with waxed paper, before frying. Allow to thaw before cooking.

1. Place fish in large frying pan with the milk, bay leaves and lemon rind

2. Add the flaked fish flesh to the freshly mashed potatoes and mix well

3. Add the anchovy essence – measure accurately, as it has a strong flavour

4. *Shape the fish mixture into eight cakes, each 3 in/7.5 cm wide x 1½ in/4 cm deep*

5. *Dip chilled fishcakes into beaten egg, then coat in fresh breadcrumbs*

6. *Shallow fry the fishcakes, a few at a time, for 4-5 mins on each side*

Pizza Margherita

This pizza has a light crisp base and is topped with tomatoes and basil, creamy mozzarella cheese, anchovies and olives. It's easy to make and ideal for supper or a light lunch for the whole family.

Calories per portion: 585 | **Serves 4**

- **1 lb/450 g strong plain white flour**
- **½ tsp salt**
- **½ oz/15 g easy-blend dried yeast**
- **2 tsp sugar**
- **2 tsp oil**
- **14 oz/397 g can chopped tomatoes**
- **1 small onion, peeled and finely grated**
- **1 tbsp freshly chopped basil or 1 tsp dried basil**
- **2 large tomatoes**
- **2 oz/50 g can anchovy fillets**
- **3 tbsp milk**
- **salt and freshly ground black pepper**
- **6 oz/175 g mozzarella cheese, sliced**
- **black olives**
- **few basil leaves to garnish**

Preheat oven to Gas 8, 450°F, 230°C, 15 mins before baking pizza. Sift flour and salt in a large mixing bowl. Stir in yeast and sugar. Mix to a soft and pliable dough with ½ pint/300 ml warm water. Knead on a lightly floured surface until smooth. Place in a clean, lightly oiled bowl. Cover with a cloth or clearwrap and leave in a warm place until doubled in size. This will take approx 1 hr.

Turn risen dough onto lightly floured surface and knead again for 5 mins. Roll out to a 9 in/23 cm circle, place on a lightly greased baking sheet. Pinch up edge to form a ½ in/1.25 cm rim.

Purée the canned tomatoes and, if preferred, sieve to remove seeds. Place in bowl with the grated onion and chopped basil. Slice the fresh tomatoes. Soak anchovy fillets in milk for 5 mins.

Spread the puréed tomato mixture over the base and top with the sliced tomato. Season. Arrange the cheese over the tomatoes. Drain the anchovy fillets and arrange in a lattice over the cheese and top with olives.

Bake in oven for 20-25 mins or until the pizza crust is golden, and cheese melted and bubbly. Garnish with basil leaves. Cut into wedges, serve immediately with a tossed salad and a red Italian wine like Chianti Classico.

Handy Tips

You can make two or three pizza bases and freeze for use later. Soaking the anchovies in milk removes any excess salt from them. Vary the topping by adding sliced salami or ham over the tomatoes, then top with sliced mushrooms and peppers before adding the cheese, anchovies and olives.

1. Sift flour into bowl, add salt, yeast and sugar, mix to a dough with water and oil

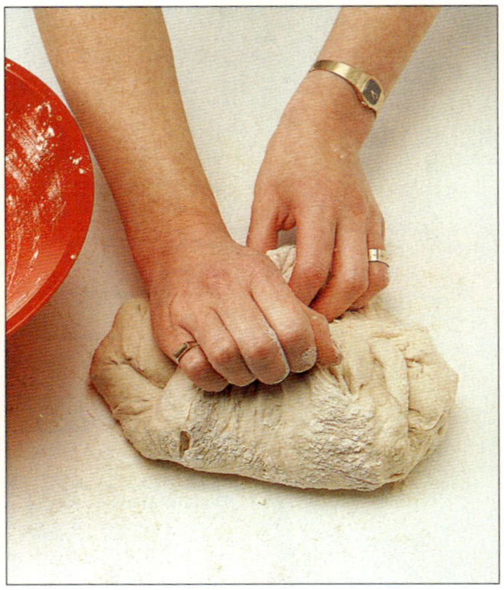

2. Knead dough on lightly floured surface until smooth and pliable. Leave to rest

3. When risen, knead, then roll out on lightly floured surface to 9 in/23 cm round

4. Place on lightly greased baking sheet and pinch up edge to ½ in/1.25 cm

5. Spread puréed tomato over base to ½ in/1.25 cm from edge. Top with tomatoes

6. Arrange sliced mozzarella over tomatoes, then anchovies. Top with olives

Meatloaf

So simple to make, this dish is delicious served hot with a chunky home-made tomato sauce, jacket baked potato and freshly cooked cabbage, or try it cold with a mixed salad. Either way, it's ideal for lunch or as a supper-time dish.

Calories per portion: 560 **Serves 6**

2 onions
2 tbsp oil
1 lb/450 g lean minced beef
1 lb/450 g lean minced lamb
1-2 garlic cloves
2 tsp paprika pepper
2-3 tbsp freshly chopped mixed herbs, such as rosemary, oregano and parsley
4 tbsp tomato purée
salt and freshly ground black pepper
6 oz/175 g fresh white or brown breadcrumbs
2 eggs, size 3

FOR THE TOMATO SAUCE:

1 lb/450 g ripe tomatoes
1 onion
1 tbsp oil
1-2 tbsp tomato purée (optional)
¼ pint/150 ml chicken or vegetable stock
1 tsp sugar
1 tbsp freshly chopped basil
salt and freshly ground black pepper

Preheat oven to Gas 4, 350°F, 180°C. Peel the onions and chop. Heat the oil in a frying pan then fry the onions for about 5 mins until soft and transparent. Drain well on absorbent kitchen paper and cool.

Place the minced meats into a large bowl then add the cooled, drained onion. Peel and crush the garlic, add to the mixture together with the paprika, chopped fresh herbs, tomato purée, salt and freshly ground black pepper and breadcrumbs. Mix well together. Beat the eggs then add to mixture. Mix well.

Pack into a 2 lb/900 g loaf tin, packing the mixture well down in the tin, both in the corners and sides of tin.

Cover with tin foil and place in a roasting tin half filled with boiling water. Cook for 1½-2 hrs or until cooked. Uncover for last ½ hr of cooking. (The meatloaf is cooked when the meat starts to shrink away from the sides of the tin.) Allow to cool for 5-10 mins before turning out.

Garnish top of meatloaf with sprigs of fresh herbs.

To make sauce, make a cross at the stalk end of the tomatoes. Place in a large bowl of boiling water. Leave for 2 mins, drain, peel and chop.

Peel onion and roughly chop. Heat the oil in a small pan then fry onion for 5 mins. Add the chopped tomatoes, tomato purée, stock, sugar, basil and seasoning. Cook gently for 10-15 mins or until the sauce is thick. Serve hot with the meatloaf.

If liked use two 1 lb/450 g loaf tins. Cook for 1 hr or until cooked. Cool and freeze one for later.

Handy tip

The meatloaf is ideal to slice and use in lunch boxes – cool quickly and store for up to two days, well covered, in the fridge.

1. Fry the chopped onion in the oil until soft and transparent, drain well

2. Mix the cooled, drained onion with minced beef and lamb in a large bowl

3. Mix all the other ingredients into the bowl then add beaten egg and stir well

4. Pack the meat mixture into the loaf tin. Press well into the sides and corners

5. Place tomatoes in a bowl of boiling water then peel. Peel onion, chop roughly

6. Just before serving, heat the prepared tomato sauce then season to taste

Pork Pie

Succulent pieces of lean pork with a subtle blend of aromatic spices, encased in crisp pastry – this classic pork pie is delicious. It's perfect for a picnic or a party. And it's a good standby for a quick supper dish too.

Calories per portion: 594 | **Serves 8**

2 lb/900 g boneless pork
½ level tsp cayenne pepper
1½ level tsp ground ginger
1 level tsp ground mace
1 tbsp freshly chopped parsley
1 tbsp freshly chopped coriander
½ level tsp salt
freshly ground black pepper
5 oz/150 g lard
½ pint/300 ml milk and water
1 lb/450 g plain flour
¼ pint/150 ml stock
1 egg, size 5, beaten
½ oz/15 g gelatine

Preheat oven to Gas 7, 425°F, 220°.

Trim pork, cut into ¼ in/6 mm cubes. Mix with the spices, herbs and the seasoning. Cover and leave on one side while preparing the pastry.

Melt the lard in the milk and water over medium heat. Sift the flour into a large mixing bowl and make a well in the centre. Pour in the lard and mix with a wooden spoon until the flour is fully incorporated. Continue to mix until cool enough to handle then knead until smooth. Cut off a third for the lid and leave covered in the bowl.

Roll out the pastry on a lightly floured surface and use to line a fluted raised pork pie tin or an 8 in/20.5 cm loose-bottomed, round cake tin. Bring sides of the pastry up to top of the tin.

Spoon the prepared pork filling into the pastry-lined tin, packing it down firmly with the back of a spoon. Pour in 3 tbsp of the stock.

Roll out remaining pastry for a lid, reserve trimmings. Brush the top edge of the pie with beaten egg and place lid in position, pressing edges firmly together. Roll out the trimmings and cut out four leaves. Place leaves in position. Brush with egg.

Make a small hole in the centre of the pie to allow the steam to escape.

Place in oven on the centre shelf and cook for 30 mins. Lower temperature to Gas 4, 350°F, 180°C, and cook for a further 1½-2 hrs. Cover the top loosely with foil halfway during cooking.

When cooked, remove and allow to cool. Dissolve gelatine in remaining stock, cool then carefully pour into pie. Leave overnight in fridge.

HANDY TIP

If using a loose-bottomed cake tin: when ready to serve, place tin on a clean can then gently ease cake tin away.

1. Cut pork into ¼ in/6 mm cubes. Place in bowl with herbs and spices

2. Pour the milk and lard into sifted flour and mix with a spoon until cool

3. When cool enough to handle, knead the pastry until it is smooth

4. Mould the hot water crust pastry carefully into the sides of the tin

5. Pack the meat firmly into the tin, making sure there are no air pockets

6. Pour the cooled gelatine stock gradually into pie, allowing liquid to settle

Bacon Pie

Whether it's supper or lunch-time, no one will be able to resist a large slice of this tasty bacon pie. With its crisp, light, golden pastry and delicious herby sauce spiced with the tang of chives, it makes a mouthwatering family favourite.

Calories per portion: 522 | **Serves 6**

FOR THE PASTRY:
12 oz/350 g plain flour
pinch of salt
3 oz/75 g butter or margarine
4 oz/100 g lard or white vegetable fat
FOR THE FILLING:
8 oz/225 g bacon, derinded
2 oz/50 g butter or margarine
2 oz/50 g plain flour
1¼ pints/750 ml skimmed milk
3 eggs, size 3
salt and freshly ground black pepper
2 tbsp freshly chopped parsley
1 tbsp freshly chopped chives
1 egg, size 5, beaten

Preheat the oven to Gas 6, 400°F, 200°C, 15 mins before cooking pie.

Sieve flour and salt into a mixing bowl, cube fats and rub into the flour until the mixture resembles fine bread-crumbs. Bind together with about 4 tbsp of cold water to give a firm but pliable dough. Knead on a lightly floured surface until smooth and free from cracks, then wrap and leave in fridge for 30 mins.

To make the filling, discard any cartilage from bacon, then dice bacon and reserve. Melt fat in pan, stir in flour, cook for 2 mins, remove from the heat, then gradually stir in milk. Return pan to heat and bring to the boil, stirring until thickened. Simmer for 2 mins. Remove from the heat, cover with a sheet of damp greaseproof and allow to cool for 30 mins.

When cool, lightly whisk eggs with seasoning then beat into the cooled sauce together with the reserved bacon, the parsley and chives. Stir until thoroughly mixed.

Roll out just over half of the pastry on to a floured surface and use to line a 2 pint/1.2 litre pie dish. Transfer the prepared filling to the pastry-lined dish. Roll out the remaining pastry to form the lid and dampen edges of pastry with a little water. Place lid in position, press edges firmly together, and pinch to form a decorative pattern around the edge. Roll out the pastry trimmings and cut out leaf-shaped decorations with a small cutter. Brush the top of the pie with the beaten egg and fix pastry decorations in place. Make two small slits in the top of the pie to allow the steam to escape.

Bake in oven for 30 mins, then remove and brush again with the egg. Reduce oven to Gas 4, 350°F, 180°C. Continue to cook for a further 20 mins, or until the pastry is cooked and golden brown.

Serve the pie hot or cold with either freshly cooked vegetables or a large mixed salad.

Handy Tip

Make pastry as described then scatter the bacon over base. Beat 4 eggs with seasoning and pour over. Cover with lid then cook for 35-45 mins or until golden brown.

1. Sieve the flour and salt into a bowl, cut fats into cubes and add to bowl

2. Using fingertips, rub fat into flour until the mixture resembles breadcrumbs

3. Once the sauce has cooled, beat in the eggs, then bacon, parsley and chives

4. Roll out just over half the pastry, then use to line a 2 pint/1.2 litre pie dish

5. Transfer the cooled, prepared bacon filling to the pastry-lined pie dish

6. Roll out remaining pastry to form lid, place on pie, brush with beaten egg

MAIN COURSES

When you want a tasty meal and time is short, why not try Chilli con Carne, Pork Escalopes or quick and easy Spaghetti Bolognese? If you're watching pennies try all-time favourites like Shepherd's Pie and Steak Puddings, and when you're out to impress, there's a host of ideas ranging from individual Beef Wellingtons to Peking Duck.

Coronation Chicken

Succulent pieces of chicken, toasted almonds and sweet, sun-ripened apricots with a delicately flavoured mayonnaise make this dish delicious for any occasion. Serve with a green salad and new potatoes.

Calories per portion: 403 **Serves 6**

3½ lb/1.5 kg oven-ready free-range chicken
2 onions, peeled
1 carrot, peeled
4 cloves
1 stick celery trimmed
few thyme sprigs
few parsley sprigs
4 bay leaves
1 tbsp oil
1 level tbsp curry powder
1½ tbsp tomato purée
¼ pint/150 ml white wine or wine and water mixed together
2 lemon slices
juice of ½ lemon
¼ pint/150 ml fromage frais
¼ pint/150 ml reduced-calorie mayonnaise
14 oz/397 g can apricots, drained
2 oz/50 g blanched almonds, toasted
4 oz/100 g no-need-to-soak dried apricots
1 ripe nectarine
salad leaves

Wash chicken thoroughly, discarding any giblets. Place chicken in a large flameproof casserole and cover with water. Add one of the peeled onions, the carrot and cloves. Cut the celery stick in half and place the thyme, parsley and 2 of bay leaves over one half. Tie the other half of celery over top to make a bouquet garni. Add to the pan. Bring to boil, cover, reduce heat and poach the chicken for 1½-2 hrs or until cooked. Cool slightly then remove from pan, drain and leave covered until cold. Strip off and discard the skin. Remove the chicken meat from the carcass and cut into small cubes. Cover while making sauce.

Heat oil in a small pan, chop the remaining onion. Fry the onion in the oil for 5 mins, add the 2 remaining bay leaves and curry powder, and continue to cook for 3 mins. Add the tomato purée, wine or water and wine with the lemon slices and lemon juice, simmer gently for 10 mins then strain and reserve the liquid.

Mix the fromage frais and the mayonnaise together, then stir in the cooled liquid. Purée the canned apricots, then stir into the curry mayonnaise with seasoning. Add the cubed chicken with 1½ oz/40 g of the almonds. Chop the dried apricots and add to the chicken mixture. Stir until all the ingredients are lightly coated. Stone the nectarine and cut into thin slices. Arrange salad leaves on serving dish then spoon the chicken into the dish. Decorate with the sliced nectarine and scatter remaining almonds on top.

Handy Tips

If preferred you can use cashew nuts instead of the blanched almonds and you can replace the nectarine with a peach.

1. Poach the chicken with the onion, carrot, cloves and bouquet garni

2. When cold, strip off the skin, remove meat from the carcass and cube

3. Fry onion for 5 mins, add bay leaves and curry powder, and cook for 3 mins

4. *Strain the sauce into a bowl. Set aside and allow the liquid to cool*

5. *Purée the canned apricots and then stir into the curry mayonnaise*

6. *Stir chicken into mayonnaise with almonds and apricots until coated*

CHICKEN KORMA

Tender chicken in a rich, creamy yogurt sauce, delicately flavoured with coriander and just the merest hint of spices, make this an excellent dish to give the whole family for an extra-special treat from the East.

Calories per portion: 407 — **SERVES 4**

3½ lb/1.5 kg oven-ready free-range chicken
1 tsp turmeric
1 tsp salt
10 green cardamom pods
4 tbsp ghee, or sunflower oil
2 onions, peeled and chopped
2 in/5 cm piece of root ginger
5 garlic cloves, peeled and crushed
5 cloves
1 cinnamon stick
¼ - ½ tsp freshly grated nutmeg
1 oz/25 g ground almonds
1 pint/600 ml natural yogurt
freshly ground black pepper
2 tbsp freshly chopped coriander
1 tbsp lemon juice

Wash chicken, then cut into eight pieces – discarding the parson's nose, the scale ends of the drumsticks, and the neck flap. Wash again, then place in a large pan with 1½ pints/900 ml water, ½ tsp turmeric, salt and 7 cardamom pods. Bring to the boil, cover, then reduce the heat and simmer gently for 45 mins, or until the chicken is tender. Then remove chicken, reserving the stock, and allow to cool slightly. Finally, skin the chicken pieces and keep covered while preparing the sauce.

Meanwhile, heat the ghee or oil in a large frying pan, add the onions and fry for 10-15 mins, stirring frequently, until golden. Remove from the pan using a slotted spoon, then drain on kitchen paper and reserve. Peel and finely chop the ginger, then add to the frying pan together with the crushed garlic, remaining turmeric, cloves, cinnamon stick, remaining cardamom pods and the grated nutmeg. Continue to fry the spices for 5 mins, then stir in the ground almonds.

Add the yogurt and ¼ pint/150 ml reserved chicken stock and bring to a gentle simmer. Cook for 15 mins or until the mixture has reduced and is of a thick consistency. Return the onions to the pan, together with the chicken pieces and a further ¼ pint/150 ml chicken stock. Ensure the chicken is well coated with the sauce, then cover the pan and cook for 15-20 mins, or until chicken is piping hot. Add the freshly ground black pepper to taste, then stir in the coriander and lemon juice. Heat for a further 5 mins, stir to ensure the flavours are thoroughly distributed. Serve with freshly cooked rice, salad and poppadoms.

HANDY TIPS

The whole spices are not meant to be eaten but should be left to one side. If there is a lot of oil floating around the edge of the sauce, spoon off and discard.

1. Cut chicken into eight pieces, place in pan with 1½ pints/900 ml water and spices

2. Fry onions until golden brown, stirring frequently, then drain and reserve

3. Add ginger, garlic and remaining spices to the pan and fry for 5 mins

4. Add ground almonds, yogurt and stock and cook for 15 mins, then stir in onions

5. Add the chicken to the pan, then stir in a further ¼ pint/150 ml reserved stock

6. Add the black pepper, then sprinkle in chopped coriander and lemon juice

CHICKEN & LEEK PIE

Poached chicken, lightly sautéed with shallots and leeks in a home-made chicken sauce, topped with a golden pastry. This Chicken & Leek Pie is a real family treat and so easy to make; just follow the easy step-by-step guide.

Calories per portion: 833 **SERVES 6**

3½ lb/1.5 kg oven-ready free-range chicken
2 large onions
2 carrots
2 sticks celery
2 bay leaves
4-6 black peppercorns
4 cloves
2 oz/50 g butter or margarine
12 oz/350 g leeks, trimmed, washed and sliced
8 oz/225 g shallots, peeled
FOR THE SAUCE:
2 oz/50 g butter or margarine
2 oz/50 g plain flour
FOR THE PASTRY:
4 oz/100 g white vegetable fat
2 oz/50 g butter or margarine
10 oz/300 g plain flour
1 egg, size 5, beaten

Preheat oven to Gas 6, 400°F, 200°C, 15 mins before baking the pie.

Remove any giblets from the chicken. Pull away and discard any fat from the inside of the bird then wash thoroughly under cold running water. Drain then place in a large saucepan. Peel the onions and carrots, trim and scrub the celery. Place in the pan with the bay leaves, peppercorns and cloves. Cover with water. Bring to the boil, cover with lid then reduce heat and simmer for 1½-2 hrs or until chicken is cooked.

Remove chicken from pan, cover and allow to cool. Strain stock and reserve 1 pint/600 ml. (The rest of the stock can be frozen for later use or stored in the fridge, covered, for 2 days.)

When the chicken is cool enough to handle, strip off meat, discarding skin and bones, chop meat into bite-sized pieces, cover and leave on one side.

Melt the butter or margarine then fry the leeks for 5 mins. Drain and reserve. Fry the shallots in the remaining fat for 5 mins or until golden, drain. To make the sauce, melt 2 oz/50 g butter or margarine in a clean pan then stir in flour and cook for 2 mins over a gentle heat. Remove from heat, stir in the reserved 1 pint/600 ml of chicken stock, return to the heat and cook, stirring throughout until thickened. Add the chicken meat, shallots and leeks with seasoning to taste. Place filling in a 1½ pint/900 ml oval pie dish.

To make the pastry, rub the fats into the flour then mix to a soft pliable

dough with cold water. Knead until smooth, wrap and chill for 30 mins. Roll out on a lightly floured surface and cut out a ½ in/1.25 cm strip, long enough to go all the way round the pie dish. Dampen edge of pie dish and place in position.

Cut out pastry lid as illustrated (in step 4), dampen pastry strip and place the lid on top, sealing the edges firmly together. Knock the edges together with the back of a round-bladed knife. Using your thumb and forefinger, pinch the edges together to form a decorative pattern around the edge of the dish and use the trimmings to decorate the top.

Make a small hole in the centre of the pastry lid to allow the steam to escape. Brush the pie lightly with the beaten egg then cook in the oven for 35-40 mins or until the pastry is golden. Serve hot with a selection of fresh seasonal vegetables.

HANDY TIP

A golden crust is achieved by lightly brushing the pastry with the beaten egg halfway through the cooking time as well as just before baking the pie.

1. Place the chicken, onions, carrots, celery and bay leaves in a saucepan

2. Sauté leeks in fat for 5 mins, then drain. Add shallots to pan and sauté

3. Melt fat in saucepan, add flour, cook for 2 mins. Stir in chicken stock

4. Roll pastry out on a floured surface to ½ in/1.25 cm thick. Cut oval for lid

5. After placing filling in dish, place strip around edge, dampen, position lid

6. Seal edges together firmly. Arrange pastry leaves as decoration in centre

ROAST CHICKEN

Although traditionally served for Sunday lunch, roast chicken is delicious for any occasion. It's tender, moist and full of flavour. Served with home-made stuffing balls, roast potatoes and fresh vegetables, it's ideal for the whole family.

Calories per portion: 569 | **SERVES 4**

3-3½ lb/1.5 kg oven-ready free-range chicken
small bunch of fresh thyme
1 small onion, peeled and halved
1½ oz/40 g butter, softened
salt and freshly ground black pepper
4 rashers streaky bacon
celery leaves for garnish, optional
FOR THE STUFFING BALLS:
1 tbsp vegetable oil
1 large onion, peeled and finely chopped
6 oz/175 g fresh white breadcrumbs
3 tbsp freshly chopped parsley
finely grated rind of 1 lemon
1 tbsp dried thyme leaves
2 sticks celery, trimmed and finely chopped
salt and freshly ground black pepper
1 egg, size 3, beaten
FOR THE GRAVY:
1 oz/25 g plain flour
¾ pint/450 ml chicken stock
gravy browning, optional

Preheat oven to Gas 5, 375°F, 190°C, 10 mins before roasting the chicken. Thoroughly wash chicken, inside and outside, in cold water. Drain well and pat dry with paper towels. Place the thyme and onion halves inside the bird.

Tuck the wings and neck flap neatly under the bird. Truss the chicken neatly with thin clean string as follows: cut a length of string, about 2 ft/60 cm long. Place the centre of the string under the parson's nose, cross the ends over and tie a tight knot. Take each end over, then under the drumsticks and tie once again with a tight knot, so that the legs are held securely together. Turn the chicken over, then take the string right along the sides of the bird and under the wings to the neck end. Bring the ends across neck flap and tie securely.

Place the chicken in a roasting tin. Smear the skin with butter and season with salt and pepper. Place the bacon rashers across the breast.

Cook the chicken in the centre of the oven for 1½-1¾ hrs, or until well done, basting frequently with the pan juices. Remove the bacon rashers for the last 30 mins of cooking.

To test whether chicken is cooked, pierce the bird with the tip of a small pointed knife at the thickest part of the thigh to allow juices to run out – these should be clear with no trace of pink.

Meanwhile, make the stuffing balls.

Heat the oil in a frying pan, add the onion and cook for 5-6 mins until softened, but not browned. Place in a bowl with the remaining stuffing ingredients. Season and mix together, roll into neat balls.

About 40 mins before the chicken is cooked, take 3 tbsp of the fat from the roasting tin and put it into a shallow ovenproof dish. Add the stuffing balls, turning them in the fat until they are evenly coated. Place in the oven, on a rack above the chicken, to cook until golden brown. When the chicken is done, remove from the roasting tin and place on serving plate, loosely cover with foil and keep warm.

To make gravy, discard the bacon rashers from roasting tin. Tilt tin to one side and carefully skim off all fat from the roasting juices left in bottom of the pan. Place roasting tin on the heat and stir in the flour. Stir in the chicken stock and gravy browning if using. Bring to the boil, stirring all the time until gravy thickens. Reduce heat and simmer for 5 mins. Strain the gravy into a serving jug. Serve chicken accompanied by the stuffing balls, bacon rolls and gravy.

HANDY TIP

Try this alternative for a change. Instead of covering chicken with the bacon and smearing with butter, pour 3 tbsp clear honey mixed with 2 tbsp water over the chicken. Cover with tin foil and cook as before.

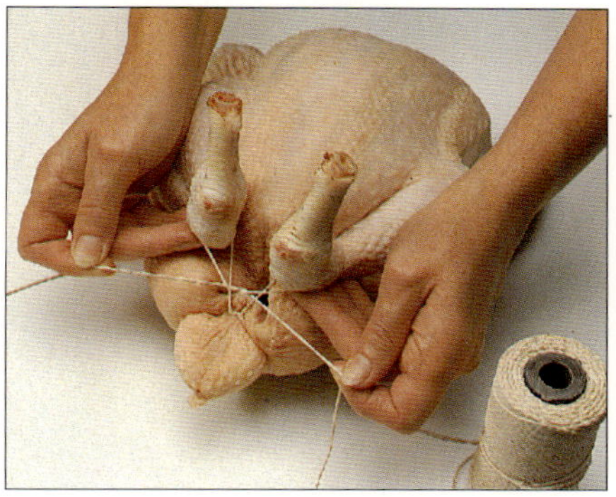

1. Truss cleaned chicken with thin string tied around parson's nose and legs

2. Turn chicken over, bring string to top of wings and tie across neck and flap

3. Place chicken in tin, smear with butter, season, place bacon across breast

4. Mix all the stuffing ingredients together, bind, and then roll into neat balls

5. For gravy, skim fat from residue left in tin and stir flour into meat juices

6. Add stock to roasting tin and bring to the boil, stirring. Cook until thickened

Chicken Cordon Bleu

Make tender pieces of chicken special by filling with smoked ham and delicious Gruyère cheese and coating in golden breadcrumbs. Easy when you follow this step-by-step guide.

Calories per portion: 568 | **Serves 4**

4 boneless chicken breasts, each approx 7 oz/200 g in weight
4 thin slices smoked ham
4 thin slices Gruyère cheese
salt and freshly ground black pepper
6 oz/175 g fresh white breadcrumbs
2 eggs, size 5, beaten
3 tbsp vegetable oil

Preheat the oven to Gas 5, 375°F, 190°C, 10 mins before cooking. Discard the skin from the chicken and trim off any small pieces of fat. Place the chicken breasts on a chopping board and cut along the long edge, without cutting completely in half.

Open out each chicken breast so that it lies flat. Place between two sheets of clearwrap or greaseproof paper and beat quite lightly with a meat mallet or rolling pin, until the breasts are completely flat. Don't beat too hard otherwise you'll end up with a pulp.

Arrange a thin slice of ham and then Gruyère cheese on top, trim the ham and cheese if necessary so that it fits inside the chicken breast once it has been folded over.

Season chicken breasts then fold over, returning them to their original shape. Place between two sheets of clearwrap or greaseproof paper and beat the edges lightly with the mallet or rolling pin so that they stick together. If necessary, secure the edges of the chicken breasts with cocktail sticks, but remove them before serving.

Put the stuffed chicken breasts on a plate, cover, then chill in the fridge for 30 mins. Place the breadcrumbs in the bottom of a clean grill pan then place under a preheated grill and toast lightly. Stir the breadcrumbs frequently to avoid burning them. Remove, allow to cool then place in a bowl.

Pour the beaten egg in a bowl large enough so that the chicken can easily be placed inside. Remove chicken from the fridge then dip each chicken breast in the beaten egg until thoroughly coated. Let any excess egg drip off into the bowl. Carefully roll the chicken breasts in the toasted breadcrumbs until they are evenly coated.

Place in a baking tin and drizzle the oil over. Cook in the oven for 20-30 mins or until the chicken is thoroughly cooked. (The time will vary slightly according to the weight of the chicken.) Serve immediately.

Handy Tips

If preferred, you can substitute brown bread instead of the white for the breadcrumbs. You can also fry the chicken breasts instead of cooking them in the oven. To fry, heat 4 tbsp oil and 2 tbsp butter together in a large frying pan. Then fry for 10 mins on each side or until cooked and the coating is crisp and golden. Drain on absorbent kitchen paper and serve immediately.

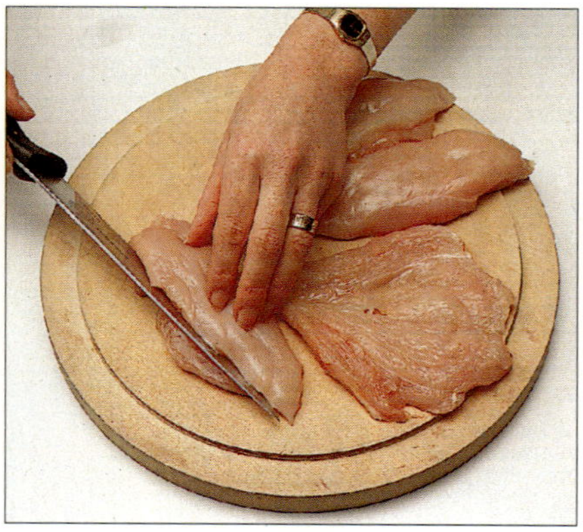

1. Place chicken on a chopping board and cut along the long edge, open out

2. Place individual breasts between sheets of clearwrap and beat lightly

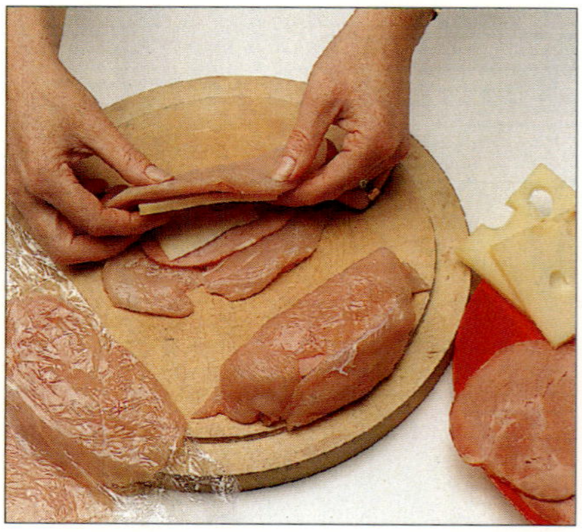

3. Open chicken breasts and place slice of ham and cheese on top, fold over

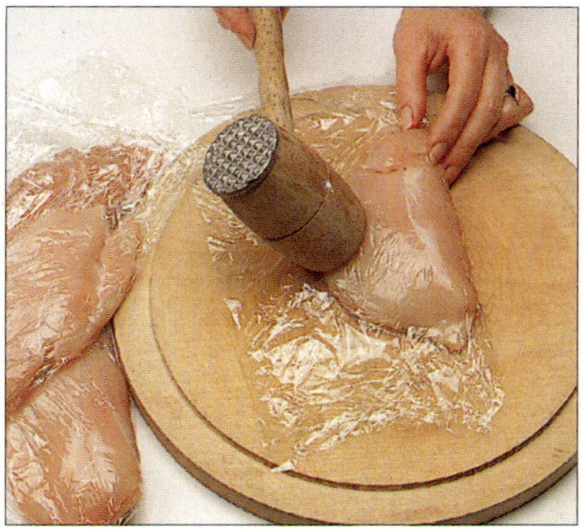

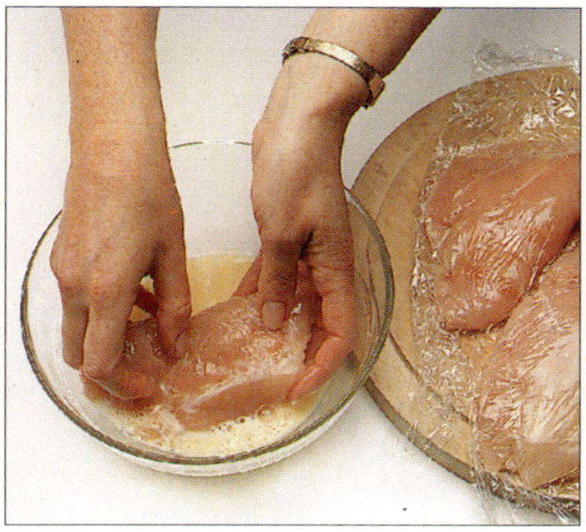

4. Replace chicken breasts between clearwrap and lightly beat the edges

5. Dip stuffed chicken breasts into beaten egg until coated, drain off excess

6. Coat chicken breasts in breadcrumbs, ensuring they are completely covered

CHICKEN MARENGO

Tender succulent chicken, gently cooked in brandy and white wine, with a subtle hint of lemon. It's said that this dish was a favourite of Napoleon's and we're sure it will be a real hit with you, too.

Calories per portion: 619 | **SERVES 4**

3½ lb/1.5 kg oven-ready free-range chicken
1 lemon
2 medium onions
3 oz/75 g butter or margarine
2 tbsp oil
3 tbsp French brandy
salt and freshly ground black pepper
¼ pint/150 ml medium dry white wine
½ pint/300 ml chicken stock
4 oz/100 g baby mushrooms, wiped
1 oz/25 g plain flour
3 tbsp single cream or crème fraîche
zested lemon rind and chopped parsley to garnish

Preheat oven to Gas 4, 350°F, 180°C, 10 mins before cooking chicken. Remove any giblets from the inside of the chicken, wash well and use to make chicken stock. Discard any fat from inside the cavity then place the chicken on a chopping board.

With a sharp kitchen knife carefully cut down along the side of the breastbone. Pull the two halves open then, using a meat cleaver, chop through the carcass to form two separate halves. (If you don't have a meat cleaver, use your kitchen knife and tap the top edge with a rolling pin to ensure a clean cut.)

Turn the halves over and cut off the scaly part of the leg. Pull the leg joint out and make a diagonal cut across to form 2 joints. Wash thoroughly under cold water and dry on absorbent paper. Cut the lemon in half and rub over the joints.

Peel and finely slice the onions. melt 1 oz/25 g of the fat with the oil in a frying pan, and fry the chicken on all sides until golden brown. Drain on absorbent paper. Place in a 4 pint/ 2.25 litre ovenproof casserole.

Fry the onions in the fat remaining in the pan for 5 mins, or until translucent. Remove from the heat, pour in brandy, add seasoning. Return to heat and cook for 1 min, then add white wine and stock. Pour over chicken then cook in oven for 1 hr or until the chicken is tender.

Meanwhile, 15 mins before end of cooking time, melt 1 oz/25 g of the remaining fat in a small saucepan. Cook mushrooms for 5 mins, drain and add to casserole. When the chicken is cooked, drain and skim, reserving stock. Place the reserved stock into a small pan and bring to the boil. Beat the remaining fat with the flour then drop small spoonfuls into the boiling stock, whisking vigorously. Cook for 2 mins or until thickened. Stir in the cream or crème fraîche, pour over chicken. Sprinkle with lemon rind and parsley.

HANDY TIPS

If watching your fat intake, use skinned chicken and olive oil instead of butter or margarine and fromage frais, not cream.

1. With a very sharp knife, cut down along the side of the chicken breastbone

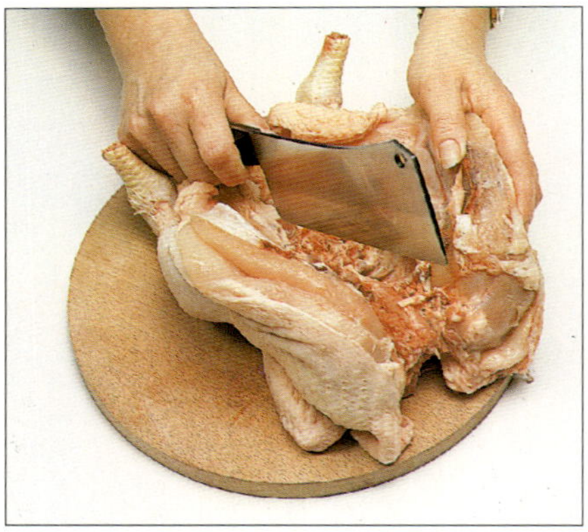

2. Pull the chicken open and, using a meat cleaver, chop completely in half

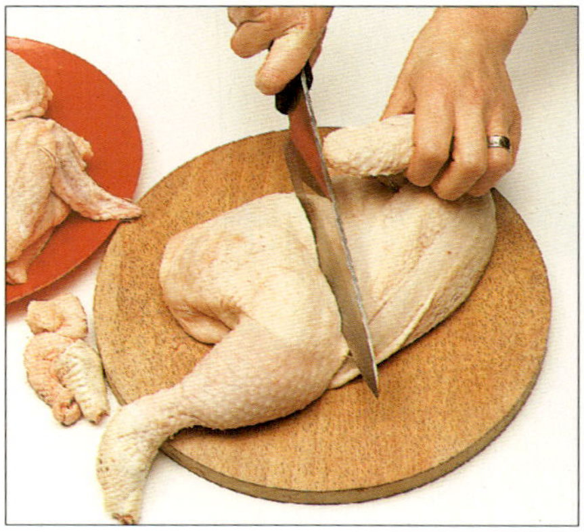

3. Take one half of the chicken, pull the leg joint out and cut in half

4. Rub the washed and dried chicken pieces all over with the cut lemon

5. Fry the chicken pieces on both sides until they are golden brown all over

6. Gently fry the onions until they are translucent, then pour in the brandy

CHICKEN CHASSEUR

Succulent chicken joints, simmered in a white wine sauce with shallots, mushrooms and just a hint of tomato. It's easy to prepare and cook and is ideal for any occasion.

Calories per portion: 595 | **SERVES 4**

4 chicken joints
2 tbsp vegetable oil
3½ oz/90 g butter or margarine
6 oz/175 g shallots or baby onions
4 oz/100 g mushrooms
½ pint/300 ml chicken stock
½ pint/300 ml white wine
1 tbsp tomato purée
1 oz/25 g plain flour
2 tbsp freshly chopped parsley
salt and freshly ground black pepper
2 bay leaves

HANDY TIPS

To freeze, prepare as above but omit thickening the sauce with the butter and flour paste. Once chicken is cooked, leave until cold, then place in a freezable container and freeze. To serve, remove from freezer and allow the chicken to thaw, preferably overnight in the bottom of the fridge. Place in casserole, heat through at Gas 4, 350°F, 180°C, for 40-50 mins. Carefully stir in the butter and flour paste halfway through re-heating.

Preheat oven to Gas 4, 350°F, 180°C, 10 mins before cooking casserole. Wipe chicken joints with a clean damp cloth, discarding any fat. Trim away any extra pieces of skin. Heat the 2 tbsp of oil and 1½ oz/40 g of the butter or margarine in pan. Fry the chicken joints until golden brown all over. Drain well on absorbent paper then place in a 4 pint/2.25 litre oven-proof casserole.

Peel shallots or baby onions, removing the root, then fry in the fat remaining in frying pan until golden. Drain and place on top of chicken. Wipe mushrooms and slice thinly, add to fat remaining in pan and cook, stirring occasionally for 3-4 mins. Drain then place on top of chicken joints and the shallots or baby onions.

Gradually pour the stock into the frying pan, stirring throughout to remove any pieces of sediment left in the pan. Stir in the wine and the tomato purée and bring to the boil. Beat the remaining 2 oz/50 g butter or margarine with the flour, then whisk in small teaspoonfuls to the boiling liquid. Whisk until smooth and thickened. Stir in the parsley, and season to taste with the salt and black pepper.

Pour the sauce over the chicken joints. Place 2 bay leaves in the sauce. Cover casserole with the lid and cook on the centre shelf for 1½-1¾ hrs or until the chicken is tender. Discard bay leaves. Check seasoning then serve sprinkled with a little extra chopped parsley and vegetables, baked potatoes, rice or tagliatelle.

1. Fry chicken joints in the oil and 1½ oz/40 g of the fat until golden brown all over

2. Add the shallots or baby onions to the pan and gently fry until golden

3. Slice the mushrooms thinly then fry in the pan for 3-4 mins or until lightly brown

4. *Whisk in small spoonfuls of the butter and flour paste*

5. *Stir in the chopped parsley to the thickened sauce*

6. *Pour the sauce over the chicken, cover casserole with a lid and cook*

PEKING DUCK

With its crisp, tangy skin, Peking Duck is the most popular of all Chinese dishes. Serve with cool cucumber, spring onion strips and a rich plum Hoisin sauce. Wrapped in featherlight pancakes, it's delicious.

Calories per portion: 964 | **SERVES 6**

5 lb/2.25 kg oven-ready duck
4 tbsp Chinese five spice powder
2 tsp salt
4 tbsp clear honey
1 tbsp white wine vinegar
1 tbsp medium dry sherry
3 tbsp light soy sauce
FOR THE PANCAKES:
8 oz/225 g strong plain flour
1 tbsp sesame oil
TO SERVE:
1 bunch spring onions
½ small cucumber
Hoisin sauce

Preheat oven to Gas 6, 400°F, 200°C, 15 mins before cooking duck.

If the duck is frozen, ensure it is thoroughly thawed before use. Rinse and pat dry with absorbent paper. Mix the Chinese five spice powder with the 2 tsp salt and sprinkle inside the duck cavity. Pinch the duck all over with the forefinger and thumb to help break down the fat and to loosen the skin from the bird.

Place the duck in a roasting tin or a large ovenproof bowl and scald by pouring boiling water over. Drain and allow to dry in a cool, airy place for at least 2-3 hrs. The longer you leave the duck to dry the crisper the skin will be. The Chinese hang them up to dry overnight before cooking.

Mix the honey, wine vinegar, sherry and soy sauce with ¼ pint/150 ml boiling water and stir until thoroughly blended. Put duck on a trivet in a roasting tin. Pour marinade over and roast for 1½-2 hrs. To test if cooked, the juices should run clear when the leg is pierced with a skewer.

Meanwhile make the pancakes: mix the flour with 6 fl oz/175 ml hot water to form a dough, knead until smooth then leave to relax for 30 mins. Cover with clean cloth. Divide dough into small pieces then roll out to 2 in/5 cm rounds. Brush one side with sesame oil and place two pancakes together, oiled sides innermost. Roll out again until the pancakes are really thin, cut each into 7 in/18 cm rounds. Heat a non-stick frying pan over a gentle heat. Fry pancakes until dry on one side, turn over and cook the other side. Repeat until all the pancakes are cooked. When it's time to eat, reheat in a steamer over gently boiling water.

Trim spring onions to 3 in/7.5 cm lengths. Take half and using a sharp knife, make very thin cuts to 1 in/2.5 cm of base. Place in a bowl of iced water for 2-3 hrs: this will make the ends curl decoratively. Shred remainder. Peel cucumber, cut into ¼ in/6 mm thin strips. To eat, shred or carve the duck. Spread a spoonful of sauce on to pancakes. Top with shredded spring onions and strips of cucumber and duck. Roll up filled pancakes to eat.

HANDY TIP

Make the pancakes in advance, then freeze until required. Thaw before using. Reheat as above, in a steamer.

1. *Pinch the duck all over with thumb and forefinger to break down the fat*

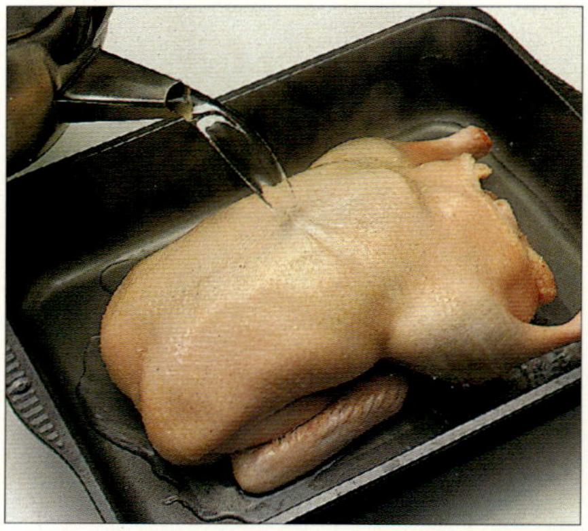

2. *Place seasoned duck in a large roasting tin, pour boiling water over, drain*

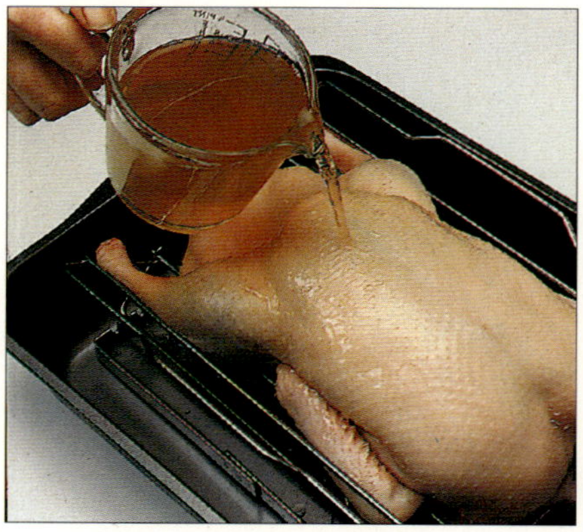

3. *Put the duck on a trivet, mix the marinade then pour over and roast*

4. *To make the pancakes: add water to the sifted flour and bind to a stiff dough*

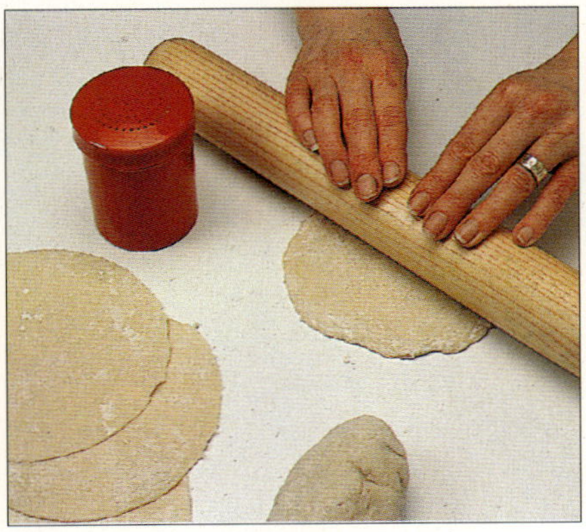

5. *Knead dough on a floured board then roll out small pieces to 2 in/5 cm rounds*

6. *Trim cleaned spring onions to 3 in/7.5 cm. Make cuts 1 in/2.5 cm from base*

Roast beef

It's great at any time of the year! Served traditionally with roast potatoes, sprouts and horseradish sauce, a roast is equally delicious with new potatoes, baby carrots and fresh peas. Try it cold next day with bubble and squeak.

Calories per portion: 760 **Serves 8**

1 piece wing rib, 2 or 3 ribs approx 3-5 lb/1.5-2.25 kg in weight
1 oz/25 g lard or white vegetable fat
salt
FOR THE YORKSHIRE PUDDING:
4 oz/100 g plain flour
2 eggs, size 3
½ pint/300 ml milk or milk and water mixed
1 oz/25 g lard or white vegetable fat or 1½ tbsp fat from roasting meat
FOR THE GRAVY:
3 tbsp fat from roasting meat
1½ -2 tbsp plain flour
½ pint/300 ml beef or vegetable stock – you can use some of the vegetable cooking water
½ -1 tsp gravy browning, optional

Preheat oven to Gas 7, 425°F, 220°C, 15 mins before roasting the beef. Weigh the joint and calculate the cooking time, allowing 20 mins per lb plus 20 mins-slightly less if rare meat is required. Cut away the bone at base of joint, but leave in place to ensure easy carving. Wipe the meat with a clean, damp cloth. Tie round the joint with string in two or three places and put in a large roasting tin, ensuring that the cut sides are exposed to the heat and the thickest area of fat is uppermost. This way, the fat keeps the meat moist during cooking.

Dot with small knobs of fat and season with salt. Roast in centre of oven for calculated length of cooking time. Towards the end of cooking time pour off 1½ tbsp fat, if using, for Yorkshire Pudding and 3 tbsp of fat for gravy.

To make Yorkshire Pudding, sift flour into mixing bowl, make a well in centre, drop in eggs. Gradually beat in milk, bringing in the flour from the sides of the bowl. Beat to a smooth batter. Heat lard or fat either in a small roasting tin 8 in x 6 in/20 cm x 15 cm or in individual patty tins until smoking. Pour in batter and return to oven, towards the top. Cook large pudding for 30-40 mins or individual puddings for 15-20 mins, or until well risen.

To make the gravy, heat fat from meat in a small saucepan, stir in flour and cook for 2 mins. Remove from heat and stir in stock, gravy browning, if using, and any of the meat juices left in the roasting tin, and seasoning to taste. Return gravy to heat and cook, stirring throughout, until smooth and thickened.

HANDY TIP

Using two eggs in your Yorkshire Pudding and ensuring that the fat is really hot and the oven temperature is correct, produces perfect results every time.

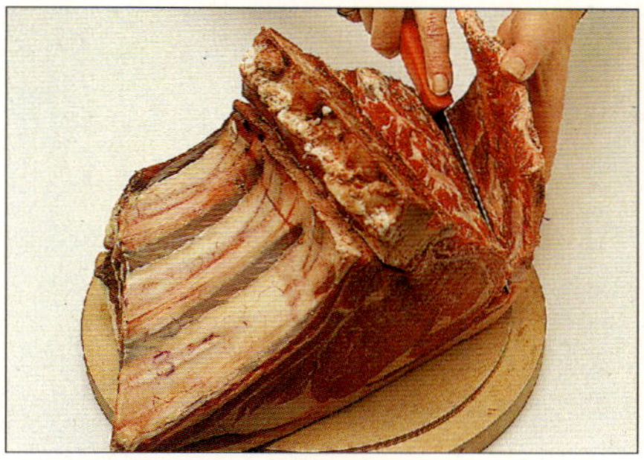

1. Cut the bone away from base of meat but leave in position for easy carving

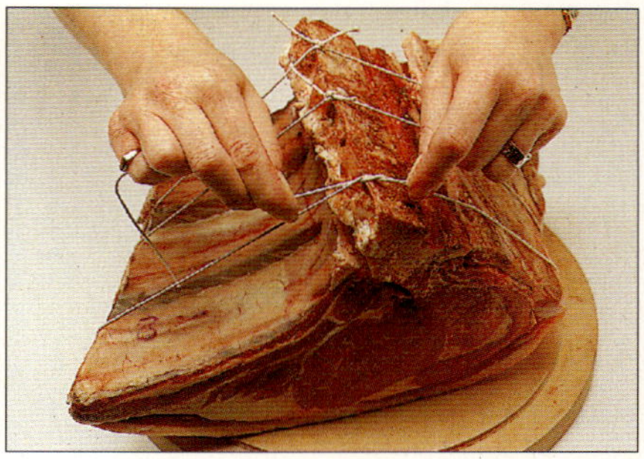

2. Tie joint in two or three places to keep meat a good shape during cooking

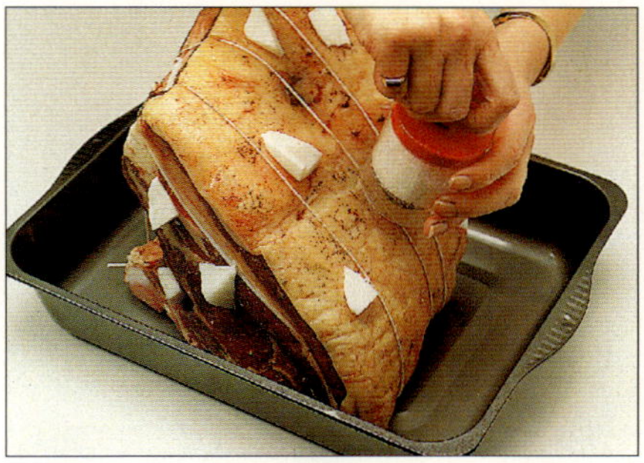

3. Place in a roasting tin. Dot with small pieces of fat and season with salt.

4. Make a well in centre of flour, drop in eggs then beat to a batter with milk.

5. Heat a little fat in the patty tins and then when smoking, pour in batter

6. Heat fat from roasting tin, stir in flour, cook for 2 mins, then slowly add stock

STEAK & STOUT PIE

Make a perfect pie of tender pieces of steak, carrots, mushrooms and tomatoes, simmered in stout, then topped with mouthwatering, crisp shortcrust pastry. Serve it with fresh vegetables to warm them up deliciously when it's cold outside.

Calories per portion: 581 | **SERVES 4**

1 lb/450 g braising steak, trimmed
2 small onions
2 carrots
2 large tomatoes
2 tbsp oil
2 tsp sugar
2 bay leaves
salt and freshly ground black pepper
2 tbsp flour
½ pint/300 ml stout
½ pint/300 ml beef stock
4 oz/100 g button mushrooms
8 oz/225 g prepared shortcrust pastry, thawed if frozen
beaten egg or milk to glaze

Preheat the oven to Gas 6, 400°F, 200°C, 15 mins before baking. Cut the beef into 1 in/2.5 cm cubes. Peel and thinly slice the onions and carrots. Make a small cross in the top of each tomato, then cover with boiling water and leave for 2 mins. Drain. Peel the tomatoes, discard seeds, then roughly chop the flesh and reserve.

Heat the oil in a large saucepan, then fry meat in small batches, stirring, until browned. Remove each batch with a draining spoon and reserve. When all the meat has been browned, add the onions and carrots to the pan, then cook gently for 5 mins, or until softened. Return the meat to the pan, then add the chopped tomatoes, sugar and bay leaves. Season. Sprinkle with the flour and continue cooking over a very gentle heat for 2 mins. Gradually stir in the stout and beef stock, bring to the boil, then cover and gently simmer for 1½ hrs, stirring occasionally.

Wipe the mushrooms, then add to the pan and continue to cook for a further 10 mins. Leave to cool. Using approx 1½ oz/40 g shortcrust pastry, roll out, on a lightly floured surface, a thin strip wide enough to fix to the edge of a 2½ pint/1.5 litre pie dish.

HANDY TIP

If preferred cook the meat in the oven at Gas 4, 350°F, 180°C, for 2 hrs, then add mushrooms and allow to cool before proceeding with the pie.

Spoon cooled filling into the pie dish, then roll out remaining pastry and cut out a lid, large enough to cover top of dish completely. Dampen pastry strip, then wrap the pastry lid round the rolling pin and place on top of pie. Pinch the edges securely together and make a decorative border around the edge. Use any pastry trimmings to decorate the top of the pie, then brush with the beaten egg or milk.

Bake in the oven for 15 mins, then brush again with the egg or milk and continue to cook for a further 15 mins, or until the pastry is golden brown. Serve hot with cooked vegetables.

1. Cut meat into 1 in/2.5 cm cubes, then peel and slice the onions and carrots

2. Fry the meat in small batches until browned, then drain and reserve

3. Return meat to pan, add tomatoes, sugar, bay leaves, seasoning and flour

4. Continue cooking for 2 mins, then stir in stout and stock and bring to the boil

5. Dampen the pastry strip and press on to rim of dish. Spoon in the filling

6. Roll out the remaining pastry, dampen the strip and place the lid on top

Beef Wellingtons

Try these delicious savoury parcels! Tender, lean steak, topped with a mouthwatering mushroom and pâté stuffing, encased in crisp, golden pastry, means every bite is a pure delight.

Calories per portion: 694 | **Serves 4**

4 x 4 oz/100 g pieces fillet steak
½ oz/15 g unsalted butter
FOR THE STUFFING:
2 shallots
1 oz/25 g unsalted butter
2 oz/50 g mushrooms
2 oz/50 g fresh white breadcrumbs
2 oz/50 g liver pâté
1 tbsp freshly chopped parsley
salt and freshly ground black pepper
1 egg, size 5
1 lb/450 g puff pastry
flat-leaved parsley to garnish

Preheat the oven to Gas 7, 425°F, 220°C, 15 mins before cooking the Beef Wellingtons. Trim off any fat from the steaks and, if necessary, trim to a good shape. Heat the butter in a frying pan, then fry the steaks on both sides until completely sealed. Remove from pan, drain on kitchen paper, cover lightly and allow to cool.

Meanwhile, make the stuffing. Peel and finely chop the shallots, then heat butter in a pan and fry shallots for 2-3 mins, or until soft. Wipe mushrooms and chop finely, add to pan and fry for a further 3 mins. Remove pan from the heat, then add the breadcrumbs. Chop the pâté finely, add to the pan with the parsley, and season to taste. Mix lightly. Beat the egg, then add enough to bind stuffing together.

Roll out the pastry on a lightly floured work surface and, using a saucer, cut out four 7 in/18 cm rounds. Reserve trimmings.

Place a spoonful of the stuffing in the centre of each pastry round, then top with a piece of steak. Brush edges of the pastry lightly with water, then bring the edges up and over to encase the steak completely. Pinch the edges firmly together, then place on a slightly dampened baking sheet, with the join underneath.

Roll out the pastry trimmings and cut out 12 thin strips with a pastry wheel. Brush the strips lightly with water, then use to decorate the parcels. Brush completely with remaining beaten egg and cook in the oven for 15-20 mins, or until pastry is golden brown and well risen. Garnish with the flat-leaved parsley and serve immediately with freshly cooked vegetables.

Handy Tip

Provided neither the steak nor the pastry has been previously frozen, you can prepare the Beef Wellingtons as instructed (but don't brush with egg), then open-freeze before cooking. Once frozen, transfer to a freezerproof container or freezer bag, seal and store until required. Allow to thaw overnight in the fridge before brushing with beaten egg and cooking.

1. Heat butter in frying pan, then seal steaks on both sides. Remove and drain

2. Melt butter in saucepan, sauté shallots for 2-3 mins, then add mushrooms

3. Roll out the pastry and, using a saucer, cut out four 7 in/18 cm rounds

4. Place a spoonful of stuffing in centre of the pastry, then top with steak

5. Dampen edges of pastry, then bring edges up and over to encase steak

6. Roll out the pastry trimmings, then cut out strips and decorate the parcels

Beef Carbonnade

There's nothing more appetizing than the smell of Beef Carbonnade as it cooks. Tender strips of beef, thinly sliced onions and a hint of garlic simmered in a delicious rich sauce.

Calories per portion: 606 **Serves 4**

1½ lb/675 g braising steak
2 large onions
2 garlic cloves, optional
3 oz/75 g butter or margarine
1½ oz/40 g flour
¾ pint/450 ml light ale
¼ pint/150 ml beef stock
1 tbsp tarragon vinegar
2 tsp sugar
2 bay leaves
salt and freshly ground black pepper
1 tbsp freshly chopped parsley

Preheat oven to Gas 4, 350°F, 180°C, 10 mins before cooking carbonnade.

Discard any fat or gristle from steak, then cut into strips 3 in/7.5 cm long x 1 in/2.5 cm wide. Remember when slicing beef – to help ensure the meat will be tender, slice across the grain. Peel onions and slice thinly. Peel and crush garlic, if using. Melt butter or margarine in frying pan, then cook the onions and garlic for 5 mins or until soft and transparent. Drain and place in an oven-proof casserole.

Fry the meat in the fat left in the pan, stirring with a wooden spoon until the meat is browned completely. Drain and place on top of onions. Sprinkle the flour into pan and cook, stirring carefully throughout until all the flour is incorporated into the juices left in the pan. Cook for a further 1 min and gradually stir in the light ale, then the stock. Bring to the boil and continue to cook until mixture thickens.

Stir in the vinegar, sugar, bay leaves, salt and freshly ground black pepper to taste. Cook for a further 2 mins. Pour over the meat and onions and mix well together.

Cover with a lid and cook in oven for 2-2½ hrs or until meat is tender – stir the carbonnade occasionally during cooking. Discard bay leaves, check seasoning and sprinkle with parsley.

In France this dish is served with plenty of bread so the rich, tasty gravy can be soaked up and none of it is wasted. Or serve with mashed or baked potatoes.

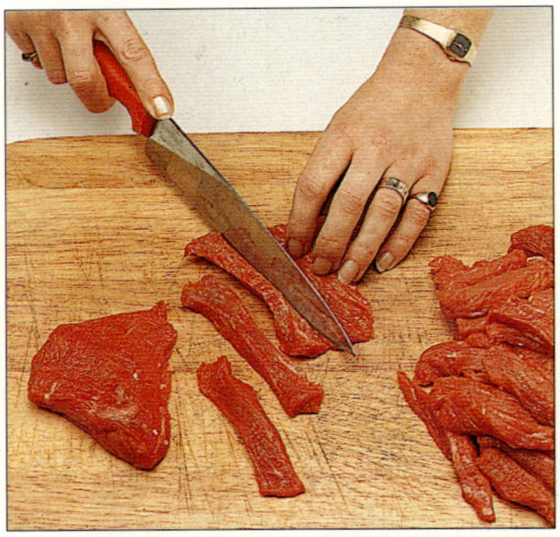

1. Trim beef, discard fat and gristle, cut into 3 in x 1 in//7.5 cm x 2.5 cm strips

2. Thinly slice the peeled onions. It's easier if you leave the root on when slicing

3. Melt the butter or margarine and fry onions until soft and transparent

Handy tip

You can make your own speciality herb vinegars quite easily. Place a sprig or two of the herb of your choice in a screw-top bottle. Fill up with either a white vinegar or wine vinegar. Leave for a couple of months before using.

4. Fry meat in fat remaining in pan until browned. Stir with a wooden spoon

5. Gradually add ale to the pan, stirring throughout to prevent lumps

6. Mix in the vinegar, sugar, salt and ground black pepper and bay leaves

Steak Puddings

Tender chunks of steak flavoured with onions and mushrooms, encased in a suet pastry, this delicious dish is a traditional family favourite. Just follow this easy step-by-step recipe for a hearty meal that everyone is sure to love.

Calories per portion: 336 **Serves 4**

6 oz/175 g self-raising flour
3 oz/75 g shredded vegetable suet
pinch of salt
FOR THE FILLING:
1 small onion
4 oz/100 g braising steak
2 oz/50 g mushrooms
1 level tbsp freshly chopped parsley
salt and freshly ground black pepper
1 tsp flour
2-3 tbsp beef stock, optional

Lightly grease four individual steamed pudding or dariole moulds. If liked, you can cut out four small rounds of greaseproof paper to fit the base of each mould (this will help when turning out the puddings).

Place the self-raising flour in a bowl, add suet and salt, mix to a soft, pliable dough with approx 9 tbsp cold water. Knead until smooth but not sticky. Roll out dough on a lightly floured surface and cut out four 4 in/10 cm rounds. Fold each round in half, then into quarters. Place inside moulds, then carefully ease the pastry into the base and up the sides, ensuring there are no air bubbles or cracks. Roll the remaining pastry together, cut out four lids and reserve.

To make the filling, peel, then finely chop the onion and place in a bowl. Trim braising steak then cut into ¼ in/6 mm cubes. Add to the onion. Wipe the mushrooms, chop finely, then add to onion and meat with the parsley and seasoning to taste. Sprinkle the flour over and toss all the ingredients together. Moisten with 2-3 tbsp beef stock, if using, or cold water.

Spoon the filling into the pastry-lined moulds, packing it down firmly. Dampen the edges of the pastry with water, then place the lids in position and pinch the edges firmly together. Cover each mould with pleated greaseproof paper and pudding cloth or foil, securing firmly with string.

Place puddings in the top of a steamer over a pan of gently boiling water. Steam steadily for 2 hrs, replenishing water as necessary.

Remove puddings from steamer and allow to stand for 3-5 mins. Using a round-bladed knife, carefully loosen around edges, then invert puddings on to a warm serving plate. Serve immediately with freshly cooked vegetables and gravy.

Handy Tip

The filling can be varied according to personal preference. Try using 1½ tsp dried mixed herbs in place of the parsley, or add 1 finely chopped or crushed garlic clove to the mixture.

1. Roll dough on a lightly floured surface, cut out four rounds and fold into quarters

2. Place each round into lightly greased mould, easing it into base and sides

3. Finely chop onion, place in bowl. Trim steak cut into cubes, then add to onion

4. Finely chop mushrooms, add to the bowl, with chopped parsley and seasoning

5. Spoon the prepared filling into pastry-lined moulds, packing it down firmly

6. Dampen edges of pastry with water, place lids in position and seal firmly

SHEPHERD'S PIE

This popular family dish is a simple and tasty way of using up cold leftover lamb. It can be served with a mixed salad or your favourite freshly cooked vegetables – either way it's just the thing for a delicious lunch or a supper treat.

Calories per portion: 427 | **SERVES 6**

2 lb/900 g potatoes, peeled
1 lb/450 g leftover roast lamb
1 large onion
2 large carrots
2 tbsp olive oil
1 oz/25 g plain flour
1 tbsp dried mixed herbs
1 tbsp tomato purée
14 oz/397 g can tomatoes, drained and chopped
½ pint/300 ml lamb stock or leftover lamb gravy
salt and freshly ground black pepper
2 oz/50g butter
2-3 tbsp milk

Preheat oven to Gas 7, 425°F, 220°C, 15 mins before cooking the Shepherd's Pie. Cut the potatoes into small pieces, cook in boiling, salted water for 15 mins, until soft.

Meanwhile, cut the cooked lamb off the bone then cut into small pieces, discarding any fat or gristle, then chop with a large knife. (To make the job quicker, use two evenly weighted knives, holding one in each hand. Chop the meat by letting the knives fall alternately and rhythmically.) Alternatively if you have a mincer, pass the meat through using the coarse cutter.

Peel the onion, then chop finely. Peel carrots, trim, then cut into small cubes. Heat the oil in a large frying pan, add the onion and carrot and cook over a low heat for 10-15 mins until softened but not browned. Stir in the flour and herbs, cook for 2 mins, then add tomato purée, tomatoes, chopped lamb and the stock or gravy. Bring to the boil, stirring all the time. Allow to simmer for 5 mins. Season well with salt and pepper. Remove from the heat and spoon into an ovenproof dish, smooth the top and set aside.

Drain the cooked potatoes, mash well, then add 1 oz/25 g butter, milk and seasoning to taste. Beat until smooth and creamy, then spread mashed potatoes evenly over the lamb. Mark the top with a criss-cross pattern using a fork or palette knife.

Melt remaining butter in a small pan then brush melted butter carefully over the potato. Cook in oven for 35-40 mins until golden brown and thoroughly heated through.

Serve with baked tomatoes and spring greens.

HANDY TIPS

Shepherd's Pie freezes really well. You can prepare the pie, but omit brushing the top with the melted butter. Allow pie to cool, then cover and label before freezing.
To cook – allow to thaw in the fridge overnight, then brush top with the butter and cook as before. If preferred, the onion and carrots can be minced coarsely as well.

1. Cut the cooked lamb off the bone in thick slices, discarding any gristle

2. Cut slices into small pieces, then chop using one or two large knives

3. Fry onion and carrots in the oil until they are softened, but not browned

4. Add the flour and mixed herbs and cook for 2 mins, stirring throughout

5. Add lamb, tomato purée, tomatoes and stock. Bring to boil, simmer 5 mins

6. Spoon lamb into an ovenproof dish, then cover with the mashed potatoes

BEEF TOURNEDOS

Delicious, tender steaks that just melt in the mouth – served on croûtons of fried bread with pâté and topped with a pat of maître d'hôtel beurre. With a rich red wine sauce, perfect for a special occasion.

Calories per portion: 810 **SERVES 6**

FOR THE MAÎTRE D'HÔTEL BEURRE:
4 oz/100 g unsalted butter
2 tbsp freshly chopped parsley
freshly ground black pepper
2-3 tbsp lemon juice
FOR THE MAIN DISH:
3 oz/75 g mushrooms
6 slices white bread
6 tournedos (fillet steak), each about 6oz/175g in weight
salt and freshly ground black pepper
2½ oz/65 g unsalted butter
2 tbsp vegetable oil
1 tbsp plain flour
8 fl oz/250 ml Madeira or red wine
6 slices smooth pâté (about 6 oz/175 g total weight)
4 tbsp double cream

Beat together all the ingredients for the maître d'hôtel beurre until well mixed. Form into a long roll about 1½ in/4 cm thick. Wrap in greaseproof paper and chill until required.

HANDY TIPS

Tournedos are small round slices of beef normally 1½ in/4 cm thick, taken from the middle of a fillet of beef. The classic tournedos recipe is served with pâté de foie gras and slices of truffle. Other names for this cut include filet mignon and châteaubriand, the latter is usually served whole.

Wipe or wash and dry mushrooms and slice thinly. Leave to one side. Cut out six 4 in/10 cm rounds from bread and leave on one side.

Lightly wash and dry the steaks, discarding any fat and trim to a neat round. Season on both sides with salt and pepper. Melt 1 oz/25 g of the butter with the oil in a frying pan then cook the steaks on both sides over a moderate heat. Cook for 2-3 mins on each side for rare, 4-5 mins each side for medium and 6-8 mins both sides for well done. When cooked, remove from pan, draining well, and keep hot.

Melt ½ oz/15 g of the remaining butter in a separate pan, add mushrooms and cook for 2 mins. Pour off all but about 1 tbsp of the butter left in pan then sprinkle in the flour. Cook, stirring for 2 mins, then gradually stir in the madeira or wine, allow to simmer for 5 mins.

Meanwhile melt the remaining 1 oz/25 g butter in the cleaned frying pan then fry the rounds of bread on both sides for 1-2 mins or until golden brown and crisp. Drain well on absorbent paper.

Cut six 4 in/10 cm rounds from the pâté then place on top of fried bread. Top with the steaks and place a knob of maître d'hôtel beurre on top. Place on a warmed serving dish.

Pour the double cream into the wine sauce and mix well. Heat through then pour around the tournedos. Serve any extra sauce separately. Serve immediately with vegetables of your choice.

1. Form butter into 1½ in/4 cm thick roll. Wrap in greaseproof paper

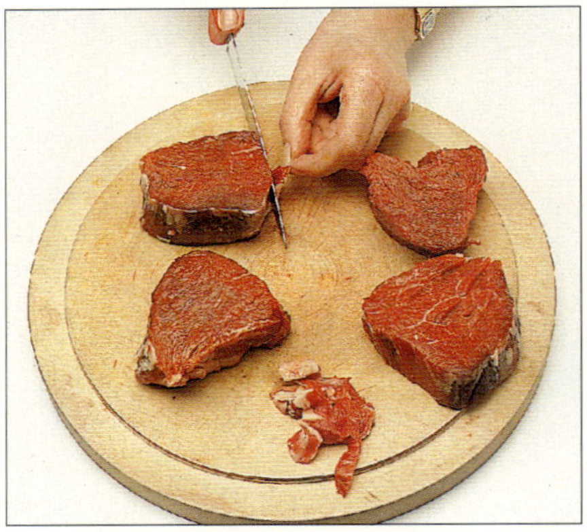

2. Trim steak with a sharp knife, discard any fat and shape into neat rounds

3. Heat butter and oil in pan. Fry steaks on both sides. Drain and keep hot

4. Cook mushrooms in remaining butter for 2 mins then slowly add the wine

5. Fry bread in cleaned pan for 2-3 mins each side, until crisp and golden

6. When ingredients are cooked, assemble tournedos, place on serving dish

CHILLI CON CARNE

This famous Mexican dish can be as fiery or as mild as you like, depending on how brave you're feeling! Made with lean minced beef, tomatoes, red kidney beans and chillies, it's an economical meal that's always popular.

Calories per portion: 440 **SERVES 4**

2-3 fresh chillies
1 lb/450 g ripe tomatoes
1-2 garlic cloves
1 large onion
1 tbsp oil
1 lb/450 g lean minced beef
1 tbsp flour
salt and freshly ground black pepper
2 tbsp tomato purée
¼ pint/150 ml beef stock
15 oz/432 g can red kidney beans
fresh coriander sprigs

Cut the tops from the fresh chillies, scoop out and discard the seeds. Wash thoroughly under cold water. (Wash your hands really well after handling fresh chillies and never touch your eyes, mouth or nose while preparing them as the seeds burn when in contact with the skin.)

Make a small cross in the top of each tomato, place in a large bowl and cover with boiling water. Leave for 2 mins, then drain. Peel and discard the skins. Cut tomatoes into quarters, scoop out and discard seeds, then chop roughly.

Peel the garlic cloves, then peel and finely chop the onion. Crush the chillies and garlic cloves in a pestle and mortar. Alternatively, chop finely, either in a food processor or on a board with a sharp knife.

Heat the oil, then fry the chopped onion with the garlic and chillies for 5 mins, or until the onion is soft and transparent. Add the minced beef and continue to fry, stirring frequently with a wooden spoon, until the beef is browned all over. Ensure the meat is well broken up and not in large lumps. Add the chopped tomatoes, then sprinkle in the flour, with salt and pepper to taste. Cook for 1 min, then stir in the tomato purée and stock. Bring to the boil, then cover and simmer for 30 mins.

Drain kidney beans and rinse under cold water, add to pan and continue to cook for a further 15 mins. Serve hot with freshly cooked long grain rice, garnished with fresh coriander.

1. Cut tops off chillies and scoop out seeds. Rinse well, then wash your hands

2. Put tomatoes in boiling water for 2 mins, peel, quarter and discard seeds

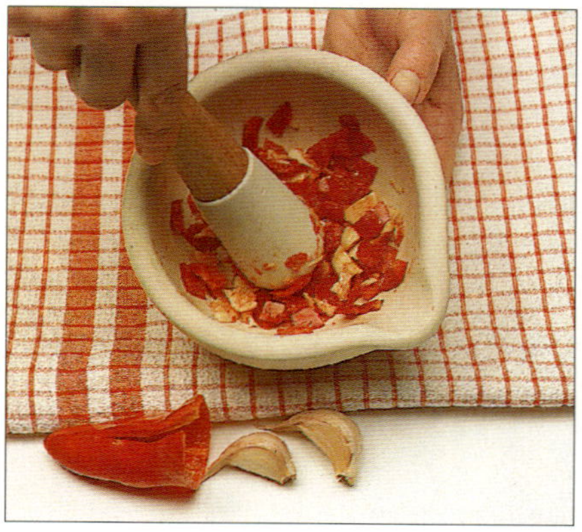

3. Crush chillies and garlic in a pestle and mortar or chop in a processor

HANDY TIPS

Dried chillies or chilli powder can be substituted for the fresh chillies. Use 1-2 tsp, depending on how fiery you like your food. You can also buy dried red kidney beans. If using these, soak overnight in cold water. Next day, drain, place in pan, cover with cold water. Bring to the boil and boil vigorously for 10 mins. Reduce heat, cover and simmer for 30 mins, drain. Add to the frying pan with the other chilli ingredients and cook for 15 mins.

4. Fry the chopped onion in oil for 5 mins with crushed chillies and garlic

5. Fry the minced beef in frying pan, stirring throughout, until browned

6. When beef is browned, add the chopped tomatoes and seasoning

Roast Lamb

This mouthwatering dish of succulent, tender slices of roast lamb, delicately flavoured with garlic and rosemary, is an ideal choice for a traditional Sunday roast. What makes this dish truly irresistible is its tangy apricot sauce.

Calories per portion: 394 | **Serves 6**

1 leg of lamb, preferably English or Welsh, approx 4 lb/1.75 kg in weight
1-2 garlic cloves
sprigs of fresh rosemary
salt and freshly ground black pepper
2 tbsp olive oil
FOR THE APRICOT SAUCE:
14 oz/397g can apricots in natural juice
1 cinnamon stick
1 oz/25g butter
3 tbsp wine vinegar
1 oz/25g demerara sugar
1 tsp freshly grated nutmeg

Preheat oven to Gas 8, 450°F, 230°C, 15 mins before roasting lamb. Wipe the lamb with a clean damp cloth and then place on a clean surface. Cut off the shank bone just above the knuckle. Turn the joint round and cut the exposed surface round the pelvic bone. Cut deep into the flesh, following the shape of the bone. When you have exposed the ball and socket joint, sever the tendons joining the pelvic bone to the thigh bone. Remove pelvic bone. Cut away any excess fat.

Peel the garlic cloves, then cut into thin slivers. Using a sharp knife, make small incisions just under the skin and insert the slivers of garlic. This will ensure that, during cooking, the flavour of the garlic penetrates the whole joint of lamb. Place small sprigs of rosemary into the cuts in which you have inserted the garlic. Season with the salt and freshly ground black pepper.

Place in a roasting tin, brush with olive oil, then roast in the oven. For your cooking time, allow 10-12 mins per 1 lb/450 g plus 12 mins for pink meat, 15-20 mins per 1 lb/450 g plus 20 mins for medium lamb, 25-30 mins per 1 lb/450 g plus 25 mins for well cooked meat. After 10 mins, reduce heat to Gas 4, 350°F, 180°C, and continue to roast for the calculated cooking time. Baste the meat from time to time during cooking. When it's cooked, remove from the oven. Pour off the juice, reserving it for gravy, and allow the joint to stand for 10 mins before carving.

To make the apricot sauce, purée the contents of the can of apricots in a food processor or blender until smooth. Pour into a small saucepan. Lightly bruise the cinnamon stick, add to the pan with the butter, wine vinegar and sugar. Finely grate the nutmeg into the pan. Heat the sauce through gently, stir occasionally and allow to simmer for 8-10 mins. Discard cinnamon stick before serving.

Handy Tips

If preferred use 8 oz/225 g no-need-to-soak apricots to make the sauce. Simmer apricots in ¼ pint/150 ml water for 10 mins then purée.

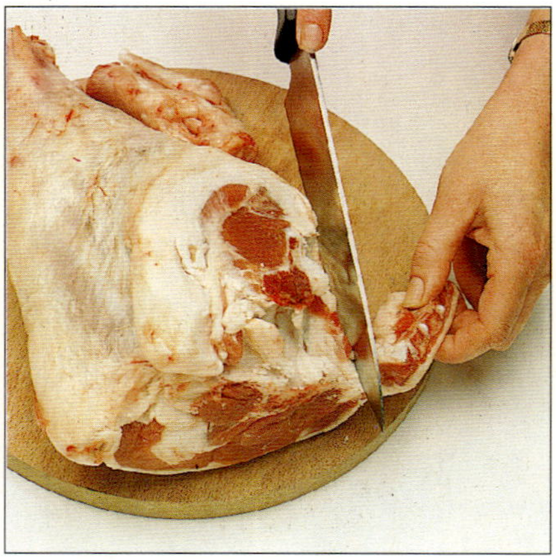

1. Cut off the shank bone just above the knuckle and small bone at pelvic end

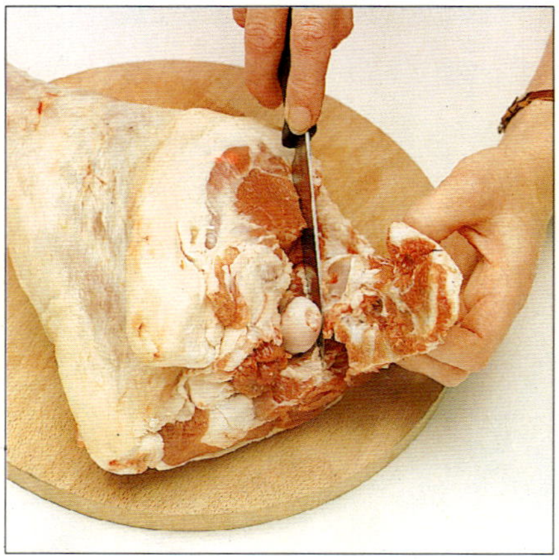

2. Remove pelvic bone, cut deep into flesh, following contours of the bone

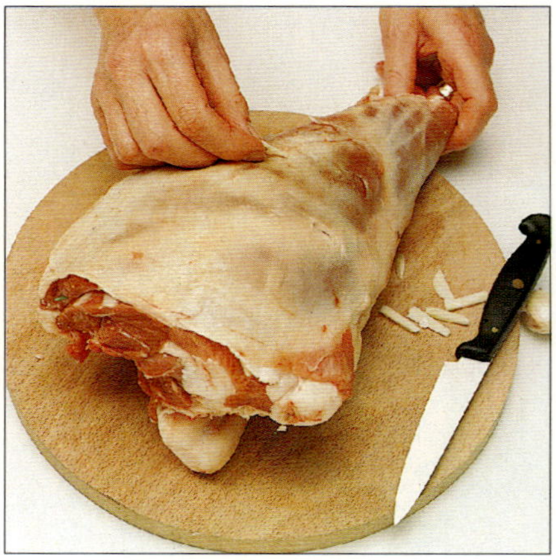

3. Cut garlic clove into slivers, then insert into lamb, just under the skin

4. Insert small sprigs of fresh rosemary into the same holes as the garlic

5. Purée apricots in a food processor or blender until smooth, pour into pan

6. Add wine vinegar, butter and sugar. Finely grate nutmeg, then add to pan

NOISETTES OF LAMB

Tender succulent cuts of lamb with a delicious creamy raspberry sauce. Perfect for a summer treat or when you want to impress. The secret is in the preparation, just follow the easy steps for a mouthwatering meal to remember.

Calories per portion: 724 **SERVES 4**

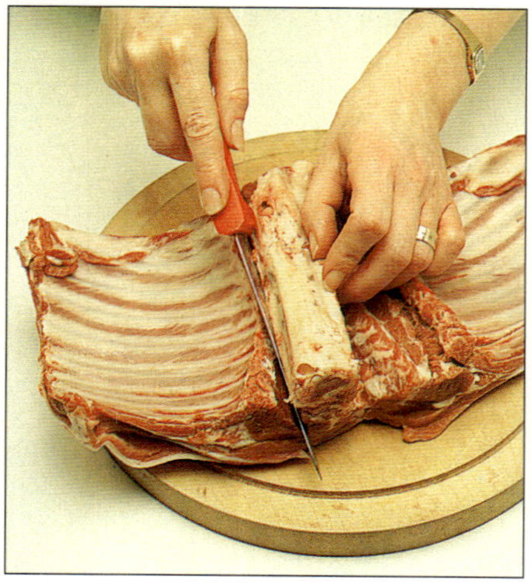

1. Ask the butcher to saw through chine bone then cut down each side, discard

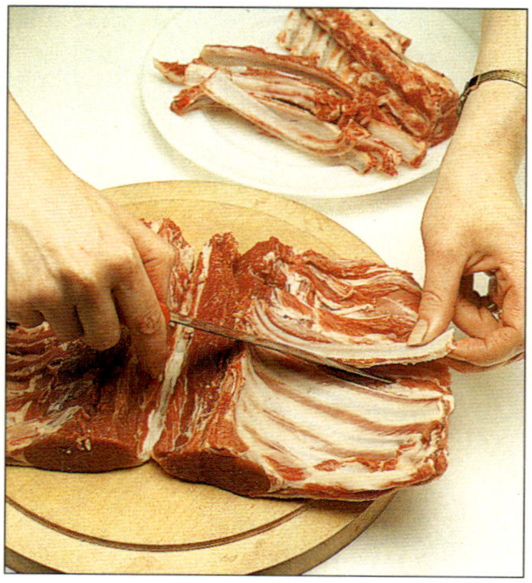

2. Cut between each rib bone and discard, leave as much meat as possible

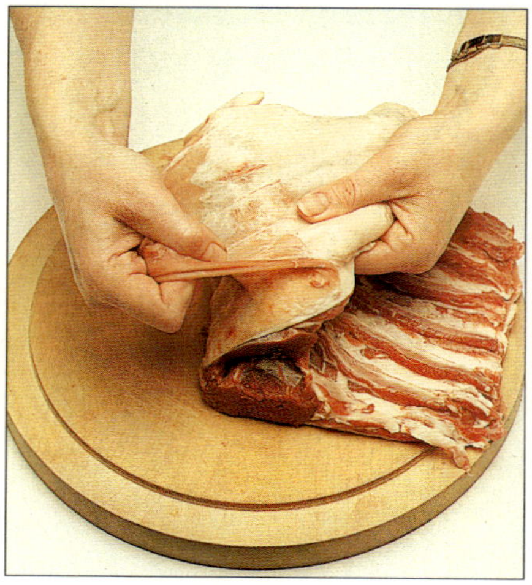

3. After boning rack of lamb, hold meat firmly then pull the skin away

1 whole English or Welsh best end of neck, approx 12-16 chops in all
salt and freshly ground black pepper
2 tbsp oil
2 tbsp flour
¼ pint/150 ml lamb or vegetable stock
12 oz/350 g raspberries
3 tbsp redcurrant jelly
¼ pint/150 ml crème fraîche
fresh mint leaves

Ask your butcher to saw through the chine bone of the lamb. Using a very sharp knife, cut down between the chine bone and the edge of the meat, then carefully remove the chine bone. Place the rack skin side down on a board, then, using a very sharp knife, carefully cut down each side of the rib bones. Ease the bone up and cut down the back of the bone, remove. Repeat this until all the bones are removed, then remove any cartilage that lies at the tip of the meat.

Turn the meat over and, holding it firmly with one hand, take the top edge of the skin and pull it away from the lamb. Don't try and cut it away as you will not get an even surface, which will affect the finished look of the noisettes. Trim away any pieces of cartilage or bone.

Cut the rack in half, season with salt and freshly ground black pepper. Place the racks, meat uppermost, then roll into neat rolls, tucking in any odd pieces of meat. Tie the meat at 2 in/5 cm intervals. Cut into four.

Brush the noisettes with a little oil. Preheat the grill, then place the noisettes on the grill rack and cook for 5-8 mins each side, depending on how thick the noisettes are and how pink you like your lamb. Remove from the rack, place on a serving plate and keep hot.

Drain off the fat from the grill pan and place in a small pan. Hull raspberries, rinse lightly. Purée 10 oz/300 g of the raspberries in a food processor then sieve to remove pips.

Heat the reserved fat, sift in the flour and cook for 2 mins. Remove from the heat and stir in the stock, raspberry purée and add redcurrant jelly. Return to the heat and cook, stirring throughout until the sauce thickens and the jelly has melted.

Season with salt and pepper then stir in the crème fraîche. Heat through until hot but do not allow to boil. Garnish noisettes with remaining raspberries and mint leaves. Serve with prepared sauce and vegetables of your choice.

Handy tip

You can buy the racks of lamb fresh from your butcher. Prepare the noisettes and then freeze, uncooked, until ready to use. To thaw, place in bottom of fridge, covered, and leave overnight.

4. Cut the meat in half then neatly roll both pieces up, tuck in any spare meat

5. Tie meat with string to form a neat roll. Use a double knot to make it secure

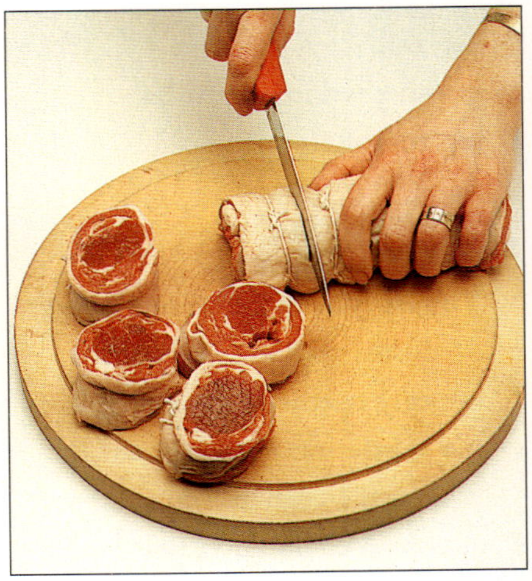

6. Using a sharp knife, cut each roll into four 2 in/5 cm thick noisettes

ROGHAN JOSH

Tasty chunks of lamb in a rich, mild yogurt sauce, with a hint of spice. This authentic curry is perfect for entertaining friends. Serve with poppadoms, tangy lime pickle, nutty rice and a cool cucumber raita for a true taste of India.

Calories per portion: 812 **SERVES 4**

2 in/5 cm piece root ginger
10 garlic cloves, peeled
¼ pint/150 ml vegetable oil
2 lb/900 g shoulder of lamb, boned, trimmed and cubed
12 green cardamom pods
2 fresh bay leaves
8 cloves
12 black peppercorns
2 in/5 cm piece cinnamon stick
8 oz/225 g onions, peeled and chopped
1½ tsp ground coriander
2½ tsp ground cumin
5 tsp paprika
1½ tsp cayenne pepper
1½ tsp salt
3 fl oz/75 ml low-fat natural yogurt
½ tsp garam masala
fresh coriander sprigs to garnish
FOR THE RICE:
1 tbsp oil
12 oz/350 g basmati rice
1 oz/25 g flaked almonds
½ tsp salt
6 green cardamom pods
1 tsp turmeric

HANDY TIPS

Yogurt is added to many Indian dishes and adds a delicate creamy texture to the dish with a subtle tartness. It must be added 1 tbsp at a time and allowed to be absorbed in the sauce before the next addition, otherwise the sauce may curdle.

Peel and finely chop the root ginger. Place in food processor with garlic and 5 tbsp water. Blend to form a smooth paste. Reserve. Heat half the oil in a large frying pan. Fry meat until sealed. Remove from pan and reserve. Place the cardamom pods, bay leaves, cloves, peppercorns and cinnamon stick in frying pan with remaining oil. Cook for 1 min. Add onions and cook for 5 mins. Stir in reserved garlic and ginger paste, coriander, cumin, paprika, cayenne and salt. Cook for 1 min, stirring well to mix the spices.

Return meat to pan. Stir well. Cook for 2 mins. Add yogurt, 1 tbsp at a time, stirring well. Cook for further 5-6 mins. Add ½ pint/300 ml water, stirring. Bring to boil. Reduce heat, cover, simmer for 1 hr. If preferred the lamb can be cooked in the oven, Gas 4, 350°F, 180°C for 1 hr.

Remove lid and cook, uncovered, for 30 mins, or until the meat is tender and liquid has reduced to form a thick reddish sauce.

Meanwhile, cook the rice. Heat the oil in a frying pan. Add rice, almonds, salt and cardamom pods. Fry for 3 mins. Add turmeric and 1½ pints/900 ml water, bring to boil, then simmer for 15-20 mins until liquid is absorbed and the rice is cooked.

Remove Roghan Josh from heat, skim off any excess oil. Place in warmed serving dish. Sprinkle with garam masala, garnish with coriander sprigs. Serve with the rice and a cucumber raita.

1. Blend ginger, garlic and water to a smooth paste in a food processor

2. Seal and brown the meat in the oil. Remove from pan and reserve

3. Add cardamom pods, bay leaves, cloves, pepper, cinnamon and onions

4. Return the meat and juices to the pan. Stir in the yogurt, 1 tbsp at a time

5. Gradually add ½ pint/300 ml water, bring to the boil, stirring, then simmer

6. Skim off any excess oil from the top of the thickened Roghan Josh

Cassoulet

Tasty chunks of bacon, lamb and sausages are combined with haricot beans, vegetables and herbs, then simmered until tender, to create this delicious traditional French dish. Make it as a mouthwatering main meal for lunch or supper.

Calories per portion: 803 | **Serves 6**

1. Place washed beans in a large bowl, cover with water and soak overnight

2. Add bacon, carrots, onion, tomatoes, garlic and bouquet garni to the pan

3. Trim lamb and cut into cubes, then melt fat in a second pan and brown meat

1 lb/450 g dried haricot beans
8 oz/225 g piece smoked bacon, rind removed
2 small carrots, peeled
1 small onion, peeled and studded with 2-3 cloves
8 medium tomatoes
4 garlic cloves, peeled
1 bay leaf
1 parsley sprig
2 thyme sprigs
1 lb/450 g boneless lamb, such as fillet
2 oz/50 g lard or white vegetable fat
1 medium onion
salt and freshly ground black pepper
1 tbsp freshly chopped thyme
2 large pork sausages, quartered
6 oz/175 g garlic sausage, thickly sliced
4 oz/100 g white breadcrumbs
flat-leaved parsley to garnish

Preheat the oven to Gas 3, 325°F, 160°C, 10 mins before baking the Cassoulet. Wash the beans, then cover in cold water and leave to soak overnight. Drain beans, then place in a large pan with the bacon, carrots and studded onion. Peel and chop 4 tomatoes, then crush 2 garlic cloves and add to the pan. Tie the bay leaf, parsley and thyme sprigs together to make a bouquet garni, then add to the pan with 3 pints/1.7 litres water. Bring to the boil, then cover and simmer for 1-1½ hrs, or until the beans are tender.

Meanwhile, trim lamb, discarding fat, and cut into cubes. Melt 1 oz/25 g fat in another large pan, add lamb and brown. Peel and slice the onion, finely chop 1 of the remaining garlic cloves, then add to the pan and cook for 3-4 mins. Add ½ pint/300 ml water. Peel and chop the remaining tomatoes, then add to the pan with seasoning and thyme. Bring to the boil, cover and simmer for 1½ hrs.

Melt the remaining fat in a pan and brown the quartered sausages. Drain, then add to the lamb with the garlic sausage for the last 10 mins of cooking time.

Remove beans from the heat, discard herbs, carrots and onion. Remove the bacon joint and cut into chunks. Rub the inside of a 4 pint/2.25 litre oven-proof casserole with the remaining peeled garlic clove. Place half of the beans in the base of the casserole. Top with lamb mixture and the bacon, then cover with the remaining beans. Sprinkle 2 oz/50 g breadcrumbs over and bake, uncovered, for 1½ hrs, stirring occasionally to prevent a crust forming, sprinkling each time with more breadcrumbs. When all the bread-crumbs have been used, increase oven temperature to Gas 4, 350°F, 180°C, 25 mins before end of cooking time, so that the top turns golden. Garnish and serve with salad.

HANDY TIPS

You can use dried red kidney beans instead of haricot beans. After soaking, place in pan, cover with water and boil vigorously for 10 mins. Drain, add bacon and rest of ingredients. Or use canned beans then there is no need to soak or cook first. Add carrots, onions, tomatoes and garlic to the lamb, before cooking.

4. Add chopped tomatoes, seasoning and thyme, cover and simmer for 1½ hrs

5. Place half the beans in casserole, top with meat, cover with remaining beans

6. Bake, uncovered, for 1½ hrs, stirring occasionally to prevent crust forming

Lamb en Croute

Tender cutlets of lamb with a delicious lemon and mint stuffing, encased in crisp, golden puff pastry. This dish is the perfect answer for a special lunch or dinner party. It's impressive, but so easy to make with this step-by-step guide.

Calories per portion: 1,160 **Serves 4**

best end of lamb joint, with 8 cutlets (ask butcher to chine them)
1 small onion
4 button mushrooms
1 oz/25 g butter or margarine
2 oz/50 g fresh white breadcrumbs
1 tbsp freshly chopped mint
grated rind of ½ lemon
salt and freshly ground black pepper
1 egg, size 3, beaten
1 lb/450 g prepared puff pastry
sprigs of fresh mint to garnish
cutlet frills (optional)

Preheat grill. Preheat oven to Gas 7, 425°F, 220°C, 15 mins before cooking. Place lamb on a chopping board. Remove the bone at base of meat, discard any fat. With a small sharp knife, trim meat and fat away from bone at top end of joint to a depth of 2 in/5 cm. Clean bones well.

Peel and finely chop the onion. Wipe and chop mushrooms. Melt butter or margarine in a small pan, then fry onion for 5 mins until soft and transparent. Add the mushrooms and fry for a further minute. Remove from heat. Stir in the breadcrumbs, mint, lemon rind and seasoning to taste. Mix well, then bind with sufficient egg to form a stiff mixture. Reserve remaining egg. Allow stuffing to cool.

Place the cutlets under the preheated grill and brown on both sides. Remove and drain on absorbent paper until cold. Roll out the pastry on a lightly floured surface and cut into eight squares, large enough to encase the cutlets. Reserve trimmings. Place chops on the pastry so that the bone protrudes over the edge of the pastry. Place a spoonful of the stuffing on the centre of the meat. Dampen pastry edges with water, then wrap round, completely encasing each cutlet.

Place on dampened baking sheet with the join underneath. Roll out trimmings and use to decorate the cutlets. Brush pastry with reserved egg, then bake in oven for 10 mins. Brush again with egg, then continue to cook for a further 15-20 mins, or until risen and golden. Turn over and cook underside for 5-7 mins, or until golden. Remove from oven and garnish with mint sprigs. If liked, place cutlet frills on the exposed bones before serving. Serve with freshly cooked vegetables or salad.

Handy tip

Roast a boned stuffed leg of lamb for 1½ -2 hrs. Cool, then encase in puff pastry, brush with egg and cook at Gas 6, 400°F, 200°C for 40-50 mins.

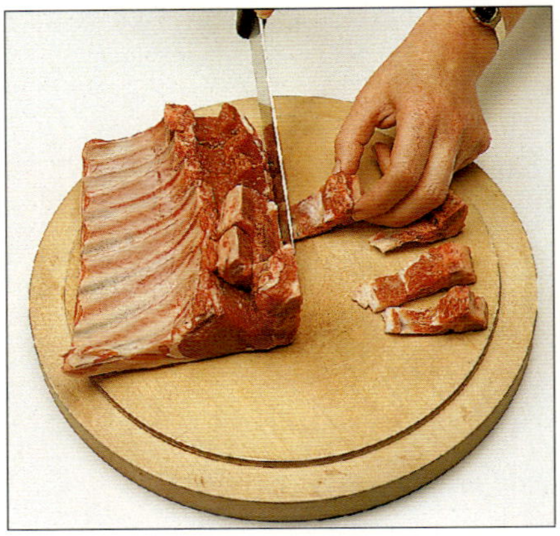

1. Carefully cut the bone away from the base of the meat with a sharp knife

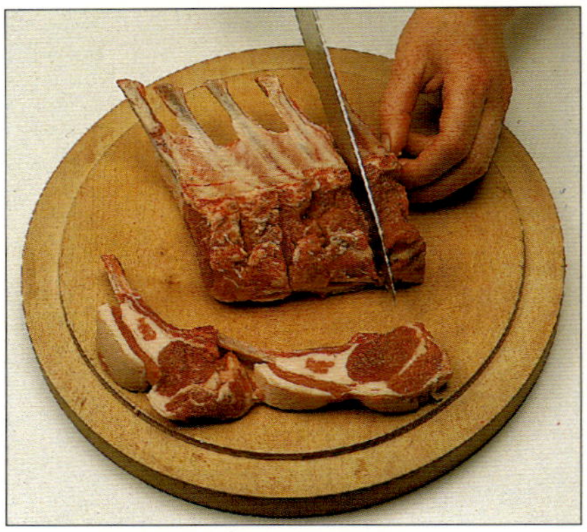

2. After trimming down the bones at the top, cut into individual cutlets

3. Add the dry ingredients to the onion and mushrooms and bind with beaten egg

4. Grill the chops on both sides until browned, then drain on absorbent paper

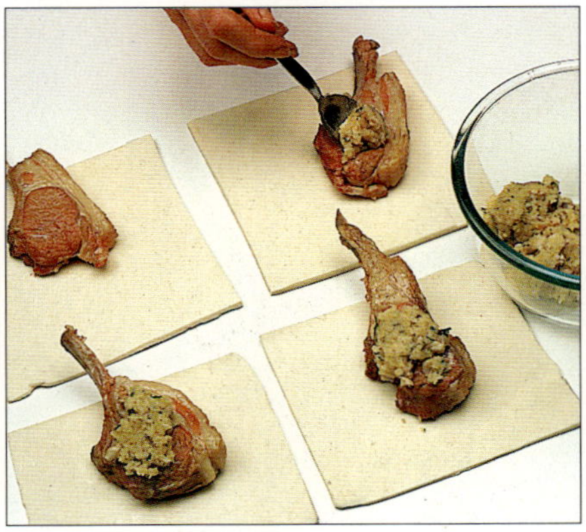

5. Place the chops on pastry squares and spoon stuffing on to centre of meat

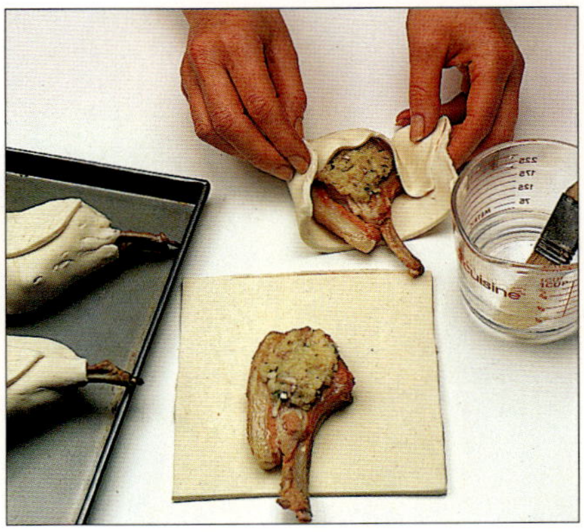

6. Dampen the edges of the pastry with water, then wrap around to encase meat

PORK ESCALOPES

Succulent pieces of pork, spiced with peppercorns and coated in breadcrumbs, then served with a creamy walnut sauce. This dish is so easy to make and so delicious, too, it's perfect when you want to serve something special.

Calories per portion: 595 | **SERVES 4**

4 x 4 oz/100 g pork steaks
2 tbsp mixed peppercorns, such as pink, green and black
2 tbsp flour
salt
1 egg, size 3
6 oz/175 g fresh, fine white breadcrumbs
2 oz/50 g unsalted butter
FOR THE WALNUT SAUCE:
½ oz/15 g unsalted butter
2 oz/50 g walnut pieces
1 oz/25 g Parmesan cheese, grated
¼ pint/150 ml single cream
1 tbsp lemon juice
salt and freshly ground black pepper
lime slices and flat-leaved parsley to garnish

Trim the pork, then place between 2 pieces of clear wrap and, using a meat mallet, beat until flattened. Place the peppercorns in a pestle and mortar, and crush. Press the crushed peppercorns on to both sides of the pork.

Place the flour in a shallow dish and season with the salt. Coat the pork steaks in seasoned flour, ensuring that they are completely covered. Beat the egg with 1 tbsp cold water and place in a shallow dish. Place the breadcrumbs in another shallow dish.

Dip the pork in the beaten egg, allow any excess egg to drip off, then completely coat the meat in the breadcrumbs. Melt butter in a frying pan and fry the pork for 5-8 mins on both sides, or until golden and cooked through. Drain well on kitchen paper and keep warm while preparing the walnut sauce.

To make the sauce, clean the pan with some kitchen paper, then add the butter. Roughly chop the walnuts, add to the pan and cook for 2-3 mins. Stir in the cheese, then the cream, and cook, stirring throughout, for 2-3 mins. Stir in the lemon juice and season to taste. Garnish the escalopes and serve.

HANDY TIPS

For an extra special occasion, add 2 tsp brandy to the sauce with the walnuts. The sauce also makes an excellent starter if mixed into freshly cooked tagliatelle, then sprinkled with extra Parmesan cheese.

1. Trim the pork, place between clearwrap, then beat with a meat mallet until flattened

2. Crush peppercorns in a pestle and mortar, then press on to both sides of the pork steaks

3. Season the flour, then coat the pork in the flour, ensuring all the pieces are completely covered

4. Dip the pork in beaten egg, allow any excess egg to drip off, then coat in the fresh breadcrumbs

5. Fry the escalopes in the melted butter for 5-8 mins on both sides, or until golden and cooked through

6. Cook the roughly chopped walnuts in butter for 2-3 mins. Stir in cheese and cream, then season

Pork Chops in Cider

Marinating meat before cooking makes it tender and flavoursome and this recipe for Pork Chops in Cider is no exception. The juniper berries and bay leaves give a subtle, yet aromatic flavour to this country-style dish.

Calories per portion: 707 | **Serves 4**

2 tbsp juniper berries
2 bay leaves
3½ tbsp olive oil
½ tsp paprika
4 tbsp clear honey
1 tbsp tomato purée
1 pint/600 ml dry cider
salt and freshly ground black pepper
4 pork loin chops, each about 6 oz/175 g in weight
2-3 tsp cornflour
7 oz/197 g can pineapple pieces in natural juice, drained
1 tbsp caster sugar
2 eating apples, cored, peeled and cut into rings

Crush the juniper berries and bay leaves using a pestle and mortar, then mix with 3 tbsp olive oil, the paprika, honey, tomato purée, 18 fl oz/500 ml cider and seasoning. Remove the rind and excess fat from the chops, place in a shallow dish and pour the marinade over them. Cover and leave to marinate in a cool place for 3-4 hours, turning the chops occasionally.

Preheat grill. Remove the chops from the marinade, drain. Cook under a moderately hot grill for 6-8 minutes each side, until well done. Brush frequently with marinade.

When cooked, place on a hot serving dish, cover and keep warm. Strain marinade into a saucepan, bring to the boil, continue boiling until marinade is reduced by half. Mix cornflour with 1 tbsp water, stir into marinade with pineapple and cook, stirring throughout until thickened.

Heat remaining oil in a wide shallow frying pan, sprinkle in caster sugar and continue cooking until sugar turns golden. Add the apple rings and turn them quickly in the caramel to brown lightly. Pour in remaining cider, bring to the boil, reduce, heat and simmer for 2-3 mins until apples are softened.

To serve, pour the cider and pineapple sauce over the chops, then garnish with apple rings. Serve with new potatoes, tossed in parsley, and a crisp green salad.

Alternatively serve with freshly cooked long grain rice, flavoured with cinnamon and stir-fried vegetables.

Handy tips

If you do not have a pestle and mortar, put the juniper berries and bay leaves into a small polythene bag and crush them with a rolling pin. Also, instead of loin chops, you could use chump chops, or try pork tenderloin.

1. Crush juniper berries and bay leaves, mix marinade ingredients together

2. Pour marinade over chops and leave covered to marinate for 3-4 hours

3. Remove chops, drain, then cook under a moderately hot preheated grill

4. Strain remaining marinade into a saucepan and boil until reduced by half

5. Mix cornflour and water, stir into marinade with pineapple. Heat through

6. Poach the prepared apple rings in cider and sugar and use to garnish chops

Baked Gammon

Lean, tender and full of goodness-gammon has that special cut-and-come-again appeal. This recipe gives it a crisp and crunchy topping which you can vary according to your taste – try orange, lemon or even glazed with honey.

Calories per portion: 894 | **Serves 10**

5 lb/2.25 kg joint gammon, preferably unsmoked
2 large onions, peeled
approx 40 cloves
10 black peppercorns
2 carrots, peeled
2 bay leaves
3 oz/75 g demerara sugar
grated rind of 1 orange

Preheat oven to Gas 6, 400°F, 200°C, 15 mins before baking gammon.

If the gammon is smoked, soak it overnight, immersed in cold water. Drain.

Place gammon in a large saucepan, and again cover with fresh cold water. Stud each of the onions with 6 cloves and add to the saucepan with the peppercorns, carrots and bay leaves. Bring to the boil, then with a draining spoon, remove any scum that rises to the surface. Lower the heat, cover then simmer gently. To calculate the cooking time allow 20-25 mins per 1 lb/450 g plus an extra 20 mins. Then simmer the joint for half the cooking time. Allow to cool in the cooking liquid for approximately 1 hr.

Remove the joint from the pan, then with a sharp knife carefully strip away the rind. If necessary remove string if used.

With a sharp knife make 1/8 in/3 mm deep cuts at 1/2 in/1.25 cm intervals across the fat. Then stud each diamond shape with a clove, using a skewer to make a hole if you have difficulty in inserting the cloves.

Mix the demerara sugar with the grated orange rind, then carefully pat into the fat, pressing firmly with the back of a spoon.

Cover the joint lightly with foil, then bake in the oven for the remainder of the calculated cooking time, but remove foil for the last 20 mins. Serve on a platter with seasonal vegetables.

HANDY TIPS

Replace the orange rind with lemon rind or try substituting a 6 1/2 oz/185 g jar of cranberry orange sauce for the demerara sugar and orange – just spoon over the top of the joint 30 mins before end of cooking time. Or pour 3 tbsp of clear honey over the clove-studded gammon, adding 3 tbsp water to the roasting tin before baking, basting with the liquid during cooking.

1. Place gammon in a pan large enough to cover joint with water. Add onions

2. When removing scum, take care not to remove the peppercorns or bay leaves

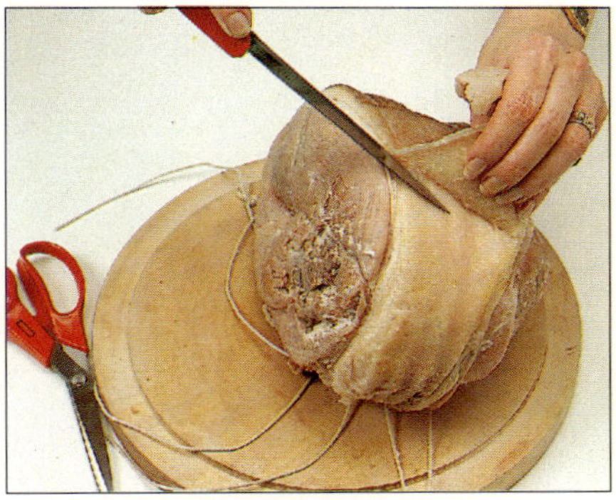

3. Carefully strip away the rind to expose the fat and trim away any excess fat

4. Make cuts 1/8 in/3 mm deep into the fat at 1/2 in/1.25 cm intervals across the joint

5. Firmly insert a clove into each diamond shape, across top and down the sides

6. Cover fat well with demerara sugar, pressing down firmly with back of spoon

PORK CHASSEUR

Tender strips of pork fillet with green and red peppers, button mushrooms that are all gently simmered in white wine and served with freshly cooked white and green tagliatelle. It's so easy to prepare and cook.

Calories per portion: 746 | **SERVES 4**

1½ lb/675 g pork fillet
12 juniper berries
1 large onion
1 green pepper
1 red pepper
6 oz/175 g button mushrooms
3-4 tbsp vegetable oil
½ pint/300 ml white wine
½ pint/300 ml pork or vegetable stock
salt and freshly ground black pepper
2 bay leaves
1½ oz/40 g butter or margarine
1½ oz/40 g flour
freshly cooked white and green tagliatelle to serve

Preheat oven to Gas 4, 350°F, 180°C. Discard any fat from pork and cut into strips 2 in/5 cm long x ½ in/1.25 cm thick. Place juniper berries in a pestle and mortar and crush lightly. Alternatively, place them in a polythene bag and crush with a rolling pin. Reserve.

Peel onion, slice thinly. Deseed green and red peppers, slice thinly into rings. Wipe or wash and dry the mushrooms.

HANDY TIP

Juniper berries are small black berries, obtainable from major supermarkets and delicatessens. They are crushed lightly to help the extraction of their fragrance and aroma. They have a slightly woody, smoky flavour and are used in the making of gin.

Heat the oil in a large frying pan then fry the pork until browned on all sides. Drain, using a slotted spoon and place in a 4 pint/2.25 litre ovenproof casserole dish. Lightly fry the juniper berries in the remaining oil for 1 min. Add the sliced onion and peppers and then continue to fry for a further 5 mins or until onion is transparent and soft. Pour in wine and stock with seasoning to taste. Bring to the boil then pour over the pork. Add the bay leaves, cover and cook in the oven for 1½-2 hrs or until pork is tender.

Half an hour before end of cooking time, fry the mushrooms in ½ oz/15 g of the butter or margarine, drain, then add to casserole. When pork is cooked, discard bay leaves and pour liquid into small saucepan. Arrange the pork and vegetables on serving dish and keep warm.

Cream the remaining butter or margarine and flour together to form beurre manié. Boil cooking liquid for 5 mins, then reduce heat and whisk in small spoonfuls of the beurre manié until sauce is smooth and thickened. Pour over the pork and vegetables and serve with the freshly cooked white and green tagliatelle.

1. Discard fat then cut pork tenderloin into 2 in x ½ in/5 cm x 1.25 cm strips

2. Lightly crush the juniper berries in a pestle and mortar to extract the flavour

3. Peel, thinly slice onion, deseed peppers, slice. Wash and dry mushrooms

4. Heat oil, fry pork until browned all over. Transfer to an ovenproof casserole

5. Fry onion and peppers for 5 mins, or until onion is soft. Add the wine

6. Place stock in saucepan. Whisk in small amounts of beurre manié until thickened

Roast Stuffed Pork

Slices of roast pork, nutty stuffing flavoured with peaches and fresh herbs and crisp golden crackling create this mouthwatering treat; ideal for a perfect Sunday lunch.

Calories per portion: 204 **Serves 12**

- **3 oz/75 g dried peaches**
- **3 lb/1.5k g pork joint, boned and scored**
- **1 oz/25 g half-fat butter**
- **1 small onion**
- **1 stick celery**
- **4 oz/100 g fresh white breadcrumbs**
- **2 oz/50 g pine kernels**
- **1½ tbsp freshly chopped parsley and rosemary, mixed together**
- **1 egg, size 5**
- **oil for brushing**
- **2 tbsp coarse rock salt**

Handy Tips

Standing the pork on a trivet or rack helps greatly in achieving crisp crackling. When carving, cut the string and discard. Cut crackling off first and divide into portions. This makes the joint easier to carve.

The best joints to use are: boned and rolled loin; boned half leg; and boned and rolled hand and spring.

For a change, try serving the apple sauce in drained, canned peach halves.

Preheat oven to Gas 4, 350°F, 180°C. Place dried peaches in a small saucepan, cover with boiling water. Cook over a gentle heat for 10 mins. Drain, allow to cool then chop. Wipe pork with a clean damp cloth and leave joint in fridge while preparing stuffing.

Melt fat in a saucepan. Peel and finely chop the onion. Trim, scrub then finely chop the celery. Cook the onion and celery in the melted fat for 5 mins or until soft and transparent but not browned. Remove from heat. Stir in the chopped peaches, breadcrumbs, pine kernels and herbs. Season to taste. Add the egg and mix the stuffing to a stiff consistency.

Lay the pork out on a clean surface or chopping board, rind side down. Place stuffing in the centre of the joint, packing it down firmly. Roll the meat up and secure with string, encasing the stuffing as much as possible. Tie the joint in several places to help keep its shape during cooking.

Weigh joint then calculate cooking time allowing 30 mins per 1 lb/450 g, plus 30 mins. Place joint on a trivet or rack and stand in a roasting tin. Brush rind with oil, then sprinkle with freshly ground rock salt.

Place on centre shelf of oven and cook for the calculated time. Thirty mins before the end of the cooking, remove from oven and grind more salt over the rind to give a really crisp crackling. Allow joint to stand for at least 5 mins before carving. Use juices from tin to make gravy.

1. Melt the fat in the pan and gently fry the onion and celery for 5 mins

2. Bind all the stuffing ingredients to a stiff consistency with the egg

3. Place the stuffing in the centre of the joint, packing it down firmly

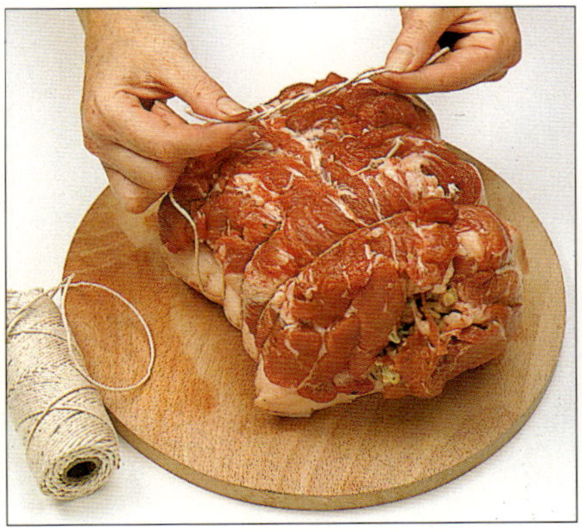

4. Tie the joint securely in several places to keep its shape during cooking

5. Place the joint on a trivet or rack in a roasting tin. Brush with oil

6. For a crisp crackling, grind rock salt over the rind before and during cooking

Oriental Pork

Succulent strips of pork gently cooked in sherry and soy sauce with colourful crunchy peppers and water chestnuts give this casserole a taste of the Orient. Serve it for a special occasion or as a family meal.

Calories per portion: 480 | **Serves 4**

- **1 small red pepper, washed**
- **1 small green pepper, washed**
- **1 small yellow pepper, washed**
- **1½ lb/675 g lean pork, preferably from leg, spare rib or fillet**
- **2 in/5 cm piece root ginger**
- **1 large onion**
- **2 tbsp vegetable oil**
- **2 tbsp soy sauce**
- **¼ pint/150 ml dry sherry**
- **1-2 tsp Chinese five spice powder**
- **¾ pint/450 ml pork or vegetable stock**
- **7 oz/227 g can water chestnuts**
- **1 oz/25 g butter or margarine**
- **1 oz/25 g plain flour**
- **spring onion tassels to garnish**
- **freshly cooked Chinese egg noodles and stir fried vegetables to serve**

Preheat oven to Gas 4, 350°F, 180°C. Cut the tops off peppers, discard seeds, cut in half lengthways, then into strips about ¼ in/6 mm thick. Discard fat and bones from pork, cut into 1 in/2.5 cm slices then cut into strips about 3 in/7.5 cm long x ½ in/1.25 cm wide. Thinly peel root ginger, then either grate or chop finely. Peel the onion and slice thinly.

Heat oil then gently fry the onion for 5 mins or until soft and transparent. Transfer to ovenproof casserole using a draining spoon. Add pork and grated ginger to oil remaining in pan and fry until meat is brown. Turn heat down, add the soy sauce, sherry, Chinese five spice powder and stock. Bring slowly to boil then pour into casserole dish. Cover and cook in oven for 1 hr or until pork is just tender.

Place peppers into large bowl, pour over boiling water to cover and leave for 2 mins. Drain thoroughly, then add to casserole, together with drained water chestnuts. Continue to cook for a further 15 mins.

Beat the butter or margarine with the flour to a beurre manié. Pour off the liquid into a small saucepan and bring to a slow boil. Drop small amounts of beurre manié into liquid and whisk vigorously until sauce is thick and smooth. Check seasoning, then pour over cooked pork and peppers.

Mix well, arrange on a warmed serving dish. Serve immediately with freshly cooked Chinese egg noodles, decorated with a spring onion tassel, stir-fried vegetables such as strips of carrot, mangetout, baby corn and bean sprouts, and extra soy sauce.

Handy Tip

For a change, add mushrooms – oyster or chanterelle are usually available. Clean, fry lightly in oil, drain and add to casserole with the peppers and water chestnuts.

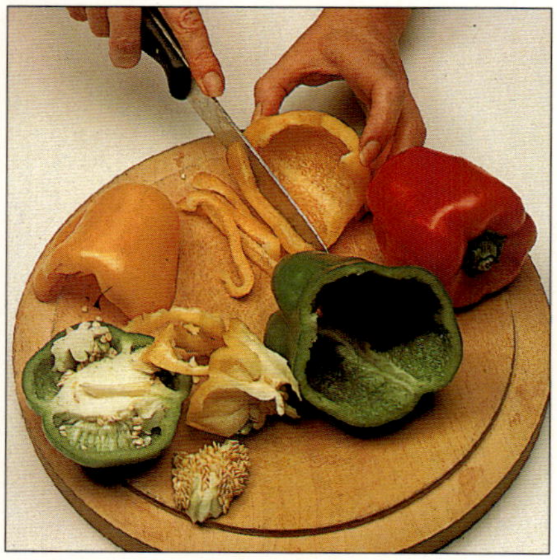

1. Cut top from peppers, discard seeds and cut in half. Cut into thin strips

2. Trim pork, discard fat and bone. Cut into 1 in/2.5 cm slices then thin strips

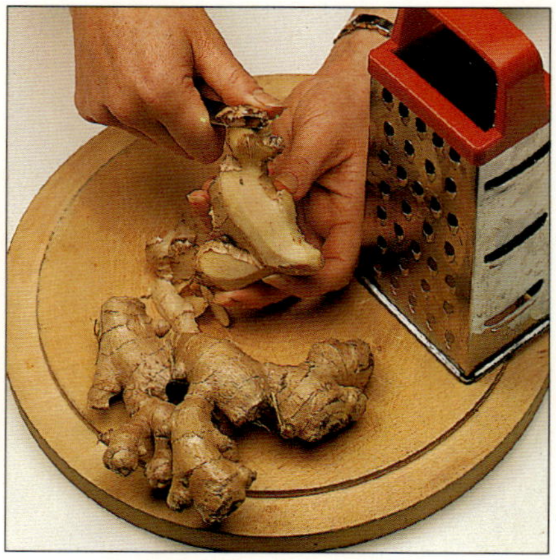

3. Thinly peel root ginger with small kitchen knife, then grate or chop

4. Fry sliced onion in oil. Using draining spoon transfer to casserole

5. Using wooden spoon, fry pork and ginger in remaining oil until brown

6. Turn heat to very low, add soy sauce, sherry, five spice powder and stock

Fish Casserole

Try this unusual combination of tender pieces of moist fish and lightly cooked vegetables, braised in beer and served in a delicious creamy sauce. Ideal for a quick and easy mid week supper dish.

Calories per portion: 512 | **Serves 4**

8 oz/225 g baby onions
8 oz/225 g carrots
2 celery sticks
6 oz/175 g courgettes
1½ lb/675 g huss fillets or monkfish
1½ tbsp seasoned flour
3 tbsp sunflower oil
2 bay leaves
½ pint/300 ml light ale
¼ pint/150 ml fish or vegetable stock
1½ oz/40 g butter or margarine
1½ oz/40 g plain flour
4 tbsp single cream
fresh chervil sprigs to garnish

Preheat oven to Gas 4, 350°F, 180°C, 10 mins before cooking the casserole. Peel the onions and carrots then cut carrots in half then into chunks approx 1 in/2.5cm in length. Wash and trim celery, cut into 1 in/2.5cm chunks. Wash and trim courgettes, cut in half then into 1 in/2.5cm chunks.

Skin fish if necessary then cut off and discard the central bone. (If using huss this is slightly to one side of the fillet. If using monkfish, the bone is located down the centre.) Wash and dry the fillets then cut into 1½ in/4 cm chunks. Coat lightly in the seasoned flour.

Heat 2 tbsp of the oil in a frying pan then gently fry the onions, carrot and celery for 10 mins. Add the courgettes and fry for a further 1 min. Drain well and place in the base of a 4 pint/ 2.25 litre ovenproof casserole. Add the remaining oil to the pan then lightly fry the fish for approx 4 mins turning the pieces over at least once. Drain then add to the casserole. Pour in the ale and stock then add the bay leaves. Cover and cook in the oven for 30-35 mins or until the fish and vegetables are cooked.

Remove from the oven and carefully drain off the liquid, discarding the bay leaves. Keep the fish and vegetables hot while thickening the sauce with the beurre manié.

Beat the fat and flour together in a small bowl and strain the liquid into a small pan. Place over the heat and bring to the boil. Drop small spoonfuls of the beurre manié into the boiling liquid, whisk vigorously. Once all the beurre manié has been used and the sauce thickened, remove from the heat, adjust seasoning then stir in the cream. Pour over the fish and vegetables and serve.

Handy tip

Look out for huss, whiting or pollack at your local fishmongers, they are cheaper than prime cod, haddock or monkfish and just as delicious.

1. Prepare the baby onions, carrots, celery sticks and courgettes and cut into 1 in/2.5 cm chunks

2. Discard bones from the fish, cut into 1½ in/4 cm chunks then coat in the seasoned flour

3. Heat 2 tbsp of the oil in a frying pan then fry the onions, celery and carrots for 10 mins. Place vegetables in casserole

4. Add the remaining oil to pan, then lightly fry the fish for 4 mins, turning the pieces over at least once

5. Add fish and bay leaves to the casserole, then pour the ale and stock over

6. Bring the cooking liquid to the boil, add small spoonfuls of the beurre manié, and whisk

GOLDEN FISH PIE

Try this appetizing dish of delicious chunks of cod mixed with smoked haddock and prawns in a creamy sauce, then wrapped in golden puff pastry. This dish is a delight for all the family.

Calories per portion: 117 | **SERVES 4**

10 oz/300 g cod fillets
10 oz/300 g smoked haddock fillets
¾ pint/450 ml milk
2 bay leaves
5 green peppercorns
5 black peppercorns
small bunch of parsley
2 oz/50 g butter or margarine
3 oz/75 g plain flour
salt and freshly ground black pepper
3 oz/75 g peeled prawns
1 lb/450 g puff pastry, thawed if frozen
1 egg, beaten, size 3

Preheat the oven to Gas 7, 425°F, 220°C, 15 mins before cooking pie. Place all the fish on a board and using a sharp knife skin the fish by holding the end of each fillet and cutting off as much flesh as possible with a sawing motion. (If you don't have a very sharp knife or find this difficult it's well worth asking the fishmonger to remove the skin for you.)

Cut the cod and haddock into small pieces. Place the milk in a frying pan or saucepan with the bay leaves, green and black peppercorns and a sprig of parsley. Add the fish to the milk and simmer for 6 mins. Strain the liquid from the pan and reserve.

Place the fat in a saucepan and heat gently until melted. Add the flour and stir over a gentle heat for 2 mins, until the fat and flour form a ball in the base of the saucepan. Remove from heat and gradually stir in the reserved milk to make a smooth sauce. Return to the heat, bring to boil and simmer for 5 mins until sauce has thickened. Season with salt and pepper, remove from the heat and allow to cool.

Stir in the cooked cod, smoked haddock and prawns. Chop the remaining parsley then add to the saucepan and mix well.

Dust a working surface with flour. Roll out pastry to a 12 in/30 cm square. Trim sides with a sharp knife. Pile the fish filling into the centre and brush all the edges of the pastry with water. Bring two corners to the centre of the square so that the two corners and sides meet as shown. Dust fingertips with plenty of flour and pinch the edges together well to seal. Repeat with remaining two corners, pinching all the edges together to encase fish filling in the pastry. Crimp all the edges with your fingers and transfer the pie to a baking sheet and brush well with the beaten egg.

Cook for 30 mins until pastry has risen and is a golden brown colour. Serve this mouthwatering dish garnished with sprigs of parsley and slices of lemon.

HANDY TIP

For a special occasion use fresh salmon instead of the smoked haddock and add two size 3 eggs, hard-boiled, shelled and chopped.

1. Prepare, weigh and measure all the ingredients before you begin

2. Cube fish and poach in pan with peppercorns, milk, bay leaf and parsley

3. Gradually add the milk to the pan and beat to a smooth sauce

4. Mix all the filling ingredients into the sauce and season well

5. Spoon filling into centre of pastry square and brush edges with water

6. Fold corners into centre, pinch and flute edges with fingertips

Salmon en Croute

Tempting flakes of fresh salmon in a creamy white wine sauce, encased in crisp golden puff pastry, a really impressive dish, ideal for all the family. It's easy to make if you follow the step-by-step guide.

Calories per portion: 544 | **Serves 8**

1 lb/450 g piece tail-end of salmon
1 small onion, peeled and sliced
small piece of carrot, peeled and chopped
2 bay leaves
few parsley sprigs
¼ pint/150 ml medium-dry white wine
1½ oz/40 g butter or margarine
1½ oz/40 g plain flour
salt and freshly ground black pepper
1 tbsp freshly chopped dill
grated rind of ½ lemon
¼ pint/150 ml single cream
4 oz/100 g cooked long grain rice
4 oz/100 g peeled prawns, optional
1 lb/450 g prepared puff pastry
1 egg, size 5, beaten
lemon and cucumber twists, whole prawns and dill sprigs to garnish

Preheat the oven to Gas 7, 425°F, 220°C, 15 mins before cooking. Remove scales from salmon, then wash well in cold water and pat dry. Place salmon in frying pan with onion, carrot, bay leaves, parsley, wine and ½ pint/300 ml water. Bring to a gentle boil, then simmer for 10-15 mins. Remove from heat, cover and cool. Strain cooking liquid and reserve ½ pint/300 ml. Skin, bone and flake salmon. Cover and reserve.

Melt fat in a saucepan, add flour and cook for 2 mins. Lower heat, then stir in the reserved cooking liquid, mixing well. Cook for a further minute until thick, smooth and glossy. Remove from the heat and stir in seasoning, dill, lemon rind, cream and rice. Mix well, then add prawns if using, and salmon. Leave until cold. Meanwhile, cut the pastry in half, then roll out into two oblongs, approx 13 in x 9 in/33 cm x 23 cm. With a round-bladed knife mark out on one the outline of a fish.

Place filling inside the fish shape and brush edges with cold water. Place the other oblong on top and press edges to seal. Using a pastry wheel, cut out fish, ¼ in/6 mm away from edge of filling. Knock up edges with a knife.

Roll out trimmings and, using a small plain round cutter, stamp out scales. Brush with beaten egg and position on fish, starting at the tail and overlapping as you go. Leave head free and fix one round for the eye. Mark tail with a sharp knife. Place on a baking sheet and brush with beaten egg.

Bake for 20 mins, then lower oven temperature to Gas 4, 350°F, 180°C, and bake for a further 20-25 mins until golden brown and risen. Garnish with lemon and cucumber twists, prawns and dill.

Handy Tips

Try using other fish, such as haddock or cod fillet instead of the salmon. You can also use fish stock instead of white wine.

1. Place salmon in pan, with onion, carrot, bay leaves, parsley, wine and water

2. Drain cooked salmon, reserving liquid, then discard skin and bones and flake

3. Melt fat in pan, add flour and cook for 2 mins. Gradually stir in the liquid

4. Mark the shape of a fish on one of the pastry oblongs and add the filling

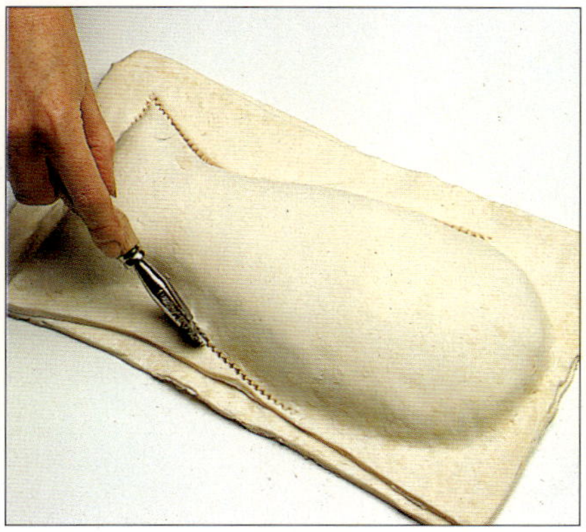

5. Dampen edge, place second oblong on top. Cut out fish shape

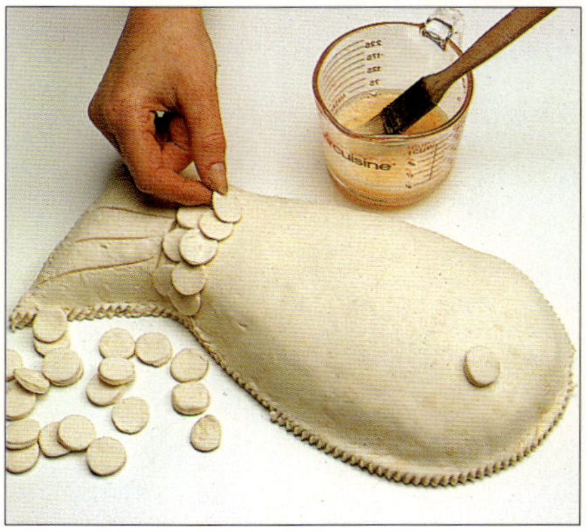

6. Brush the small pastry rounds with beaten egg, then place in position

PAUPIETTES OF SOLE

Delicate sole fillets are simply delicious stuffed with a mixture of prawns, mushrooms and pine nuts, gently cooked in white wine with a hint of orange. They make an impressive main meal or starter.

Calories per portion: 274 **SERVES 4**

4 lemon sole fillets
1 oz/25 g fresh white breadcrumbs
2 spring onions
1½ oz/40 g peeled prawns, thawed if frozen
1 dill sprig
1½ oz/40 g button mushrooms, wiped
1 tbsp pine nuts
salt and freshly ground black pepper
1 egg, size 5
2 bay leaves
¼ pint/150 ml medium-dry white wine, optional
1 orange
¼ pint/150 ml double cream
1 egg yolk, size 3
dill sprigs and orange slices to garnish

Preheat the oven to Gas 4, 350°F, 180°C, 10 mins before cooking the fish. Lightly grease an ovenproof dish. Wash fish under cold water, dry with kitchen paper, then skin.

Place breadcrumbs in a bowl. Trim the spring onions and chop finely, then add to bowl. Dry prawns with kitchen paper and chop. Chop dill and add to the breadcrumbs with the prawns. Chop mushrooms finely, stir into mixture with the pine nuts and seasoning to taste. Bind mixture together with the egg to form a soft but not sticky mixture.

Lay the fillets out on a chopping board and halve lengthways. Divide prepared filling evenly between fillets, spreading it to within ½ in/1.25 cm of each end. Roll up fish, starting from the tail end, then place in the ovenproof dish. Add bay leaves to dish, then pour in the wine and ¼ pint/150 ml water (use all water or fish stock if not using wine). Using a zester, cut approximately 1 tsp of rind from orange, then scatter rind over fillets.

Cover and cook in preheated oven for 15-18 mins or until cooked. Remove from the oven and drain off the cooking liquid into a saucepan. (Keep the fish hot while preparing the sauce.)

Boil cooking liquid until reduced by half. Beat the cream and egg yolk together, stir into the liquid and continue to cook gently, stirring throughout until sauce is of a creamy consistency. Do not allow the sauce to boil. Adjust the seasoning, then pour round fish and garnish with dill and orange slices.

HANDY TIP

If you're worried about the paupiettes unrolling during cooking, carefully tie them with fine thread or secure with cocktail sticks. Don't forget to remove the thread or sticks before serving.

1. Wash the sole fillets under cold water, dry with kitchen paper, then skin

2. Trim and chop spring onions, add to breadcrumbs. Chop prawns and dill

3. Divide filling evenly between halved fillets to within ½ in/1.25 cm of each end

4. *Starting from the tail end, roll up each fillet, then place in ovenproof dish*

5. *Add bay leaves, pour in wine, ¼ pint/150 ml water, scatter orange rind over*

6. *Boil cooking liquid until reduced by half, then stir in cream and egg yolk*

PLAICE FLORENTINE

Tasty plaice fillets filled with a tangy lemon and mustard stuffing and coated with a creamy cheese sauce, served on a bed of chopped spinach. This dish makes an ideal special treat for all the family.

Calories per portion: 571 | **SERVES 4**

2 large plaice
2 onions, peeled
few bay leaves
1-2 celery stalks, trimmed
few peppercorns
2½ oz/65 g butter or margarine
1 lemon, scrubbed
2 oz/50 g button mushrooms, wiped or washed and chopped
2 oz/50 g fresh white breadcrumbs
1 egg, size 5, beaten
1 lb/450 g cooked spinach
1½ oz/40 g plain flour
½ pint/300 ml milk
2-3 oz/50-75 g Cheddar cheese, grated

Preheat oven to Gas 6, 400°F, 200°C, 15 mins before cooking fish. Ask the fishmonger to fillet and skin the plaice for you. Keep the trimmings. Place the trimmings in a frying pan with one of the onions, sliced, bay leaves, celery, roughly chopped, and the peppercorns. Cover with water, bring to the boil, then simmer gently for 10 mins. Strain and allow the fish stock to cool.

HANDY TIP

This can be prepared to the stage of pouring over the sauce. If doing this store, covered, in a cool place for no more than 6-8 hrs. It will then need longer in the oven to ensure that the fish is thoroughly heated through.

Chop the remaining onion then sweat in 1 oz/25 g butter or margarine until soft and translucent. Remove from the heat. Add grated rind from lemon. Add mushrooms with the breadcrumbs and seasoning. Bind with sufficient egg to give a stiff consistency.

Place the fillets skinned side down and season. Place the prepared stuffing in centre, roll up to form a neat shape. Secure with cocktail sticks. Place in a lightly buttered ovenproof dish, cover with ½ pint/300 ml of the fish stock. Cover with lid or foil and cook in oven for 10-15 mins or until the fillets are just cooked.

Meanwhile, arrange finely chopped spinach in the base of an ovenproof dish and make the sauce. Melt remaining fat in a saucepan, stir in flour and cook for 2 mins. Remove from heat and gradually stir in the milk. Return to heat then cook, stirring throughout until sauce thickens. Remove from heat, add seasoning and cheese, stir until cheese has melted.

Arrange fillets on top of spinach, and discard cocktail sticks. Pour the prepared cheese sauce over then return to the oven to cook for a further 10 mins or until golden brown and bubbly. Serve immediately.

1. Place fish trimmings in pan with onion, bay leaves, celery and peppercorns

2. Sweat chopped onion in fat for 5 mins. Remove from heat, add lemon rind

3. Place stuffing in centre of fillets, roll up, secure with cocktails sticks

4. Pour over the cooled fish stock. Cover with foil, cook for 10-15 mins

5. Transfer the cooked fillets with a slice on to spinach. Discard cocktail sticks

6. Coat fish with cheese sauce, return to oven and cook until golden brown

Paella

One of Spain's most popular dishes, paella, packed full of appetizing fish, shellfish, chicken and pork. Paella makes a perfect meal for the whole family or is ideal for an informal supper party.

Calories per portion: 568 | **Serves 6**

1 lb/450 g fresh mussels or 6 oz/175 g shelled, cooked mussels
1½ lb/675 g piece monkfish
1 large red pepper
1 large Spanish onion
2-3 garlic cloves
8 oz/225 g tomatoes
few saffron strands or ½-1 tsp turmeric
1 lb/450 g pork tenderloin
12 oz/350 g chicken breasts
2-3 tbsp olive oil
1 sprig rosemary
12 oz/350 g Valencia or risotto rice
¼ pint/150 ml dry white wine
1½ pints/900 ml fish stock
salt and freshly ground black pepper
3 oz/75 g peas
4 oz/100 g peeled prawns
2 oz/50 g whole prawns

Handy tips

You can vary the ingredients of a paella to suit your palate and availability. Try adding chorizo (a spicy continental sausage), squid, Mediterranean prawns and, for a special occasion, lobster. For a change, cook your Paella over a barbecue – follow the recipe as above, but increase the amount of liquid as it will evaporate when cooked in the open.

Discard beards from the mussels and scrub thoroughly in cold water. Throw away any mussels that are open. Leave covered in a bowl of cold water.

Skin the monkfish, cut down centre and discard bone. Cut the flesh into 1 in/2.5 cm pieces. Wash and dry pepper, deseed then slice thinly. Peel, then finely chop onion. Peel and crush garlic. Wash and dry tomatoes, slice.

Place saffron in a small bowl, pour boiling water over and leave to infuse for at least 10 mins. Trim off any fat or gristle from the pork and chicken, cut in 1 in/2.5 cm pieces.

Heat the oil in a paella pan or large frying pan and fry the meat for 5 mins until browned, stir occasionally. Add the onion, garlic, tomatoes and sliced red pepper.

Lightly crush the sprig of rosemary, add to the pan together with the rice. Cook for 5 mins, stirring to prevent the ingredients sticking to the bottom of the pan. Add the monkfish, white wine and stock with seasoning. Bring to the boil then simmer for 10 mins.

Strain the saffron liquid into the pan (if using turmeric blend with 2 tsp cold water) and add the mussels, peas and peeled prawns and continue cooking for 8 mins or until the rice, meat and fish are cooked and the mussels have opened. Add a little extra stock if the paella is too dry.

Turn off heat, cover with a clean cloth or foil and leave for 3 mins. Discard any mussels that have not opened. Decorate with whole prawns.

1. Discard beards from mussels and scrub in cold water, discard any that are open

2. Skin monkfish, cut down centre, discard central bone, cut into 1 in/2.5 cm pieces

3. Prepare pepper, onion and tomatoes, crush garlic, infuse saffron in water

4. Heat olive oil in pan, fry diced meat until browned all over, stir occasionally

5. Add onion, garlic, tomatoes, rosemary, sliced pepper, stir then pour in the rice

6. After cooking rice, add monkfish and mussels, pour in wine and stock

Cannelloni

A delicious combination of grated mozzarella cheese, minced beef and fresh pasta, topped with a smooth, creamy béchamel sauce go to make this classic Italian dish.

Calories per portion: 435 **Serves 6**

1 pint/600 ml milk
2 small onions
1 small carrot
1 stick celery
4-5 peppercorns
2-3 fresh bay leaves
1 garlic clove
1 tbsp olive oil
10 oz/300 g lean minced beef
½ small red pepper
½ small green pepper
2 tbsp tomato purée
2 tbsp freshly chopped chervil
salt and freshly ground black pepper
¼ pint/150 ml Italian red wine or beef stock
4 oz/100 g mozzarella cheese, coarsely grated
12 fresh lasagne sheets
12 oz/350 g ripe tomatoes
2 oz/50 g butter or margarine
2 oz/50 g flour
1-2 tbsp Parmesan cheese, finely grated

Preheat the oven to Gas 5, 375°F, 190°C, 10 mins before baking the cannelloni. Place the milk in a saucepan. Peel 1 of the onions, peel carrot. Scrub celery, trim and discard ends. Place the onion, carrot and celery into the milk with the peppercorns and bay leaves. Heat gently to just below boiling point. Remove from heat, cover and leave to infuse for 30 mins. Strain, reserving the milk.

Peel and finely chop the remaining onion, peel and crush the garlic. Place in a frying pan with the oil and fry for 5 mins. Add the minced beef and continue to fry, stirring until the meat is browned. Deseed peppers, chop finely. Add to the minced beef and continue to cook for 5 mins. Then add tomato purée, 1 tbsp chervil and seasoning. Pour in wine or stock, cook gently for 10 mins. Cool slightly.

Place small spoonfuls of mozzarella cheese and beef mixture on the pasta sheets then roll up. Continue until all the sheets have been filled. Slice tomatoes and arrange in base of an ovenproof dish. Sprinkle with remaining chervil and seasoning. Arrange filled pasta on top, keeping the joins underneath.

Melt the butter or margarine in a small saucepan, stir in the flour, cook for 1 min. Remove from heat then gradually stir in the reserved milk. Return pan to heat and cook, stirring, until the sauce thickens. Add seasoning to taste. Pour over the pasta and sprinkle the top with the Parmesan cheese. Cook in the oven for 30-40 mins until golden brown. Serve immediately with a green salad.

Handy Tip

If you can't buy fresh lasagne sheets, buy dried ones and cook them first, with a little oil added to the water to prevent them sticking together.

1. Place milk in pan with onion, carrot, celery, peppercorns and bay leaves

2. Add chopped peppers to minced beef, continue to cook for 5 mins

3. Fill the pasta sheets with the grated mozzarella and the beef mixture

4. *Roll up the filled sheets. Place with joint side down in an ovenproof dish*

5. *Spoon or pour the freshly made sauce over the filled pasta to cover*

6. *Sprinkle top liberally with grated Parmesan cheese and cook until golden*

SPAGHETTI BOLOGNESE

A tempting rich meaty tomato sauce with tasty vegetables, just a hint of wine and freshly chopped basil. Spaghetti Bolognese is probably one of Italy's best known and loved dishes.

Calories per portion: 297 **SERVES 4**

1. Prepare ingredients, wash celery, carrots, mushrooms. Peel, chop onion

2. Dry fry the minced beef over a gentle heat, stirring frequently until browned

3. Fry onion and bacon in the olive oil, then add remaining chopped vegetables

1 large onion
2 large sticks celery
2 large carrots
8 oz/225 g tomatoes
4 oz/100 g mushrooms
12 oz/350 g lean minced beef
2 oz/50 g back bacon
2 tbsp olive oil
¼ pint/150 ml dry white wine
½ pint/300 ml beef stock
1-2 tbsp tomato purée
salt and freshly ground black pepper
1 tbsp freshly chopped basil
12 oz/350 g spaghetti
freshly grated Parmesan cheese

Peel the onion and chop finely. Trim and wash celery, chop finely. Scrape or peel the carrots, trim and chop. Make a small cross in the top of each tomato, place in a bowl and cover with boiling water. Leave for 2 mins, drain, then peel and chop. Wash and dry mushrooms, chop.

Place the minced beef in a frying pan and dry fry over a gentle heat until browned. Stir frequently as this will help to break up the mince and keep the meat separate. When browned, drain through a colander to remove any excess fat. Wipe the pan with absorbent paper.

Derind the bacon and cut into small strips. Heat the oil in the pan, then gently fry the bacon and chopped onion for 5 mins or until the onion is soft and transparent. Add the chopped celery and carrots and continue to fry for a further 3 mins.

Return the mince to the pan with the chopped tomatoes and mushrooms. Fry for a further 5 mins then pour in the wine and stock. Blend tomato purée with 2 tbsp of water and stir into pan, together with seasoning and the freshly chopped basil. Bring to the boil, then simmer gently for 35-45 mins or until the meat is cooked and the vegetables are tender but not mushy. Adjust seasoning.

Meanwhile, bring a large pan of lightly salted water to a rapid boil. Holding the spaghetti in a bundle, gently lower into the boiling water. As the spaghetti softens it will gradually curl around the pan. Cook for 10-12 mins or until it is 'al dente' (this is when the spaghetti is soft but still has a slightly chewy texture). Drain well. Mix the bolognese sauce into the cooked spaghetti and serve immediately with freshly grated Parmesan cheese.

If you wish to cook the sauce in the microwave, place meat in a shallow dish and microwave on high (uncovered) for 5 mins. Drain off meat, reserve 3 tbsp of juices in dish. Add prepared vegetables, stir and microwave uncovered on high for 3 mins. Stir after 1½ mins. Return meat to dish with remaining sauce ingredients. Stir well. Cover and microwave on high for 10-12 mins or until sauce is thick.

If liked, you can include 4 oz/100 g chopped, cleaned chicken livers in the recipe – just add them to the mince when browning.

Handy Tip

Pasta dishes which use spaghetti or tagliatelle need to be eaten immediately. Always serve in warmed dishes to help keep them hot.

4. Return the beef to the frying pan, then add the peeled chopped tomatoes

5. After adding the mushrooms to the pan, pour in the wine and then the stock

6. Bring a pan of lightly salted water to a rapid boil, slowly add spaghetti

Lasagne

We've adopted some great classics from Italy and this is certainly one of them. This tasty dish is made from a rich meaty sauce, flavoured with tomatoes, garlic and basil, layered between pasta and topped with a cheese sauce.

Calories per portion: 522 | **Serves 4**

1 large onion
8 oz/225 g tomatoes
2 sticks celery
2 garlic cloves
12 oz/350 g lean minced beef
2 tbsp freshly chopped basil or 2 tsp dried basil
salt and freshly ground black pepper
2 tbsp tomato purée
¼ pint/150 ml Chianti or red wine
¼ pint/150 ml beef stock
8-10 sheets pre-cooked lasagne
1½ oz/40 g butter or margarine
1½ oz/40 g plain flour
1 tsp mustard powder
½ pint/300 ml milk
3 oz/75 g mature Cheddar cheese, grated
1-2 tbsp Parmesan cheese, grated

Preheat oven to Gas 6, 400°F, 200°C, 15 mins before baking the lasagne. Peel onion and chop finely. Make a small cross in stalk end of tomatoes, cover with boiling water and leave for 2 mins. Drain. Peel tomatoes, then chop. Trim and wash celery, chop finely. Peel garlic and crush.

Place the beef with the onion, celery and garlic in a frying pan and fry over a moderate heat, stirring frequently until browned all over. Drain off any fat that may have run out while cooking. Stir in chopped tomatoes, basil, seasoning to taste, tomato purée, wine and stock. Bring to the boil, then simmer gently for 30 mins, stirring occasionally.

Place a layer of the minced beef mixture in the base of an oblong ovenproof dish. Cover with half the lasagne sheets. Top with remaining beef then cover with rest of lasagne.

To make the cheese sauce, melt the butter or margarine in a small saucepan, add the flour and the dried mustard, then cook for 2 mins. Draw off the heat and gradually stir in the milk. Return the pan to the heat and cook, stirring throughout until the sauce thickens and coats the back of a spoon. Add seasoning to taste and stir in the grated Cheddar cheese.

Beat until the cheese has melted, then pour over the lasagne, ensuring

HANDY TIPS

Any type of lasagne can be used for this. If using lasagne that has not been pre-cooked, just cook in boiling salted water with 2 tsp oil for 10 mins before using as instructed. Alternatively, follow instructions on the packet if using commercially made fresh lasagne.

that the pasta is completely covered. Sprinkle with the Parmesan, then cook in the oven for 25 mins or until the top is golden brown and bubbling.

1. Peel onion, leave root intact, chop finely. Blanch tomatoes in boiling water

2. Fry beef onion, celery, garlic, until beef is brown, and onion and celery soft

3. Add tomatoes, basil, seasoning, tomato purée, wine and stock, mix thoroughly

4. Place layer of cooked beef in ovenproof dish, cover with half the lasagne sheets

5. Make sauce, then add Cheddar cheese. Beat well to ensure smooth sauce

6. Cover last layer of lasagne with sauce, ensuring pasta is completely covered

DESSERTS

There's a dessert to suit everyone here. Choose from Profiteroles with a velvety thick chocolate sauce and Hazelnut Vacherin, or real family favourites such as Jam Roly Poly and Apple Dumplings. Chocoholics will love the rich Chocolate Cheesecake or the luscious Chocolate Roulade that is simply irresistible, and the more adventurous can try creating Croquembouche – the classic French wedding cake or a spectacular Mount Vesuvius dessert.

CREME CARAMEL

This delicious dessert is a combination of smooth, creamy egg custard, coated in a delicious golden caramel sauce, and is really simple to make when you follow this easy, step-by-step guide. Serve it chilled with fresh fruit, biscuits and cream.

Calories per portion: 257 | **SERVES 4**

4½ oz/120 g caster sugar
3 eggs, size 3
¾ pint/450 ml milk
½ tsp vanilla essence
whitecurrants to decorate

Preheat the oven to Gas 3, 325°F, 160°C. Place 4 oz/100 g caster sugar and ¼ pint/150 ml water in a heavy-based pan. Place pan over a gentle heat, and stir until the sugar has dissolved. Bring to the boil and boil vigorously for about 8-10 mins until a golden caramel has been formed.

While boiling the caramel, you should have ready a pastry brush and a measuring jug filled with cold water. As a sugar crust begins to form around the pan, just above the level of the syrup, dip the pastry brush into the cold water and use to push the crust from the sides of the pan down into the boiling liquid caramel.

Having made the caramel, pour it into a 6 in/15 cm soufflé or ovenproof dish. Using oven gloves or a cloth, rotate the dish carefully, so that the caramel coats the base and sides of the dish. Take care not to burn yourself with the hot caramel. Put the dish to one side while preparing the custard.

Whisk the eggs and remaining sugar together. Warm the milk to blood heat (this is when a clean finger dipped into the milk feels just warm); then gradually whisk into the egg and sugar mixture. Stir in the vanilla essence then, using a sieve, carefully strain the custard mixture into the caramel-lined soufflé dish. Place dish in a roasting tin, filled with sufficient hot water to come halfway up the sides of the dish.

Place in the centre of the oven and cook for approx 1 hr or until set and firm to the touch. (To check if the custard is set, carefully insert a round-bladed knife into the centre – if the knife is completely dry when you remove it and no liquid seeps out, the custard is ready. Remove from the oven, cool, then chill overnight in the fridge.

Remove from fridge 30 mins before serving. To turn out, using your fingertip, loosen the outside edge of the custard carefully. Place a serving dish over the top, then invert the dish, shaking slightly if necessary. Leave the soufflé dish on inverted top until all the caramel has drained out. Decorate and serve with fresh fruit, cream and home-made biscuits.

HANDY TIP

Make individual puddings using four ¼ pint/150 ml ramekin dishes. Proceed as above then cook for 25-35 mins or until set.

1. Stir caster sugar and water over a gentle heat until the sugar has dissolved

2. Brush sugar crust from the sides of the pan down into the boiling caramel

3. Swirl the caramel round a 6 in/15 cm soufflé dish, to coat the base and sides

4. Beat the eggs and remaining sugar, then gradually whisk in the warmed milk

5. Using a sieve, strain custard mixture into the caramel-lined soufflé dish

6. Place dish in a tin filled with hot water to come halfway up sides, then cook

SULTANA CHEESECAKE

This tempting cheesecake is crammed full of sun-ripened sultanas, with creamy ricotta cheese that's been flavoured with orange and encased in an orangey pastry then topped with tangy sweet currants.

Calories per portion: 502 | **SERVES 12**

FOR THE PASTRY:
10 oz/300 g plain flour
5 oz/150 g butter or margarine
1 oz/25 g sugar
grated rind 1 orange
1 egg yolk, size 3
2-3 tbsp orange juice
FOR THE FILLING:
1½ lb/675 g ricotta cheese
4 oz/100 g caster sugar
1 orange
3 eggs, size 3
8 fl oz/250 ml double cream
4 oz/100 g sultanas
FOR THE TOPPING:
10 oz/300 g red and blackcurrants, thawed if frozen, cleaned if fresh
3 oz/75 g caster sugar
2 tsp arrowroot

Preheat oven to Gas 4, 350°F, 180°C, 10 mins before baking the cheesecake. To prepare the pastry, sieve the flour into a mixing bowl, then add the fat. Mix in the sugar and orange rind then rub the fat in until the mixture resembles fine breadcrumbs. Add the egg yolk and orange juice and mix to form a smooth and pliable dough. Knead lightly on a floured surface then wrap and chill leave to relax for 30 mins. Roll out and use to completely line an 8½ in/21.5 cm spring form tin. Leave in the fridge while preparing the filling.

To prepare filling, push the ricotta cheese through a fine sieve into a bowl and add the sugar. Finely grate the rind from the orange and squeeze out the juice. Add the orange rind to the bowl and beat well until the mixture is smooth. Gradually add the eggs, beating well between each addition to ensure the mixture remains smooth, then stir in the orange juice and lastly the double cream. Fold in the sultanas. Pour the mixture into the pastry-lined tin then bake in the oven for 1½ hrs or until the cheesecake is firm to the touch. Turn the oven off and leave the cheesecake in for ½ hr. Remove from the oven, allow to cool then chill for at least 4 hrs, preferably overnight.

To make the topping, lightly wash the currants if using fresh. Drain well. Dissolve the sugar in 4 tbsp of water then boil for 5 mins. Remove from the heat and add the currants. Return to the heat. Blend the arrowroot with 2 tsp of cold water then stir into the fruit. Cook stirring until the mixture clears and thickens. Remove from heat and allow to cool. Remove the cheesecake from the tin and if necessary trim the top of the pastry to form a neat edge. Spoon the prepared topping over then leave for 2 hrs to set. Serve if liked with cream.

HANDY TIP

Vary the topping according to taste and availability of the fruit – why not try coarsely grated chocolate or chocolate curls for a real treat, then dust top lightly with sieved icing sugar.

1. Place flour in bowl with the sugar and fat, add grated orange rind. Rub in until mixture resembles breadcrumbs

2. Roll the pastry out on a lightly floured surface then use to line an 8½ in/21.5 cm spring form tin

3. Push the ricotta cheese through a fine sieve into a bowl, add the sugar and finely grated orange rind. Beat well

4. Beat the mixture together until smooth then gradually add the eggs, beating well after each addition

5. Stir in the orange juice, the double cream and lastly fold in the sultanas. Mix lightly together

6. Pour the mixture into the pastry-lined case then bake in the oven for 1½ hrs, or until firm to the touch

BREAD & BUTTER PUDDING

Slices of thinly buttered bread, layered with dried fruit and almonds, with a subtle hint of orange and cooked in custard, it makes a popular family pud.

Calories per portion: 543 | **SERVES 4**

8 thin slices white bread
2 oz/50 g softened butter or low-fat spread
grated rind of 1 large orange
2 oz/50 g sultanas
2 oz/50 g seedless raisins
3 oz/75 g flaked almonds
1 oz/25 g unrefined granulated sugar
3 eggs, size 3
¾ pint/450 ml semi-skimmed milk
¼ pint/150 ml single cream
2-3 tbsp Grand Marnier, optional
2 tsp caster sugar

Preheat oven to Gas 4, 350°F, 180°C. Thinly spread the bread with the butter or low-fat spread and cut each slice diagonally into four. Use half of the bread to line the base and sides of a lightly greased 2 pint/1.2 litre oval ovenproof dish, then sprinkle with grated orange rind. Reserve the remaining bread slices.

Mix the sultanas, raisins and 2 oz/50 g of the flaked almonds together and scatter over top of bread in dish. Sprinkle with the granulated sugar. Then arrange the reserved bread across the top of the fruit.

Beat the eggs, slightly warm the milk, then beat into eggs with the cream and Grand Marnier, if using. Pour over the bread, taking care not to spill the milk over the sides of the dish. Leave to stand for at least 30 mins.

Sprinkle with remaining 1 oz/25 g flaked almonds. Place on the centre shelf of the preheated oven and bake for 45-55 mins or until the filling is lightly set and the top is golden brown and crisp. Sprinkle with caster sugar. Serve immediately with custard or cream.

For a delicious Osborne Pudding spread thin sliced brown bread with butter or low-fat spread, then with a portion of your favourite marmalade. Cut into quarters then arrange in a lightly greased ovenproof dish. Omit the fruit and nuts and use 1 oz/25 g of sugar.

Pour the beaten egg and milk over the bread and leave to stand for 30 mins before cooking as before. Sprinkle with a little demerara sugar before serving. If preferred, you can line 4-6 small ramekin dishes with the buttered bread. Proceed as above, then bake for 25-35 mins or until set.

HANDY TIPS

This pudding is ideal for using up stale bread but if the bread is really stale leave the mixture to stand a little longer before cooking.

Don't forget you can always vary the type of dried fruits or nuts according to personal taste. Try using dates, cherries, chopped no-need-to-soak apricots, mixed peel, as well as walnuts, hazelnuts, unsalted peanuts or pine kernels.

Try varying the bread as well. You can mix white and brown bread, fruit tea breads, or even malt bread or lardy cake.

1. Spread the slices of bread thinly with butter or low-fat spread

2. Cut the bread diagonally into quarters and use to line an ovenproof dish

3. With a zester remove rind from the large orange and sprinkle over the bread

4. *Scatter the chopped mixed fruit, almonds and sugar over the bread*

5. *Warm the milk to blood heat, then whisk into the beaten eggs with liqueur*

6. *Pour egg mixture over pudding, leave for at least 30 mins before baking*

JAM ROLY POLY

This pud must definitely be everyone's favourite! Crisp golden suet pastry, oozing with delicious raspberry jam. And it's not too naughty, as semi-skimmed milk and vegetable suet have been used, so it's a whole lot lighter on calories.

Calories per portion: 333 including custard | **SERVES 6**

6 oz/175 g self-raising flour
2 oz/50 g plain flour
a pinch of salt
1 tbsp caster sugar
3 oz/75 g vegetable suet
¼ pint/150 ml semi-skimmed milk, plus a little extra for brushing
2 tbsp raspberry jam, or low-sugar raspberry conserve
1 tbsp golden caster sugar
FOR THE CUSTARD:
3 eggs, size 3
1 tbsp caster sugar
2 tsp cornflour
½ tsp vanilla essence
½ pint/300 ml semi-skimmed milk

Preheat oven to Gas 7, 425°F, 220°C. Lightly grease a baking tray. Sift the flours, salt and caster sugar into a mixing bowl and then add the vegetable suet and mix together. Pour in the milk and mix to form a soft, but not sticky, dough. Knead lightly on a floured surface until smooth and free from cracks.

Roll the dough out to an oblong roughly 9 in x 11 in/23 cm x 28 cm. Spread the raspberry jam over the dough, leaving a 1 in/2.5 cm clear border all round. Brush the border with milk, then roll up the dough to completely enclose the jam. Pinch the ends firmly together to seal.

Place the roll, with the seam side down, on the greased baking tray. Brush with milk then sprinkle with the golden sugar.

Bake for 35-45 mins until risen and golden brown. (It is natural for a roly poly to crack along its length as it cooks.) Meanwhile, make the custard.

HANDY TIP

Try varying the flavour, by using apricot or blackcurrant jam or even marmalade.

Put the eggs, caster sugar, cornflour and vanilla essence into a bowl and mix. Heat the milk until it comes almost to the boil, then whisk it into the eggs.

Place the bowl over a saucepan of simmering water and cook, stirring continuously until the custard thickens. (Alternatively, cook the custard in a microwave oven, on High for 2½-3 mins, stirring every 30 secs with a wire whisk.) Immediately the custard thickens, pour it through a nylon sieve into a serving jug. Keep warm.

Serve the jam roly poly hot, with the custard.

1. Sift flours, salt and sugar into a mixing bowl, then add the vegetable suet

2. Add milk and mix to a soft, not sticky dough. Knead lightly until smooth

3. Roll dough on a floured surface to an oblong roughly 9 in x 11 in/23 cm x 28 cm

4. Spread jam evenly over dough with a spatula to within 1 in/2.5 cm of edge

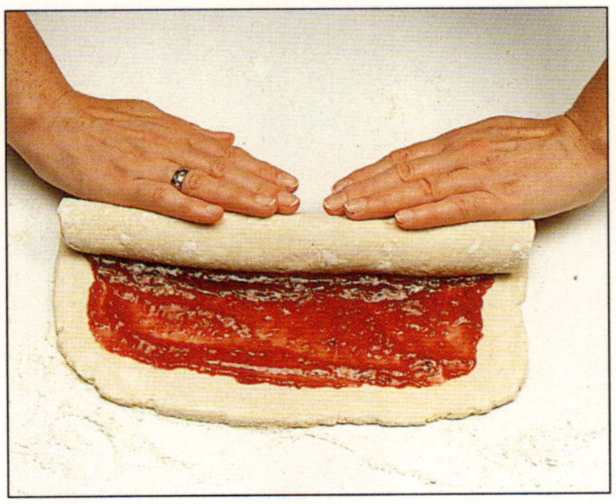

5. Brush border with milk, then roll up from long edge. Completely tuck in ends

6. Place on baking tray, seam side down. Brush with milk, sprinkle with sugar

Lemon Meringue Pie

It's light and crisp with a deliciously tangy lemon filling. So it is no wonder this great melt-in-the-mouth pudding has been a favourite for years. Follow this guide, for a perfect result.

Calories per portion: 467 | **Serves 6**

FOR THE PASTRY:
8 oz/225 g plain flour
5 oz/150 g butter or margarine
1 oz/25 g caster sugar
1 egg yolk, size 3
FOR THE FILLING:
juice and rind of 3 lemons
2 oz/50 g butter
3 oz/75 g cornflour
3 egg yolks, size 3
2-3 oz/50-75 g caster sugar
FOR THE MERINGUE:
3 egg whites, size 3
6 oz/175 g caster sugar

Preheat the oven to Gas 6, 400°F, 200°C. Place flour in a mixing bowl and rub in the butter or margarine until mixture resembles fine breadcrumbs. Stir in the sugar, beat egg yolk with 1 tbsp cold water then use to bind the pastry. Knead until smooth, wrap in greaseproof paper or clearwrap and chill for 30 mins.

Roll pastry out on a lightly floured surface and use to line a 9 in/23 cm loose-bottomed flan tin. Place a sheet of greaseproof paper in the base and cover with baking beans. Bake blind for 10-12 mins. Remove the greaseproof paper and baking beans and discard. Return the flan to the oven for a further 3-5 mins.

Make up the juice of 3 lemons to 1¼ pints/750 ml with water. Place in saucepan with the lemon rind and the butter. Bring to the boil. Blend the cornflour with 4 tbsp of water then stir into the boiling liquid. Cook over a gentle heat for 2 mins or until it is thickened.

Allow the liquid to cool then beat in the egg yolks and sugar. Pour into flan case. Return to the oven for 8-10 mins, or until the filling is set.

Whisk the egg whites until stiff and standing in peaks then add half the sugar and whisk until very stiff. Fold in the remaining sugar. Place the mixture in a piping bag fitted with a large star nozzle and pipe over the top or swirl on top of the flan with a spoon. Reduce the oven temperature to Gas 3, 325°F, 160°C, and bake the lemon meringue pie for a further 25-30 mins. Serve either hot or cold.

Handy tip

For an alternative filling, try chocolate. Melt 4 oz/100 g plain chocolate in a bowl over a pan of gently simmering water. Allow to cool. Leaving out the lemon juice and rind, beat the chocolate into the thickened cornflour mixture (use same quantities of water and cornflour as for lemon filling). Add the butter, cool, then beat in egg yolks and sugar. Pour into the flan case and proceed as for Lemon Meringue Pie.

1. Make pastry, chill, roll out and use to line flan tin. Bake blind

2. Assemble ingredients for the filling, make and pour into the baked flan case

3. Whisk egg whites until stiff (tip up bowl and meringue should not move)

4. Add half the sugar, whisk until very stiff, then add the remaining sugar

5. Swirl meringue topping on to flan, using back of spoon, lift upwards to form peaks

6. Lower oven temperature, return flan to the oven and bake for 25-30 mins

Apple Pie

It's everybody's favourite – just like Mum used to make. A crisp light pastry that melts in your mouth, tender sweet apples with a hint of spicy cloves. And, if you use organically grown apples, you can help to look after our environment.

Calories per portion: 226 | **Serves 6**

10 oz/300 g plain flour
pinch of salt
2½ oz/65 g white vegetable fat
2½ oz/65 g margarine
1½ lb/675 g cooking apples
juice of ½ lemon
6-10 cloves
3 oz/75 g golden granulated sugar
2 tsp caster sugar

Preheat oven to Gas 6, 400°F, 200°C. Sieve the flour into a large mixing bowl and add the salt. Cut the white fat and margarine into small pieces then add to the flour. Rub the ingredients together, using your fingers until the mixture resembles fine breadcrumbs. Mix to a soft and pliable, but not sticky, dough with 5 tbsp cold water. Turn out on to a lightly floured surface and knead until smooth and free from cracks. Wrap, then chill in the fridge for 20-30 mins. (By allowing the pastry to relax it has less of a tendency to shrink away from the sides of the dish.)

Remove from the fridge. Cut pastry in half. Roll out one half on a lightly floured surface and use to line a 9 in x 1½ in/23 cm x 4 cm deep glass pie dish. Ease pastry carefully around sides of dish and allow to come up about ¼ in/6 mm over outside edge. Trim neatly. Roll out remaining pastry for lid. Any extra pastry can be used for decoration.

Wash and dry the apples, peel then core. Cut into ¼ in/6 mm slices and leave immersed in a bowl of water to which you've added the juice of ½ lemon (the lemon juice will help prevent the apples turning brown). Drain, then arrange the apple slices in pastry-lined dish. Sprinkle with the cloves and granulated sugar.

Dampen edges of pastry with cold water then carefully lift pastry lid on top, ensuring that you don't stretch the pastry otherwise it will shrink during cooking. Trim and seal edges firmly together. Make a decorative edge by using your thumb or forefingers.

Brush the top of the pie lightly with a little water and make a hole in the centre to allow the steam to escape. Roll out the leftover pastry trimmings and cut into leaf shapes and place on top of pie. Sprinkle lightly with the caster sugar.

Bake in the oven for 20 mins, then reduce oven temperature to Gas 4, 350°F, 180°C, and continue to bake for 15-20 mins or until the filling is cooked and the pastry is golden brown.

This is delicious served hot with custard or with cream when cool.

Handy Tips

If you fancy a change use some other flavourings instead of the cloves. Try 1½ tsp cinnamon powder, or grated rind of a lemon or a small orange. Or you can add 2 oz/50 g sultanas or even mixed peel. They're all delicious!

1. Assemble ingredients for pastry, then sieve flour into a large mixing bowl

2. Cut fat into pieces and rub into flour until mixture resembles breadcrumbs

3. Peel cooking apples, core then cut into ¼ in/6 mm slices. Leave in water

4. Arrange apples in pastry-lined dish, add sugar and cloves, cover with pastry lid

5. Brush edges of pastry, seal firmly then pinch around edge with thumbs

6. Brush top with water, make a small hole in top, decorate with leaves

Treacle Pudding

Go on, tempt them with their favourite pud, they just won't be able to resist this delicious light sponge, oozing with a mouthwatering golden syrup. This great recipe is sure to impress and is guaranteed to satisfy the heartiest of appetites.

Calories per portion: 403 **Serves 6**

9 tbsp golden syrup
6 oz/175 g butter or margarine
6 oz/175 g caster sugar
2 eggs, size 3
2 egg whites, size 3
8 oz/225 g self-raising flour, sifted
1 tbsp skimmed milk
1 large lemon, scrubbed
2 tbsp cornflour

Grease a 2½ pint/1.5 litre pudding basin, then line the base with a small round of greased greaseproof paper.

Spoon 3 tbsp of the golden syrup into the bottom of the basin. Cream together the fat and sugar until light and fluffy. Beat together the whole eggs and the egg whites, then gradually beat them into the creamed mixture, beating well between each addition. (If the mixture starts to curdle, beat in 1 or 2 tbsp of the self-raising flour.) Carefully fold in the flour with a metal spoon. Add enough milk to give a soft dropping consistency. Spoon mixture into the pudding basin, on top of the syrup.

Cover basin with a large sheet of lightly greased foil, pleated in the middle to allow for expansion, and making sure that the foil is tightly tucked under the rim of the basin. Fold a long piece of foil, about 24 in/51 cm long, lengthways four times to form a sling. Put the basin in the centre of the foil sling, then carefully lower it into a large saucepan.

Pour in boiling water until it comes halfway up the side of the basin. Cover the saucepan with a tightly fitting lid and cook the pudding on a low heat for 2½ hrs, replenishing the water from time to time.

About 15 mins before serving the pudding, remove the rind from the lemon with a lemon zester, or a grater, and put into a small saucepan with the remaining golden syrup and the strained juice of the lemon made up to ½ pint/300 ml with cold water. Stir over heat until the syrup melts and blends smoothly with the lemon juice.

Blend cornflour with 2 tbsp water. Stir into sauce, boil gently until thick. Pour into a serving jug, keep warm.

To unmould pudding, use the foil sling to remove the basin from the saucepan and remove the foil from the top. Place a large plate on top of the basin, then invert the basin and plate together. Carefully lift the basin, wearing oven gloves for protection. Remove the small round of greaseproof paper from top of pudding.

Serve hot with lemon and syrup, and/or custard. A little extra syrup may be spooned on top of the pudding after turning out if desired.

Handy Tips

A few slices of lemon added to the water in the saucepan will help prevent the pan discolouring. You will find the syrup easier to measure if you warm it first.

1. Beat margarine and sugar together until the mixture is pale and fluffy

2. Gradually add the beaten eggs, beating well between each addition

3. Sift in the self-raising flour, then fold in carefully with a metal spoon

4. *Put syrup in bottom of greased basin, then spoon sponge mixture on top*

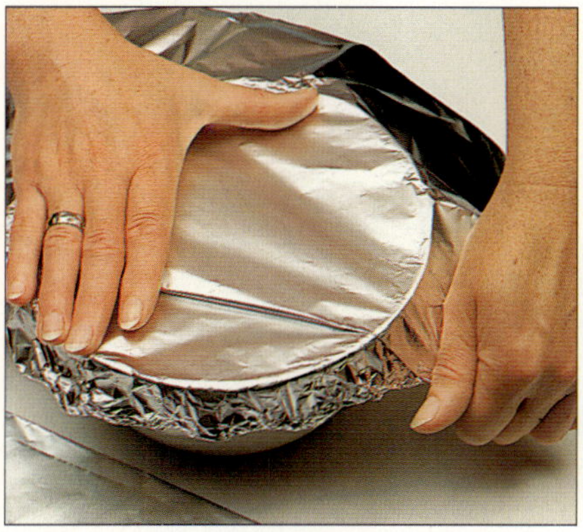

5. *Cover basin tightly with a foil sheet, pleated to allow for expansion*

6. *Using oven gloves for protection, turn pudding out on to a warmed plate*

Sussex Pond Pudding

An old-fashioned recipe originating from the South of England, this pudding gets its name as during cooking the lemon bursts and combines with the butter and sugar, making a delicious sauce.

Calories per portion: 581 | **Serves 6**

10 oz/300 g self-raising flour
pinch of salt
5 oz/150 g shredded suet
4 oz/100 g soft brown sugar
4 oz/100 g butter
1 large lemon or 2 small lemons, preferably unwaxed
custard to serve

Sieve the flour and salt into a mixing bowl then stir in the suet. Mix with approximately 8 fl oz/250 ml cold water to form a soft but not sticky dough. Turn out on to a lightly floured surface and knead until smooth. Reserve one third of the pastry for lid, then roll out the remainder to a 14 in/35 cm circle.

Lightly grease a 2½ pint/1.5 litre basin and line with the rolled-out pastry, easing the pastry with the fingertips to ensure a smooth, even fit. Trim the edge neatly with a round-bladed knife.

Place half the sugar in the basin, top with half the butter, cut into small cubes. Scrub and dry the lemon then prick all over with a skewer or point of a sharp knife. (This will ensure that the lemon softens and bursts and you will achieve the delicious pond of sauce in the finished pudding.) Sprinkle the remaining sugar over and add the rest of the butter, cut into small cubes.

Roll out the reserved pastry into a circle for the lid. Dampen edge of the pastry in the basin then place lid in position. Trim neatly then seal edges firmly. Cover with a double sheet of aluminium foil, pleated in the centre to allow for expansion. You can use a pudding cloth if preferred. Place basin on a double strip of foil (to enable you to lift the pudding out of the steamer easily). Place in a steamer.

Bring a pan of water to the boil, place the steamer on top. Steam steadily for 4 hrs, replenishing as necessary with boiling water. The water in the pan should be at least halfway up the sides.

When cooked, serve pudding straight from the basin, so everyone gets a portion of lemon and toffee-flavoured sauce. Serve with custard.

HANDY TIP

Use one large orange instead of the lemon in the filling.

1. Place sieved flour and salt into bowl, add suet. Mix to a soft dough with water

2. Reserve one third of pastry. Roll out remainder and use to line the basin

3. Trim round the pastry edge neatly. Prick lemon all over with a skewer

4. Add half the sugar and butter, cut into cubes, then place lemon on top

5. Add remaining sugar and butter. Roll reserved pastry into a circle for lid

6. Cover pudding with a double sheet of aluminium foil, pleated in the centre

PROFITEROLES

Deliciously crispy small choux buns, filled with lightly whipped cream and topped with a rich, velvety smooth chocolate sauce... just heavenly. No-one will be able to resist this special dessert!

Calories per portion: 796 | **SERVES 6**

3½ oz/90 g unsalted butter
5 oz/150 g plain flour
pinch of salt
4 eggs, beaten, size 3
½ pint/300 ml whipping cream
FOR THE CHOCOLATE SAUCE:
8 oz/225 g plain chocolate
3 oz/75 g unsalted butter
4 tbsp milk

Preheat oven to Gas 6, 400°F, 200°C. Melt the butter in a small pan with ½ pint/300 ml water. Bring to the boil, then remove from heat and add all the flour and salt. Beat with a wooden spoon until all the flour has been incorporated and the mixture forms a ball in the centre of the pan. Cool slightly, then gradually add the eggs a little at a time, beating well between each addition.

Place the mixture in a piping bag fitted with a 1½ in/4 cm plain piping nozzle, and pipe about 16-20 small buns on to a dampened baking sheet – leave a little space between each bun to allow for expansion.

Bake on the shelf above centre of oven for 15-20 mins or until well risen and golden brown. Remove from the oven and, with a sharp knife, make a small slit in the side of each bun. Return to the oven for 3-5 mins to allow the buns to dry out. Transfer to a wire cooling rack and leave until cold.

Whip the cream until thick, then place in a piping bag fitted with the small plain nozzle, and fill each bun with the cream. Place on the serving dish, to form a pyramid.

Break the chocolate into small pieces, place in a bowl with the butter, and melt over a pan of gently simmering water. Stir with a wooden spoon until smooth, glossy and free from lumps. Remove the bowl from the pan and gradually beat in the milk. Continue to beat until the chocolate sauce is completely smooth and glossy. Pour attractively over the choux buns and serve immediately.

HANDY TIPS

If liked, flavour the whipped cream with a little Tia Maria to taste. You can also use real chocolate or vanilla soft scoop ice-cream, instead of the cream, to fill the choux buns.

1. Gently melt the butter in the water in a small pan, then bring to the boil

2. Add the flour and salt all at once and beat well with a wooden spoon

3. Beat thoroughly until mixture is smooth and glossy and forms a ball in pan

4. Add the beaten eggs a little at a time, beating well between each addition

5. Using a piping bag with a plain nozzle, pipe small buns on to a baking sheet

6. Fill the cooled profiteroles with the whipped cream just before serving

Chocolate Roulade

Why don't you spoil all the family with this wickedly delicious dessert? It's full of velvety smooth chocolate, sweet juicy satsumas and lashings of whipped cream.

Calories per portion: 490 | **Serves 8**

6 oz/175 g plain chocolate
4 tbsp brandy, rum or fruit juice
8 oz/225 g caster sugar
5 eggs, size 3, separated
2 tbsp icing sugar, sieved
¾ pint/450 ml whipping cream
7½ oz/220 g can satsuma segments in natural juice
1 satsuma, peeled and segmented
2 limequats or 1 lime

Preheat oven to Gas 4, 350°F, 180°C. Lightly grease a 12 in x 9 in/30 cm x 23 cm Swiss roll tin. Line the base and sides with one complete sheet of greased greaseproof paper. The paper needs to stand at least 2 in/5 cm above the sides of the tin.

Break chocolate into pieces and place in a small heatproof bowl with the brandy, rum or fruit juice. Place over a pan of gently simmering water and stir until the chocolate has melted. Beat lightly until smooth and free from lumps. Allow to cool.

In a large bowl, add the sugar to the egg yolks and beat with a wooden spoon until thick, creamy and doubled in volume. Beat in the cooled chocolate and mix well.

Whisk the egg whites until stiff and standing in peaks. Carefully fold into the chocolate mixture in a figure of eight movement. Be careful not to over mix but do ensure the egg white is completely incorporated. Pour into the prepared tin, tap lightly to remove any air bubbles and so that mixture is spread evenly in the tin.

Bake on shelf above the centre for 20-25 mins, or until the top is set and a crust has formed. Remove from oven. Cover the surface with a sheet of damp greaseproof paper and a damp clean tea towel. Leave overnight or for at least 8 hrs.

Next day sprinkle a large sheet of greaseproof paper with the icing sugar. Turn the roulade out on to the paper and carefully discard the lining paper.

Whip the cream until thick, then spread one third of the cream over the roulade to within ¼ in/6 mm of the edge. Drain the satsumas and dry on absorbent kitchen paper, then arrange over the cream leaving a gap at the bottom, top and sides. Holding the greaseproof paper with one hand, carefully roll up the roulade.

Place the roulade on a serving platter, then cover completely with the remaining cream. Mark the top and sides with a fork. Arrange the fresh satsuma segments along the bottom edges of the dish. Cut the limequats into thin slices or the lime into quarters and arrange on top of the cream.

Handy tip

You must use a sheet of greaseproof paper when lining the tin or the roulade will break in the middle when rolling up.

1. Break chocolate into pieces, place in bowl with brandy, rum or juice. Melt

2. Beat the cooled chocolate into the egg mixture until thoroughly mixed

3. Fold whisked egg whites into the chocolate mixture using a spatula

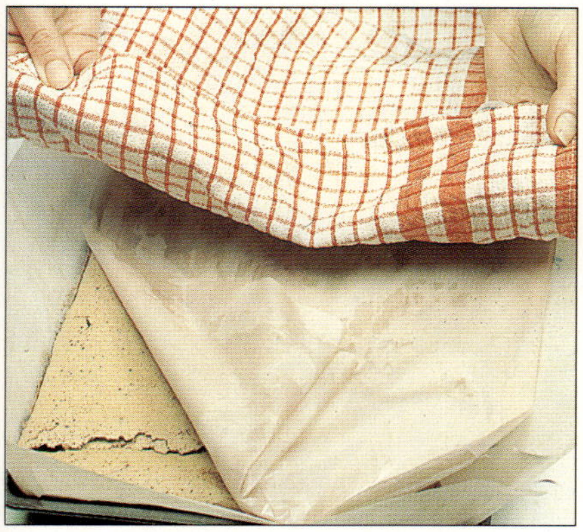

4. Cover cooked roulade with damp greaseproof paper and a damp tea towel

5. Arrange satsumas over cream leaving a gap at bottom, top and sides

6. Holding the greaseproof paper with one hand, gently roll up the roulade

CHOCOLATE SOUFFLE

Don't think you can't make a perfect soufflé – it's so much easier than you'd imagine. Just follow this step-by-step guide, and you'll have delicious results every time. So treat everyone to the lightest chocolate pud ever.

Calories per portion: 509 **SERVES 4**

4 oz/100 g plain chocolate
3 tbsp brandy, rum or water
¾ pint/450 ml milk
2 oz/50 g caster sugar
1½ oz/40 g plain flour
1 oz/25 g butter
4 eggs, size 3

Preheat oven to Gas 4, 350°F, 180°C. Lightly butter a 7 in x 3 in/18 cm x 7.5 cm deep soufflé dish. Place a baking sheet in the oven 10 mins before baking the soufflé – this will help the soufflé to rise.

Break the chocolate into small pieces and put into a bowl. Add the brandy, rum or water and place over a saucepan of gently simmering water. Stir until chocolate has completely melted and is smooth.

Heat all but 4 tbsp of the milk to blood heat then gradually stir the warmed milk into the melted chocolate. Stir in the sugar. Blend the flour with the reserved milk to make a smooth paste. Using a balloon whisk, gradually whisk the flour paste into the chocolate mixture.

Pour mixture into a clean saucepan, place over a gentle heat and stir continuously until thickened and smooth. Cook for a further minute. Add butter, stirring gently throughout until it has been thoroughly incorporated. Remove from the heat and allow mixture to cool slightly.

Separate the eggs and place the egg whites into a large clean bowl. Add the yolks one at a time to the cooled chocolate mixture beating well after each addition. Whisk the whites until stiff and standing in peaks. Carefully fold into the mixture using a spatula or metal spoon. Take care not to over mix otherwise you will remove the air you have whisked in.

Turn the mixture into the prepared soufflé dish and place on the preheated baking sheet. Bake for 35-45 mins or until well risen and firm to the touch. Serve the soufflé immediately with cream or fromage frais.

HANDY TIP

This pudding, if liked, can be prepared up to the stage before whisking the egg whites. When ready to cook the soufflé whisk the egg whites until stiff, fold into the cold chocolate mixture, turn into the prepared dish and cook as before. Do not keep opening the oven door during cooking as this can cause soufflés to sink. For a hot mocha soufflé, substitute 3 tbsp of strong black coffee for the brandy, rum or water, then proceed as before.

1. Melt the chocolate pieces in bowl over pan of gently simmering water

2. Gradually stir in the warmed milk, beating well after each addition

3. Blend flour to a smooth paste with the reserved milk, whisk into mixture

4. In a clean pan, gently heat chocolate mixture until thick, add butter

5. Cool slightly, add yolks one at a time. Beat well after each addition

6. Whisk egg whites until stiff, then gradually fold into the mixture

CHOCOLATE CHEESECAKE

Make the richest, delicious cheesecake ever! With a crisp chocolatey biscuit base, a tangy orange and creamy chocolate cheese filling and just a little more chocolate to top it off.

Calories per portion: 396 — **CUTS INTO 12 SLICES**

FOR THE BASE:
2½ oz/65 g unsalted butter
4 oz/100 g plain chocolate
8 oz/225 g digestive biscuits
FOR THE FILLING:
3 eggs, size 5, separated
3 oz/75 g caster sugar
grated rind and juice of 1 large orange
1 lb/450 g low-fat cream cheese
4 oz/100 g plain chocolate
2 tbsp brandy
1 oz/25 g gelatine
¼ pint/150 ml double cream
chocolate curls and icing sugar to decorate

Lightly butter sides and base of an 8 in/20.5 cm loose-bottomed cake tin. To make base, place butter and chocolate in a heavy-based pan over a gentle heat and allow chocolate to melt, stirring occasionally.

Draw the pan to one side and sir until smooth and free from lumps. Place the biscuits in a polythene bag and, using a rolling pin, crush finely. Stir the biscuits into the melted chocolate, then mix well. Spoon into the buttered tin and, using the back of a spoon, press into the base and sides. Chill.

Place the egg yolks and caster sugar in a bowl and whisk until thick and creamy, then whisk in the orange rind and juice. Add the cream cheese to the mixture, then whisk again until thoroughly mixed. Melt the chocolate and brandy together in a bowl over a pan of gently simmering water, stir well, until smooth, leave to one side.

Dissolve gelatine in 4 tbsp hot water, allow to cool slightly. Whisk reserved egg whites until standing in peaks. Whip cream until softly peaking.

Once the gelatine has cooled, pour into the cream cheese mixture in a thin, steady stream. Fold in the cream, then the egg whites. Mix lightly together until all ingredients are incorporated.

Divide the mixture in half, then stir the melted plain chocolate into one half and mix lightly together. Spoon the two mixtures alternately into the prepared cheesecake base and carefully smooth over the top. Leave to set in the fridge for at least 4 hrs.

When ready to serve, remove the cheesecake from the tin and place on serving plate. Arrange chocolate curls on top, then dust with sieved icing sugar. Serve with fruit.

HANDY TIP

Try adding 3 oz/75 g chopped toasted shelled hazelnuts to the chocolate mixture for an added crunch!

1. Melt butter and chocolate in a pan. Add finely crushed biscuits and mix well

2. Using the back of a spoon, press biscuit mixture into base and sides of tin

3. Whisk egg yolks and caster sugar together, whisk in orange rind and juice

4. After adding the cream cheese, stir in the gelatine in a thin steady stream

5. Divide the mixture in half, then fold one half into the melted chocolate

6. Spoon the two mixtures alternately into the chilled biscuit case and smooth top

Chocolate Toffee Pud

Lashings of delicious toffee sauce poured over a steaming hot chocolate pudding makes this a treat no one can resist. Follow this easy step-by-step guide to enjoy a perfect pudding every time.

Calories per portion: 764 | **Serves 6**

3 oz/75 g plain chocolate, broken into squares
6 oz/175 g butter
6 oz/175 g caster sugar
3 eggs, size 3, beaten
2 tbsp milk
¼ tsp vanilla essence
5½ oz/165 g self-raising flour
½ oz/15 g cocoa
FOR THE SAUCE:
2 oz/50 g soft brown sugar
2 oz/50 g butter
¼ pint/150 ml double cream
1 tsp lemon juice
1 tsp arrowroot

Grease a 2 pint/1.2 litre pudding basin with a little butter or oil. Place the chocolate in a small bowl and place over a pan of simmering water until melted. Stir until smooth.

Cream the butter and sugar together until pale and fluffy with either a wooden spoon or an electric mixer.

Gradually add eggs to the creamed mixture, beating well between each addition. Add the milk, vanilla essence and melted chocolate and mix well to a soft consistency. Sift the flour and cocoa together and carefully fold into the chocolate mixture then spoon the mixture into the greased pudding basin.

Cut a 10 in/26 cm double circle of greaseproof paper. Make a double pleat across the centre of the paper circle and place over the basin. Using string, tie the paper securely to the basin, round the rim. Cover with a sheet of pleated foil and tie securely.

Half fill a large pan with water and bring to the boil. Place a steamer over the pan and, using a folded strip of foil to lift it, place the basin inside. Cover tightly with a lid. Steam for 2 hrs until light and well risen.

To make the sauce, place soft brown sugar and butter in a heavy-based saucepan and gently heat, stirring occasionally until the sugar has dissolved and the butter melted. Bring to the boil without stirring until the mixture is a golden brown colour. Add the cream and lemon juice.

Place the arrowroot in a small bowl and mix with 1 tbsp water to a smooth paste. Add to the pan and heat, stirring constantly, until thickened. Remove the toffee sauce from the heat and then immediately pour it over the hot chocolate sponge. Serve at once.

HANDY TIP

Try serving the pudding with a different sauce, such as chocolate or melba.

1. Weigh out ingredients before starting to prepare the pudding

2. Melt the chocolate in small bowl over a pan of simmering water

3. Thoroughly cream the butter and sugar together until light and fluffy

4. Sift the flour and cocoa together and carefully fold into the mixture

5. Cover basin with a sheet of pleated foil and tie securely round rim

6. Place a folded strip of foil under basin to lift in and out of steamer

Tarte Tatin

This classic French dessert is a real culinary masterpiece! Crisp, light pastry is placed on top of thickly sliced, caramelized apples, then the tarte is turned upside down after cooking and sprinkled with icing sugar.

Calories per portion: 446 | **Serves 8**

FOR THE PATE SUCREE:
8 oz/225 g plain white flour
1½ oz/40 g caster sugar
6 oz/175 g unsalted butter
1 egg yolk, size 3
FOR THE TOPPING:
4 oz/100 g vanilla or caster sugar
2 oz/50 g butter
2 lb/900 g firm dessert apples
1 tsp ground cinnamon
1 tsp icing sugar

Preheat the oven to Gas 7, 425°F, 220°C, 15 mins before baking.

First, make the pâte sucrée: in a large bowl, sieve flour, then stir in 1½ oz/40 g caster sugar. Either leave in the bowl or turn out on to a clean surface and form into a mound. Make a hollow in the centre, then add unsalted butter, egg yolk and 2 tsp chilled water. Using your fingertips, bring mixture together to form a soft dough. (If making pâte sucrée on a work surface, carefully draw the flour in from the sides of the mound to prevent egg and water escaping.)

Knead the dough lightly, then wrap in greaseproof paper and chill while preparing the topping.

Sprinkle 1½ tbsp vanilla or caster sugar over the base of an 8 in/20.5 cm cake tin. Melt the butter and reserve. Peel the apples, cut into quarters, then core and slice thickly. Arrange a layer of apples over the base of the cake tin in a decorative pattern. Sprinkle with half the remaining sugar, drizzle half the melted butter over, then dust lightly with half the cinnamon. Repeat with the remaining apples, sugar, butter and cinnamon.

Place tin over a gentle heat and allow the sugar to melt, then caramelize, taking care not to burn the apples. (This process can take up to 20 mins, depending on how watery the apples are. Firm eating apples work best. You'll be able to tell when the sugar begins to caramelize as it will start to bubble up between the apples.) Remove from heat and set aside.

Meanwhile, on a lightly floured surface, roll out the chilled pâte sucrée to the size of the tin. Using the rolling-pin, carefully place the pastry over the apples and press lightly round the edge of tin.

Bake in preheated oven for 20 mins, or until pastry is cooked. If top is browning too quickly, cover with foil. Remove from the oven and invert on to a serving plate. Sprinkle the icing sugar over and serve hot or warm with the cream.

Handy tip

To make vanilla sugar, place a vanilla pod in a screw-top jar, then fill the jar with caster sugar. Secure the lid and leave for at least one week. Top up with sugar as you use it.

1. Form flour and sugar into mound, make a hollow, add butter and egg yolk

2. Sprinkle 1½ tbsp vanilla or caster sugar over the base of an 8 in/20.5 cm cake tin

3. Peel apples, cut into quarters, core and slice thickly, then arrange over base of tin

4. Sprinkle apples with half the remaining sugar and drizzle half melted butter over

5. Place the cake tin over gentle heat and allow the sugar to melt, then caramelize

6. On a lightly floured surface, roll out the pâte sucrée and use to cover the apples

PEAR & ALMOND TART

Crisp, almond pastry encases a mouthwatering combination of creamy custard and juicy pears in a delicious dessert. Serve with cream for an extra special family treat.

Calories per portion: 640 | **SERVES 6**

3 ripe pears
juice of 1 lemon
2 oz/50 g caster sugar
FOR THE PASTRY:
8 oz/225 g plain flour
¼ tsp salt
6 oz/175 g unsalted butter or margarine, softened slightly
2 oz/50 g ground almonds
1 oz/25 g caster sugar
1 egg, size 3, separated
FOR THE CUSTARD CREAM:
4 egg yolks, size 3
2 oz/50 g caster sugar
few drops of almond essence
1 tbsp cornflour
2 tbsp plain flour
¾ pint/450 ml milk
1 tbsp warmed apricot jam, sieved
toasted flaked almonds and lemon zest to decorate

Preheat oven to Gas 5, 375°F, 190°C, 15 mins before baking. Lightly grease a 9 in/23 cm loose-bottomed flan tin.

Core, peel and quarter pears, and sprinkle with lemon juice to avoid discolouration. Place pears in pan with sugar and pour in 1 pint/600 ml water and heat until sugar is dissolved. Poach pears gently for 15 mins until tender. Allow to cool in liquid.

Meanwhile, make pastry. Sift flour and salt into a bowl and rub in fat until mixture resembles breadcrumbs. Stir in almonds and sugar and bind together with egg yolk and 2 tsp cold water to form a firm dough. Knead gently on a lightly floured surface until smooth. Wrap and chill for 30 mins.

Roll pastry out on a lightly floured surface to fit greased flan tin and gently press into tin. Using a small leaf cutter stamp out enough shapes from the trimmings to go round the pastry rim. Stick the shapes on to pastry rim with lightly beaten egg white. Prick base and chill for 30 mins. Brush all over with egg white and bake for 15-20 mins until golden. Allow to cool.

To make custard cream, whisk together egg yolks, sugar and almond essence until pale and thick, and stir in cornflour and flour. Gradually blend in the milk and place in a heatproof bowl over a pan of simmering water or a double saucepan. Stir until thickened. Cover surface of custard with greaseproof paper to prevent a skin forming and allow to cool.
Remove pastry case from tin and stand on serving board. Spoon in custard cream and smooth over top. Drain pears and arrange on top of custard. Brush with apricot jam and serve sprinkled with almonds and lemon zest, accompanied with cream.

HANDY TIP

When buying pears for cooking, choose fairly firm, unblemished and even shaped fruit. Prepare and use immediately to prevent discolouration.

1. Core, peel and quarter pears and sprinkle with lemon juice to avoid discolouration

2. Place pears in pan with sugar and pour in 1 pint/600 ml water. Heat until sugar is dissolved

3. Stir in almonds and sugar and bind together with egg yolk and 2 tsp water to form a firm dough

4. *Using a small leaf cutter stamp out shapes from the trimmings. Stick the shapes on to pastry rim with egg white*

5. *Whisk together egg yolks, sugar and almond essence until pale and thick. Stir in cornflour and flour*

6. *Remove pastry case from tin and stand on serving board. Spoon in custard cream and smooth over top*

Blackberry Charlotte

Make the most of the late-summer fruits and serve your family and friends a delicious taste of the country with this simply mouth-watering dessert, full of juicy blackberries and sweet apples. It's a really super treat.

Calories per portion: 464 | Serves 8

1 lb/450 g blackberries, washed and patted dry
1 lb/450 g cooking apples
finely grated rind and juice of 1 lemon
1 tsp ground cinnamon
6 oz/175 g light brown sugar
4 tbsp cake crumbs
¾ large loaf white bread
4 oz/100 g butter or margarine, melted
1 egg, size 5, beaten
1 tbsp demerara sugar
a few blackberries and leaves to decorate

Preheat the oven to Gas 5, 375°F, 190°C. Lightly grease a 2½ pint/1.5 litre charlotte mould or a 6 in/15 cm round cake tin.

Place the blackberries in a large pan. Peel, core and thickly slice the apples and add to saucepan along with the lemon rind and juice and cinnamon. Cook gently for 10 mins until the apples have softened slightly. Stir in the brown sugar and cake crumbs.

Cut the bread into ½ in/1.25 cm thick slices and remove all the crusts. Trim two slices to fit the base of the tin and brush both sides of each slice with some melted butter or margarine. Fit into tin base. Reserve two slices for the top. Trim the remaining slices to fit the side of the tin. Dip both sides of each slice in the melted fat and arrange them closely around the side of tin, overlapping them as you go. Brush over the joins with some of the beaten egg.

Spoon in the stewed fruit and cover with the reserved slices of bread. Trim to fit and then brush the top with beaten egg. Bake for about 1 hr, or until golden brown.

Remove from the oven. Run a palette knife around the edge of the charlotte and invert on to a warmed serving plate. Sprinkle demerara sugar over the top and serve immediately, decorated with a few blackberries and leaves and accompanied by fruit-flavoured fromage frais decorated with mint.

HANDY TIP

Substitute 1 lb/450 g blackberries with prepared mixed black and redcurrants, proceed as instructed.

1. Stir the light brown sugar and cake crumbs into the stewed blackberry and apple mixture

2. Cut the ¾ loaf of white bread into ½ in/1.25 cm thick slices and remove the crusts

3. Dip slices in the melted fat and arrange around side of tin, overlapping as you go

4. Once you have arranged the bread, brush over joins with some of the beaten egg to help seal the joins

5. Spoon in stewed apples and blackberries and cover with reserved slices of bread

6. Run a palette knife around edge of charlotte and invert on to a warm serving plate. Serve sprinkled with demerara sugar

ORANGE SOUFFLE

Light as a feather, this delicious dessert has a wonderfully refreshing orange flavour that will get the taste buds tingling. Follow this easy step-by-step guide and cook the best soufflé ever.

Calories per portion: 405 **SERVES 4**

2 large oranges
½ oz/15 g unsalted butter, melted
1½ oz/40 g butter or margarine
1½ oz/40 g plain white flour
2 oz/50 g caster sugar
2 tbsp Grand Marnier or Cointreau
4 eggs, size 3
1 tbsp icing sugar
orange zest to decorate
assorted sweet biscuits to serve

Preheat oven to Gas 4, 350°F, 180°C, 10 mins before cooking the soufflé. Place a baking sheet in the oven 5 mins before cooking the soufflé. (By placing the soufflé dish on to the hot baking sheet the heat from the baking sheet will give the soufflé an initial burst of heat thus ensuring that the soufflé rises well.)

Scrub and thoroughly dry the oranges then grate the rind finely. Add the grated rind from half an orange to the melted butter to use to brush the sides and base of a 2 pint/1.2 litre soufflé dish. Leave to one side while preparing the soufflé. Squeeze the juice from the two oranges, strain and if necessary make up to ¼ pint/150 ml with water.

Melt the 1½ oz/40 g fat in a small pan then add the flour and cook over a gentle heat for 2 mins, stirring throughout. Turn off or remove from heat, gradually stir in strained orange juice. Return the pan to the heat and cook, stirring throughout until the mixture thickens. Remove from the heat and stir in the sugar and Grand Marnier or Cointreau. Allow the mixture to cool. Separate the eggs and once the mixture has cooled, beat in the egg yolks, one at a time, beating well between each addition. Place the egg whites in a large mixing bowl. (Ensure that the bowl is completely clean, otherwise the whites will not whisk properly.) Whisk the whites until stiff and standing in soft peaks. Fold 1 tbsp of the egg white into the mixture, followed by half the remaining whites then the other half. (Take great care when folding in that you do not beat out all the air you have so carefully whisked in. Use a figure of eight movement when folding in, this ensures that the egg white is folded in evenly.)

Tap the soufflé lightly on the surface to remove any air bubbles then place on the preheated baking sheet in the oven and cook for 30-35 mins or until the soufflé is well risen and golden brown. Have ready the icing sugar in a small sieve and the orange zest.

As soon as the soufflé is cooked, remove from oven, sieve over icing sugar, decorate with zest and serve.

HANDY TIP

If liked divide the mixture between six ¼ pint/150 ml ramekin dishes, prepare as instructed then cook in the oven for 15-20 mins or until cooked. Serve at once.

1. Stir the grated rind from half an orange into the melted butter and use to brush the sides and base of dish

2. Melt the fat in a small pan then add the flour and cook over a gentle heat for 2 mins

3. Turn the heat off then gradually stir in the strained orange juice. Return to the heat and cook until thickened

4. Once the mixture has thickened, allow to cool then add the egg yolks one at a time

5. Whisk the egg whites until stiff, add 1 tbsp to the orange mixture then the remaining egg whites in two stages

6. Pour the prepared soufflé mixture into the dish and place on the preheated baking sheet and cook

APPLE STRUDEL

Deliciously light pastry filled with chunks of apple, flavoured with lemon, cinnamon and nutmeg. Don't be frightened of making strudel pastry – it's really easy, and the smell as it's cooking will start everyone's taste-buds tingling.

Calories per portion: 366 **SERVES 6**

FOR THE PASTRY:
8 oz/225 g plain flour
½ tsp salt
1 egg, size 3
2 tbsp vegetable oil
FOR THE FILLING:
1 lb/450 g cooking apples
1½ oz/40 g flaked almonds
2 oz/50 g seedless raisins
1 tbsp grated lemon rind
½ tsp freshly grated nutmeg
½ tsp ground cinnamon
2-3 oz/50-75 g sugar
1½ oz/40 g butter, melted

Preheat oven to Gas 5, 375°F, 190°C, 10 mins before baking the strudel. Sift the flour and salt into a large mixing bowl. Make a well in the centre, add the egg with 4-5 tbsp of tepid water and the 2 tbsp oil. Mix to a pliable dough and continue to knead for about 15 mins until the dough is silky smooth and very elastic.

If liked, the dough can be made in a food mixer using the dough hook attachment – the pastry will take about 5 mins. Shape into a round ball then leave in a lightly oiled polythene bag for about 1 hr.

Meanwhile, prepare the filling. Peel, core and slice the apples. Place in a bowl with ½ oz/15 g of the flaked almonds, the raisins, lemon rind, nutmeg, cinnamon and sugar. Mix together lightly.

Roll the relaxed pastry out as thin as you can on a lightly floured surface with a warmed rolling pin. Then, lift the pastry up and gently stretch it from the centre towards the edge, taking care not to tear it. Cut into two 12 in x 10 in/30 cm x 26 cm oblongs and place on to individual sheets of greaseproof paper. Divide the prepared filling between each pastry oblong, brush all edges well with melted butter then carefully roll up each strudel, tucking each end into the centre and keeping the roll a neat shape.

Lift on to a greased baking sheet, with the join underneath and brush each strudel with remaining melted butter. Sprinkle with remaining almonds and bake just above the centre for 20-25 mins or until golden brown. Allow to cool slightly before dusting with a little sifted icing sugar. Serve this delicious dessert cut into slices, hot or cold with custard or cream.

HANDY TIPS

When making the strudel pastry, use a warm, flour dusted rolling pin to prevent the pastry sticking. Add the filling and roll up immediately to prevent the pastry drying out. You can use whatever sugar you prefer – caster, soft light brown or dark brown sugar, for a rich flavour.

1. Sift the flour and salt into the bowl, add the egg, then the water and oil

2. Peel and slice apple, add almonds, raisins, rind, nutmeg, cinnamon, sugar

3. Roll relaxed dough out on a lightly floured surface, using a warm rolling pin

4. Cut dough into two 12 in x 10 in/30 cm x 26 cm oblongs and arrange the filling

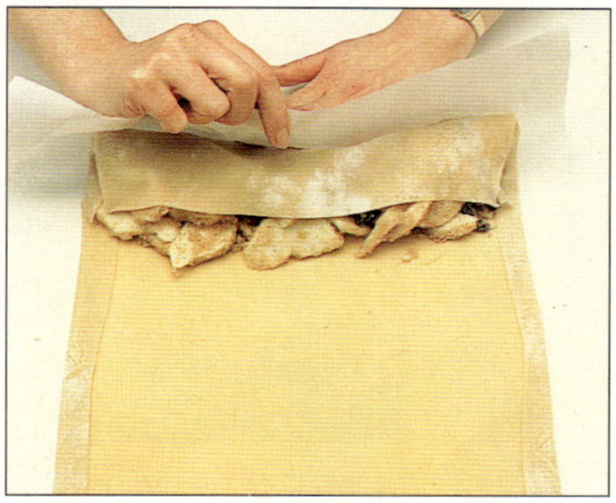

5. Lift greaseproof paper and carefully roll strudel, ensuring filling is encased

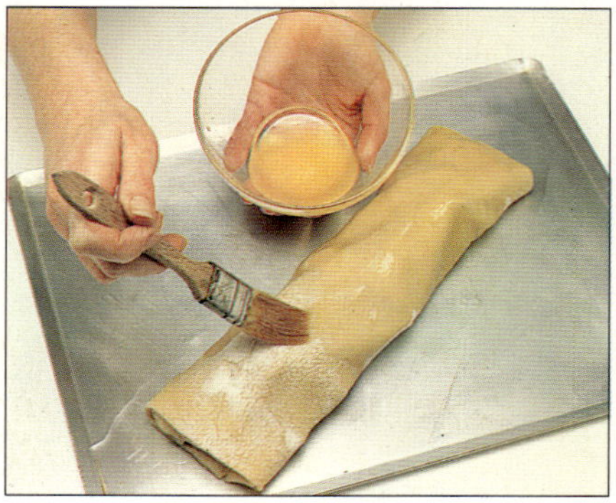

6. Place on a lightly greased baking sheet, brush with the melted butter

Pears in Red Wine

This classic French recipe provides a perfect ending to any meal. The pears are gently poached in a light sugar syrup with red wine, cinnamon and lemon until they are tender and have become a beautiful red colour.

Calories per portion: 162 | **Serves 6**

1 lemon, preferably unwaxed
6 firm pears such as William or conference – choose good even shaped pears and ones that are not damaged or bruised
6 oz/175 g caster sugar
1 cinnamon stick
8 fl oz/250 ml full-bodied red wine
cinnamon sticks and lemon peel to garnish
cream and sweet biscuits to serve

Using a vegetable peeler carefully remove a long thin strip of peel from the lemon and reserve. Cut the lemon in half and squeeze out the juice. Place the juice in a large mixing bowl and fill it with cold water. Using the vegetable peeler, peel the pears thinly but leave the stalks intact. Place the peeled pears as soon as they are peeled in the bowl of water. (The lemon juice in the water helps to ensure that the pears do not discolour before cooking.)

Place the sugar in a heavy-based pan with 6 fl oz/175 ml of water. Add the lemon peel. Lightly bash (bruise) the cinnamon stick and break in half, add to the pan. Place over a gentle heat and cook, stirring until the sugar dissolves. Bring to the boil then boil steadily for 2 mins.

Drain the pears then add to the pan, cover with a lid then poach the pears for 20-30 mins or until the pears are tender, turning the pears occasionally during cooking. (The length of time will depend on the ripeness of the pears.) Test the pears with a skewer. If the skewer is easily inserted the pears are cooked.

Once cooked add the red wine and continue to poach the pears for a further 10 mins turning them occasionally very gently with a wooden spoon. (This will allow the pears to absorb the flavour and colour of the wine.)

Carefully remove the pears from the pan and place them in a dish. Increase the heat under the pan and bring the syrup to the boil. Boil steadily for 10 mins or until the liquid is reduced by half and has become the consistency of thick syrup. Discard the lemon rind and cinnamon stick.

If serving the pears warm, place them upright in a dish, pour over the syrup and garnish with thin strips of lemon peel and cinnamon sticks.

If serving the pears cold, pour the syrup over the pears and leave to become cold. Turn the pears frequently in the syrup. (You will get a deeper colour if the pears are served cold as they have longer sitting in the red wine syrup.) Serve pears with cream and sweet biscuits.

Handy tip

For a change, try using a medium dry white wine instead of the red wine, and orange peel instead of the lemon. Stir in 2 tbsp Cointreau or Grand Marnier as well for an added indulgence.

1. Using a vegetable peeler, peel the pears thinly then place in the water mixed with lemon juice

2. Place the sugar, lemon peel and cinnamon stick in a heavy-based pan with 6 fl oz/175 ml water

3. Drain the peeled pears then carefully add to the pan taking care not to damage them

4. *Cover the pan with a lid then poach the pears for 20-30 mins or until tender. Test with a skewer*

5. *Once the pears are cooked, pour the red wine over and continue to poach for 10 mins*

6. *Remove the pears from the syrup then increase the heat and boil steadily until a thick syrup consistency is reached*

Lemon Syllabub

A classic dessert that dates back to Elizabethan times, rich and creamy with a subtle tang of white wine and lemons. Simple to make, it's the perfect answer for occasions when you want a treat.

Calories per portion: Syllabub 379; Biscuits 55 **Serves 4**

1 large lemon
¼ pint/150 ml dry white wine
3 oz/75 g caster sugar
½ pint/300 ml double cream
zested lemon rind to decorate
TUILLE BISCUITS:
2 fl oz/50 ml double cream
1 egg, size 3 separated
4½ oz/120 g icing sugar
1½ oz/40 g plain flour
½ tsp baking powder
1 oz/25 g flaked almonds

To make the syllabub, scrub the lemon and dry thoroughly then finely grate the rind and place in a bowl. Squeeze out the juice and strain into the bowl then stir in the wine. Add the sugar and stir then cover. Place in the fridge and leave to infuse for 3-4 hrs.

Add the cream to the infused liquid then gently whip together until the mixture thickens and forms soft peaks.

Spoon the mixture into four individual glass dishes and then chill for a further 3-4 hrs before serving with the tuille biscuits and decorated with zested lemon rind.

To make the tuille biscuits, preheat oven to Gas 6, 400°F, 200°C, 15 mins before baking the biscuits. Well grease 2-3 baking sheets with oil. Beat the cream and egg yolk together in a bowl until thoroughly mixed together. Sift the icing sugar then gently stir into the bowl, ensuring that there are no lumps. Sift the flour and baking powder together then add to the mixture and fold in using a metal spoon. Whisk the egg white until stiff then fold into the mixture. Place in a piping bag fitted with a small plain potato nozzle then pipe 1½ in/4 cm lengths onto the baking sheets. (Only pipe a few onto each baking sheet, as they spread.) Sprinkle the biscuits with 4-5 flaked almonds then bake in the oven for 5-7 mins or until cooked. To tell if they are cooked, the biscuits should be completely pale golden in colour. Remove from the oven, leave for a couple of seconds then gently wrap round the handle of some clean wooden spoons. Leave for a few minutes to harden, before cooling on a wire cooling rack. This amount of mixture should make 18 biscuits. Serve with the Syllabub.

Handy tip

You can vary the flavour of the syllabub by substituting orange or lime rind and juice for the lemon, or try a mixture of them both.

1. Scrub the lemon and dry then grate the rind finely. Place in bowl with the juice, wine and sugar

2. Pour the double cream into the chilled infused wine and lemon juice, stirring throughout

3. Gently whisk the mixture until it thickens and forms soft peaks. Spoon into glasses and chill

4. Whisk the egg white until stiff then carefully fold into the tuille mixture. Place in a piping bag

5. Pipe 1½ in/4 cm lengths onto the greased baking sheets and sprinkle with flaked almonds

6. Allow tuilles to cool for a couple of seconds. Remove from baking sheet and shape round a wooden spoon

FRUIT CRUMBLE

Make the most of fruit and cook up a scrumptious crumble. This one with apples and delicious sun-ripened apricots is an appetizing pudding for the whole family, served with custard or ice cream it's bound to be a real favourite.

Calories per portion: 550 | **SERVES 4**

FOR THE FILLING:
2 lb/900 g cooking apples
2 cinnamon sticks
grated rind and juice of 1 large orange
3-4 oz/75-100 g golden granulated sugar
6 oz/175 g, no-need-to-soak apricots
FOR THE TOPPING:
6 oz/175 g plain flour
3 oz/75 g butter or margarine
2 tbsp bran, optional
2 oz/50 g unrefined granulated sugar

Preheat oven to Gas 6, 400°F, 200°C, 15 mins before baking crumble. Peel the cooking apples and core. Slice thinly and place in a saucepan. Lightly bruise the cinnamon sticks and add to pan with the grated rind and juice of the orange and sugar to taste. Place over a gentle heat and cook for 12-15 mins or until apples are soft and pulpy. Stir the apples occasionally during cooking to prevent them burning on base of pan. Remove from heat and discard cinnamon sticks. Beat to form a purée.

Chop or snip the apricots with scissors and add to the apples. Spoon into a shallow ovenproof dish.

To make the topping: Sift the flour into a mixing bowl. Add the fat then rub in, using fingertips, until mixture resembles fine breadcrumbs. Stir in the bran if using then the sugar.

Spoon the mixture over the apple and apricots ensuring that the filling is completely covered. Press topping down lightly with the back of a spoon. Place dish on a baking sheet and bake on the centre shelf for 30-35 mins or until topping is golden. Remove from oven and serve hot with custard or ice cream.

Variations: here are some ideas for varying the fruit filling. Add 6 oz/175 g blackberries or raspberries to the apple purée. Try stewing 1½ lb/675 g rhubarb with 1 tsp ground ginger and 2-3 tsp ginger wine with sugar to taste until soft. Or wash 1½ lb/675 g plums, cut in half and discard the stones. Simmer gently with 2-3 oz/50-75 g of sugar. Stir in 3 oz/75 g washed, dried and halved, natural coloured glacé cherries.

HANDY TIP

Make double the quantity of crumble topping. Place half in a container or polythene bag. Either freeze or store for up to one week in the fridge for a quick pudding when time is short.

1. Thinly peel the apples then carefully core, slice and place in saucepan

2. Simmer the apples with the cinnamon, sugar and the orange rind and juice

3. Beat the apples to a pulp then add the apricots – no need to soak them first

4. Stir the apple and apricots together, then spoon into a shallow ovenproof dish

5. Sift flour into a bowl, add the butter or margarine, rub in with fingertips

6. Spoon topping over the filling, pressing it down with the back of a spoon

Apple Dumplings

Who can resist the taste of these delicious fluffy apples, filled with nuts and cherries, then covered in a light, crisp golden pastry that melts in your mouth. Serve them with a thick creamy custard or cream.

Calories per portion: 890 | **Serves 4**

4 firm cooking apples, each about 6 oz/175 g in weight
strained juice of ½ lemon
2 oz/50 g glacé cherries
1 oz/25 g whole blanched almonds
grated rind 1 orange
2 oz/50 g sultanas
2 oz/50 g unrefined granulated sugar
1¼ lb/550 g prepared shortcrust pastry, thawed if frozen
1 egg white, size 5, beaten
2 tsp caster sugar

Preheat oven to Gas 6, 400°F, 200°C, 15 mins before cooking dumplings. Choose firm and unblemished apples. Wash the fruit thoroughly under cold running water and dry well. Dip an apple corer into strained lemon juice, then use to core apples. Make a reasonably large cavity to ensure all the core has been removed. Brush the cut surface on the inside of the apples with lemon juice to prevent the apple discolouring.

Wash and dry cherries, then chop. Chop the almonds. Place the cherries, almonds, orange rind, sultanas and sugar in a small bowl. Mix together.

Roll the pastry out on a lightly floured surface to ½ in/1.25 cm thick, then cut out four 8 in/20.5 cm rounds. Reserve trimmings.

Place an apple in the centre of each pastry round. Fill cavity of each apple with the prepared filling, packing it down firmly. Dampen the edge and then carefully mould the pastry round the apple. Make sure that it's completely encased.

Place on a baking sheet, with the join underneath. Roll out the trimmings and cut out pastry leaves. Dampen the underneath of each leaf, then place in position on the top of each apple. Brush completely with beaten egg white and sprinkle with caster sugar.

Place on shelf above centre of oven and cook for 30 mins or until pastry is golden. If liked, halfway through cooking, brush again with egg white and sprinkle with a little more caster sugar. Serve hot.

If preferred, peel apples completely then after removing the core, brush all cut surfaces with lemon juice before filling and covering with pastry.

Handy Tips

If liked, you can make a double quantity – prepare the apples and cover in pastry, then freeze before cooking, for future use. If cooking from frozen, cook for 40-45 mins, or until the pastry is golden and the apple is cooked. You can also vary the filling. Try chopped dates with muscovado sugar and ground cinnamon, chopped walnuts with stem ginger and 2 tbsp clear honey or raisins with mixed spice, unsalted peanuts and demerara sugar.

1. Wash the apples, core and brush centres with strained lemon juice

2. Chop the cherries and almonds. Add to sugar and sultanas with orange rind

3. Roll pastry out. Cut into 8 in/20.5 cm rounds. Place cored apples in centre

4. Fill the apples with nut and cherry mixture, packing it down firmly

5. Dampen pastry edges with water. Bring sides up to encase apples

6. Seal pastry firmly. Place sealed side down, on baking sheet, decorate top

SUMMER PUDDING

In the summer when there's so many tasty soft fruits around, the time is ripe to make this tasty traditional pudding, full of currants, strawberries, plums, apples and raspberries. It's easy to prepare, looks impressive, and is perfect as a special treat.

Calories per portion: 193

SERVES 6

8 thin slices white bread, preferably one day old
4 oz/100 g redcurrants
8 oz/225 g blackcurrants
4 oz/100 g raspberries
6 oz/175 g ripe plums
4 oz/100 g strawberries
6 oz/175 g cooking apples
4 oz/100 g caster sugar
fresh mint leaves to decorate
fresh cream to serve

Place the thinly-sliced bread on a chopping board, trim off the crusts and discard them. Reserve 2 of the slices and use the remainder to line the base and sides of a 1½ pint/900 ml pudding basin. Ensure that there are no gaps in the bread.

Wash and dry the red and blackcurrants lightly, discarding any leaves or under-ripe fruit, then prepare the currants by stripping them off the stalks. Place them in a saucepan with the raspberries. Reserve a few currants to decorate. Wash the plums, cut in half and discard the stone, chop roughly and add to the pan. Hull the strawberries, wash lightly, then chop roughly and add to pan. Peel the cooking apples, and discard the cores, chop roughly and add to pan with the sugar and 2 tbsp of cold water.

Bring slowly to the boil, lower the heat, and simmer very gently for 5 mins or until the fruits are soft but still retain their shape. Cool slightly for 3-4 mins then place the lightly stewed fruit into the bread-lined pudding basin. Pack down firmly with the back of a spoon or spatula, taking care not to squash the fruit too much. After filling basin to the top with fruit, carefully place reserved bread slices on top, ensuring fruit is completely covered.

Place a saucer or small plate – which will just fit inside the basin – on top of the bread, then weigh down with some heavy weights or a large, clean can. Place in the fridge, preferably overnight, to allow the juices from the fruit to soak into the bread and give the pudding its colour.

To serve, carefully invert the basin on to a flat serving plate and shake lightly to remove the basin.

Decorate the summer pudding with the reserved currants and mint leaves, and serve with cream.

HANDY TIPS

If you find that you have trouble removing the basin, carefully run a round-bladed knife between the bread and the basin to loosen the pudding. Vary the fruits according to availability and own personal tastes. For a healthier version of this pudding, try substituting brown bread for white.

1. Place the thinly sliced bread on a chopping board, trim crusts and discard

2. Line the base and sides of a 1½ pint/900 ml pudding basin with the bread

3. Prepare the red and blackcurrants, place in pan, then peel cooking apples

4. Place the lightly stewed fruit into the bread-lined basin, pack down firmly

5. After filling basin with the fruit, place the reserved bread slices on top

6. Place a saucer or small plate on top, then weigh down with heavy weights

HAZELNUT VACHERIN

Layers of delicious nutty meringue sandwiched together with whipped cream and fresh fruit make this scrumptious dessert. It's just ideal for those special occasions or when you simply want to give your family a super treat.

Calories per portion: 437 | **SERVES 8**

4 oz/100 g hazelnuts
4 egg whites, size 3
8 oz/225 g caster sugar
FOR THE FILLING:
½ pint/300 ml whipping cream
1-2 tbsp kirsch, optional
8 oz/225 g strawberries
8 oz/225 g raspberries

Preheat the oven to Gas 5, 375°F, 190°C, 10 mins before skinning hazelnuts. Lightly oil and line three baking sheets with vegetable parchment paper. Draw a circle in the centre of each sheet by inverting a 6 in/15 cm plate on top and tracing round it.

Skin hazelnuts, if necessary, by placing on an unlined baking sheet and baking in oven for 10 mins. Remove and cool. Rub off skins by placing in a clean tea towel and rubbing between hands. Place in a food processor or blender and blend until finely ground.

Place egg whites in a clean, grease-free glass bowl. Whisk until stiff. Add half the sugar, 1 tbsp at a time, whisking after each addition, bringing the mixture back to its original stiffness each time. Fold in remaining sugar, using a metal spoon or spatula and taking care not to over mix.

Lightly fold in the ground hazelnuts using a figure of eight movement. Place an equal amount of mixture in the centre of each drawn circle, smoothing out to the edges with a palette knife. Place in oven and bake for 15 mins. Reduce oven temperature to Gas 2, 300°F, 150°C, and continue to cook for 20-30 mins, or until meringue is firm to touch. You may need to swap the positions of the baking sheets to ensure even browning.

Remove from oven and allow to cool for at least 15 mins before transferring to wire racks. Peel off paper when cold. Whip the cream until thick, then stir in the kirsch, if using. Hull the strawberries and raspberries and rinse lightly. Leave to dry on absorbent kitchen paper. Spread cream over each meringue layer, top with fruit, then sandwich layers together. Reserve a little cream and fruit for decoration.

Place reserved cream in a piping bag fitted with a star nozzle and pipe rosettes around edge. Decorate the top with fruit, serving any remaining fruit separately.

HANDY TIPS

The meringue can be made beforehand and stored for up to two days in an airtight tin. If liked, ground almonds can be used instead of hazelnuts. Vary the fruit according to taste and availability.

1. Lightly oil and line three baking sheets, draw a circle in the centre of each

2. Whisk egg whites until stiff, whisk in half the sugar, then whisk again

3. Using a metal spoon, carefully fold in the finely ground hazelnuts

4. Place an equal amount of mixture in the centre of each drawn circle

5. Using a palette knife, spread the meringue mixture to edge of each circle

6. When cooked, remove from oven. Allow to cool, then transfer to wire racks

CREME BRULEE

Make any occasion special and cook this classic dessert. It's naughty but truly delicious, made with thick double cream and flavoured with a hint of vanilla then topped with a crunchy caramel topping. Serve with fresh fruit and sweet biscuits.

Calories per portion: 522 | **SERVES 6**

1 pint/600 ml double cream
1 tsp vanilla essence or
1 vanilla pod
4 egg yolks, size 3
6 oz/175 g caster sugar

Preheat the oven to Gas 2, 300°F, 150°C. Pour the cream into a large mixing bowl or into the top of a double saucepan. Place over a pan of gently simmering water. Stir in the vanilla essence or add the vanilla pod. Heat through gently until almost at boiling point, then remove from heat and, if using the vanilla pod, discard.

Whisk the egg yolks with 2 oz/50 g of the sugar until doubled in size and thick and creamy. It's thick enough when the whisk leaves an impression as it's lightly drawn across the surface. Gradually whisk the warmed cream into the egg mixture, mix well.

Pour the mixture into six individual ovenproof dishes or ramekins to within ½ in/1.25 cm of the top. Place in a roasting tin then carefully pour in boiling water so that the level of the water comes halfway up the sides of the dishes.

Bake in the oven for about 1-1½ hrs, or until set. Top up the water as necessary. Take care not to allow the skin on the top of the custard to colour. When set, the top will have a slightly crusty appearance and will feel firm when pressed lightly with a finger. Remove roasting tin from the oven and take out the individual dishes. Leave until cool then refrigerate overnight.

Next day, preheat grill. Cover the custard (in each dish) with the remaining sugar, ensuring that the surface is completely covered. Tap the dishes lightly to level out the sugar. Place under the preheated grill for 4-5 mins, or until the sugar caramelizes. Take great care at this stage not to burn the sugar. Turn the dishes to ensure even browning. Remove from grill and leave to cool, then chill.

HANDY TIPS

This dish is not suitable for freezing or cooking in a microwave. If liked, fresh fruit such as raspberries or strawberries can be placed in the dishes before pouring over the custard and baking. It can also be made in a larger ovenproof dish, such as a soufflé dish – this will then need to be cooked for at least 1½ -2 hrs.

1. Place cream in bowl over pan of simmering water, add vanilla essence

2. Cream egg yolks and sugar until thick, gradually whisk in warmed cream

3. Pour the cream mixture into six individual ovenproof or ramekin dishes

4. Place dishes in roasting tin, pour boiling water to reach halfway up sides

5. Sprinkle the brûlées with caster sugar to at least ¼ in/6 mm in depth

6. Place under a preheated grill until sugar turns to caramel. Turn occasionally

MOUNT VESUVIUS

This spectacular pudding is made with delicious apricots, raspberry sorbet and vanilla ice cream, covered with super-light meringue. But what makes it really special is how you serve it – topped with lit sparklers!

Calories per portion: 527 **SERVES 8**

FOR THE SPONGE CAKE:
2 eggs, size 3
2 oz/50 g caster sugar
2 oz/50 g plain flour
FOR THE FILLING:
6 oz/175 g no-need-to-soak apricots, chopped
¼ pint/150 ml unsweetened orange juice
1¾ pint/1 litre tub vanilla ice cream
17½ fl oz/500 ml raspberry sorbet
FOR THE MERINGUE:
3 egg whites, size 3
4½ oz/120 g caster sugar
FOR THE DECORATION:
2 oz/50 g whole blanched almonds
2 tbsp demerara sugar
sparkler or dessert candle

Preheat the oven to Gas 5, 375°F, 190°C. Grease and line the base of a 7 in/18 cm sandwich tin. Whisk eggs and caster sugar until pale and thick. Sieve flour, carefully fold into egg mixture with a metal spoon, with 1 tbsp tepid boiled water. Pour into tin and bake for 20-25 mins, or until firm to the touch. Turn out on to a wire rack to cool.

To prepare filling, place apricots in pan with orange juice, bring to boil and simmer for 10 mins until soft. Leave to cool. Place the vanilla ice cream in a 2½ pint/1.5 litre pudding basin and mould up the sides using the back of a metal spoon. Freeze for approx 30 mins to harden. Mould sorbet in same way to form a layer inside ice cream. Fill centre with cooled apricots and freeze for 30 mins, or until frozen.

When ice cream is frozen, place basin in a bowl of hot water for 10 secs and loosen edges with a palette knife. Place sponge over top of dessert, turn out, then return to freezer for a further 30 mins.

Increase the oven temperature to Gas 8, 450°F, 230°C. Whisk egg whites until stiff and standing in peaks, then whisk in half the caster sugar. Whisk again until stiff, then carefully fold in remaining sugar. Place the ice cream and sponge on to a lightly greased baking sheet then spoon over the meringue, ensuring ice cream and sponge are completely covered. Press almonds into the meringue and sprinkle with the demerara sugar.

Bake in the oven for 3-4 mins or until the tips of the meringue are light brown and the meringue is set. Serve immediately with cream, decorated with a sparkler or candle, which should be removed before cutting the dessert.

HANDY TIP

Instead of using the sparkler or candle, place a metal eggcup in the top of the meringue before flash-baking. Once cooked, half fill with warmed brandy then ignite and serve.

1. Whisk the eggs and sugar in a mixing bowl until creamy, then fold in flour

2. Mould the ice cream and sorbet up the sides of a basin. Fill with apricots

3. Place the frozen dessert carefully in a bowl of hot water for 10 secs

4. Loosen with palette knife. Place sponge over dessert and turn out of basin

5. Refreeze, then place on greased baking sheet. Swirl meringue over to cover

6. Press whole almonds into meringue, sprinkle with sugar and bake

Sherry Trifle

Light sponge cakes laced with sherry, covered with fruit and a creamy custard, topped with lashings of whipped cream. That's what makes this sherry trifle so delightful. Make two and freeze one for that special occasion.

Calories per portion: 555 **Serves 6**

1 pkt trifle sponge cakes
6 tbsp raspberry jam
6-8 tbsp medium dry sherry
14 oz/397g can fruit cocktail
1 pint/600 ml milk
3 tbsp plain flour
2 eggs, size 3
1 oz/25 g caster sugar
½ tsp vanilla essence
½ -1 oz/15-25 g butter
½ pint/300 ml whipping cream
6 glacé cherries, halved
1 oz/25 g flaked almonds

Cut the sponges evenly in half, spread with the raspberry jam and sandwich together. Place in the base of a glass serving dish, arranging the cakes so that the base of the dish is completely covered. If necessary, cut the sponge cakes in half so that there are no gaps.

Pour the sherry evenly over the sponge cakes. Drain the can of fruit, reserving 2-3 tbsp of the juice. Arrange the fruit over the cakes and pour the juice over. The sponge cakes should be well moistened but not swimming in excess liquid. If necessary, use less sherry or juice depending on how potent you want the trifle to be. Leave the soaked sponge cakes to one side while you are preparing the custard.

Heat the milk to blood heat (you can test this by dipping a clean finger into the milk – it should feel the same temperature as your finger).

Meanwhile, place the flour in a bowl, add the eggs and beat with a wooden spoon. Gradually stir in the warm milk and return the mixture to the pan. Heat gently until thickened.

At this stage it is very important to stir continuously to prevent the custard from becoming lumpy. If lumps do appear once the custard has thickened, strain it through a fine sieve. When the custard has thickened, cook for 1 min, remove from the heat then beat in the sugar, vanilla essence and butter. Beat until the butter has melted then pour over the sponge cakes and fruit. Leave until cooled. Place the trifle in the fridge or a cool place until the custard is completely cold.

Whip the cream until it is stiff and standing in soft peaks. Spoon into a piping bag fitted with a star nozzle and pipe a pattern across the top. Decorate the top with halved glacé cherries and flaked almonds.

Handy tip

Whipped cream freezes very well, so if freezing, prepare the trifle in a freezable dish, omitting the glacé cherries and flaked almonds. Thaw and decorate before serving.

1. Spread the halved sponge cakes with jam. Use to line the base of the dish

2. Moisten sponge cakes with sherry. Use extra sherry or fruit juice if liked

3. Spoon fruit over in an even layer. For a change, vary fruit and jam used

4. Beat eggs into flour. Heat milk to blood heat then stir into egg mixture

5. Remove thickened custard from heat. Beat in sugar, vanilla essence and butter

6. When custard is completely cold, whip cream until thick then pipe over top

TIRAMISU

When the occasion calls for an extra special treat, or even when you just want to spoil the family this stunning Italian dessert fits the menu perfectly. A combination of creamy cheese, sponge biscuits and a wicked hint of brandy, it's irresistible.

Calories per portion: 793 | **SERVES 4**

2 egg yolks, size 3
2 tbsp caster sugar
2 tsp vanilla sugar, or ½ tsp vanilla essence, plus 2 tsp caster sugar
14 oz/400 g mascarpone cheese
2 tbsp brandy or coffee liqueur
4 tbsp strong black coffee
20 sponge finger biscuits
2 tsp cocoa powder, sieved
FOR THE MOCHA CREAM:
2 oz/50 g plain chocolate
1 tbsp coffee essence
¼ pint/150 ml double cream
1 tsp icing sugar, sieved
chocolate coffee beans to decorate

Place the egg yolks, caster sugar and vanilla sugar – or vanilla essence and the 2 tsp caster sugar – in a mixing bowl. Whisk until the mixture is thick and creamy. Add 2 tbsp mascarpone cheese to the whisked mixture and fold in gently. Gradually add the remaining cheese, folding it in gently to form a smooth, thick cream.

Place the brandy, or the coffee liqueur, and coffee in a shallow dish. Dip the sponge finger biscuits into the coffee for a couple of seconds. The biscuits need to absorb the flavour of the coffee but still remain firm enough to prevent them disintegrating, so only dip a few biscuits in the coffee at a time as you begin to assemble the dessert.

In either four individual serving dishes or one large bowl, arrange alternate layers of biscuits and cheese mixture, finishing with a layer of the cheese mixture. Dust with the sieved cocoa powder, then chill in the fridge until set.

Meanwhile, make the mocha cream. Break the chocolate into small pieces, then place chocolate and coffee essence in a heatproof bowl over a pan of gently simmering water. Ensure that the bottom of the bowl does not touch the water. Stir until the chocolate is smooth. Remove from the pan and leave to cool for 5 mins.

Whip the cream until just beginning to form soft peaks, then gradually fold it into the cooled melted chocolate. Cover and chill for 30 mins.

Just before serving, top the set Tiramisu with spoonfuls of the mocha cream and dust lightly with icing sugar. Decorate with chocolate coffee beans..

HANDY TIP

For a change, decorate with brandy-flavoured whipped cream.

1. Place the egg yolks and sugars in a mixing bowl and whisk until creamy

2. Add 2 tbsp mascarpone cheese to the whisked mixture and fold in gently

3. Place the brandy or coffee liqueur in a shallow dish and dip in the sponge fingers

4. Arrange alternate layers of biscuits and cheese mixture in serving dishes

5. Gradually fold the whipped cream into the cooled melted chocolate

6. Top set Tiramisu with spoonfuls of mocha cream, then dust with icing sugar

CHRISTMAS PUDDING

Make this deliciously light Christmas pudding, laden with dried fruit and flavoured with brandy a month in advance and give it time to mature. Using breadcrumbs instead of suet makes it healthier and also ideal for vegetarians.

Calories per portion: 698 | **SERVES 8**

8 oz/225 g butter or margarine
8 oz/225 g muscovado sugar
3 eggs, size 3, beaten
4 tbsp golden syrup
grated rind and juice 1 lemon
8 oz/225 g fresh brown breadcrumbs
1 tsp ground cinnamon
1 tsp ground nutmeg
1 tsp ground ginger
8 oz/225 g sultanas
8 oz/225 g seedless raisins
8 oz/225 g currants
4 oz/100 g cut mixed peel
4 oz/100 g self-raising wholemeal flour
3 fl oz/85 ml brandy, sherry or fruit juice

Cream butter or margarine and sugar together until light and fluffy. Gradually beat in the eggs, syrup, grated rind and lemon juice. Stir in fruit, mixed peel, then flour and brandy, sherry or fruit juice. Stir in the breadcrumbs, then spices, ensuring that they are thoroughly mixed in. Cover the bowl and leave to stand overnight.

Next day cut out two small rounds of greaseproof paper to fit the base of two 2 pint/1.2 litre pudding basins. Grease basins lightly. Stir the mixture with a wooden spoon and make a wish! If you want to put in little Christmas novelties, now's the time, but make sure that they are suitable. DON'T use our present day coinage, they are not suitable – coins must be silver.

Divide the mixture between the two pudding basins to within 1½ in/4 cm of the top. Cover with either greaseproof paper and a pudding cloth or a double sheet of tin foil. Tie cloth securely or fold the tin foil firmly under rim. Place in top of a steamer and place over a pan of gently simmering water and steam for 6 hrs (top up with boiling water as necessary). Allow to cool, then recover and store in a cool dark place until required.

Before serving, steam for 2-3 hrs, then serve with brandy butter or cream and caster sugar. The earlier you make your pudding, the better, as this gives the pudding time to mature.

HANDY TIPS

Place a cut lemon in the base of the steamer – this will prevent the pan from turning black. For a delicious brandy butter, cream 3 oz/75 g unsalted butter with 5 oz/150 g caster sugar, then gradually beat in 3-4 tbsp of brandy. Cover and freeze if making in advance. This will keep in the fridge for up to one week.

1. Gradually add the beaten eggs to the creamed butter and sugar mixture a little at a time

2. Stir in the dried fruit and chopped mixed peel, ensuring they are thoroughly mixed in

3. Stir in the fresh brown breadcrumbs to create a much lighter pudding, ensuring they are well mixed in

4. Next day, divide the mixture between the prepared pudding basins to within 1½ in/4 cm of the rim, smoothing the top

5. Make a pleat in the tin foil to allow for expansion, use a long strip of foil for easy removal

6. Place the pudding in the top of the steamer, over a pan of gently simmering water and steam for 6 hrs

ICED ORANGE BOWL

This unusual, stunning dessert is a true masterpiece – an ice bowl, filled with juicy, tangy oranges, covered with smooth, golden caramel and decorated with fresh flowers.

Calories per portion: 208 **SERVES 4**

FOR THE ICE BOWL:
approx 36 ice cubes
fresh flowers and foliage
FOR THE CARAMELIZED ORANGES:
6 large oranges
4 tbsp Cointreau
4 oz/100 g caster sugar
mint sprigs, to decorate

Before you start, prepare a large enough space in your freezer for a 3 pint/1.7 litre glass bowl to stand upright, without tipping over. Adjust the freezer to rapid freeze.

Place a few ice cubes in the base of a 3 pint/1.7 litre glass bowl (one that's suitable for freezing – not a crystal glass bowl!). Next, place a 1½ pint./900 ml glass bowl on top of the ice cubes and decide where you'd like to position the flowers. Then break off the flower heads and small pieces of foliage and arrange in between the two bowls, wedging in position with ice cubes. Continue until you have filled the space between the bowls with flowers and ice cubes. Weigh down the smaller bowl by placing some heavy weights (about 1½ lb/675 g in total) inside it. Carefully pour sufficient cold water in between the two bowls to cover the flowers and ice cubes completely. Place the bowls in the freezer for at least 3 hrs, until frozen solid.

When completely frozen, remove the bowls from the freezer and return the freezer to its usual setting. Remove the weights from the smaller bowl, then using a hot damp cloth, rub the inside of the smaller bowl until it loosens sufficiently for you to remove it.

Place the larger bowl in a sink or washing-up bowl, half-filled with hot water for 10 secs, taking care not to flood the centre. Slip out the ice bowl from the glass bowl. (You may need to repeat this process if it doesn't work the first time.) Place ice bowl on a freezer-proof plate. Return to the freezer until required.

To prepare caramelized oranges, carefully peel the oranges, using a small sharp knife, ensuring that none of the bitter white pith remains. Slice the oranges thinly, place in a bowl and pour the Cointreau over the fruit.

Place the caster sugar in a heavy-based saucepan with 8 tbsp water. Heat gently, stirring occasionally, until the sugar dissolves. Increase the heat, then boil the sugar syrup until it bubbles and turns golden brown.

Remove from the heat instantly and dip the base of the pan into cold water to stop the caramel cooking and to cool it quickly.

Remove the prepared ice bowl from the freezer and fill with the oranges, then drizzle the caramel over. Serve decorated with mint sprigs.

HANDY TIP

As an alternative, fill the ice bowl with scoops of ice cream.

1. Place a few ice cubes in a 3 pint/1.7 litre bowl. Place 1½ pint/900 ml bowl on top

2. Arrange flower heads and foliage in between bowls; wedge with ice cubes

3. Place weights inside smaller bowl, cover flowers with water, then freeze

4. Using a hot, damp cloth, rub the inside of the small bowl until it loosens

5. Carefully peel the oranges, ensuring none of the bitter white pith remains

6. Boil the sugar syrup in a pan until it bubbles and turns golden brown

CREPES SUZETTES

Wonderfully light pancakes, flavoured with lemon and orange butter, then flamed in brandy, make this classic dessert. Just follow this easy step-by-step recipe for perfect results – and serve up a delicious extra-special treat.

Calories per portion: 221 | **SERVES 12**

4 oz/100 g plain flour
pinch of salt
3 eggs, size 3
8 fl oz/250 ml milk
1 oz/25 g butter, melted
4 oz/100 g butter, preferably unsalted, softened
3 oz/75 g icing sugar
grated rind of 1 lemon
grated rind and juice of 1 orange
2-3 tbsp Cointreau
1½ oz/40 g clarified butter or 1-2 tbsp oil for frying
2-3 tbsp brandy
orange zest to decorate

Sieve the flour and salt into a mixing bowl, make a well in the centre, then break in the eggs. Using a balloon whisk, whisk flour into eggs, gradually drawing in flour from the sides of the bowl. Adding the milk, a little at a time, continue whisking until a smooth batter is formed. Then whisk in the melted butter. Leave for 30 mins (this will help the starch in the flour to soften and expand in the liquid, resulting in a lighter crêpe).

Place softened butter in a bowl. Sieve icing sugar, add to butter. Beat until pale and creamy. Add lemon and orange rind, together with 2 tbsp orange juice. Beat well, then gradually beat in the remaining orange juice and the Cointreau. Cover and reserve.

When you are ready to cook the crêpes, heat a small knob of clarified butter or 1 tsp oil in a non-stick crêpe pan or small frying pan. When the pan is hot, swirl the melted butter or oil carefully around the pan, then pour off any excess. Pour 2 tbsp batter into the pan, again swirling the pan gently to allow the mixture to cover the base. Cook for 2-3 mins, or until the crêpe has set and is beginning to come away from the sides of the pan. Using a palette knife or spatula, turn the crêpe over and cook for a further 2 mins, or until the crêpe is cooked through and pale golden brown in colour.

Repeat until all the batter has been used. Stack the crêpes on a plate with sheets of greaseproof or baking parchment between them. Keep the crêpes warm.

When ready to serve, fold four crêpes into quarters. Melt 2½ oz/65 g of the orange and lemon butter in a non-coated pan (it's inadvisable to flambé in a coated pan) and add crêpes. Heat through, spooning butter over. Pour in a little brandy, allow to heat through gently, then remove pan from heat and carefully ignite. Once the flames have subsided, decorate the crêpes with orange zest and serve. Repeat until all the crêpes have been used.

HANDY TIP

The crêpes will freeze very well. Thaw, then reheat for a little longer than if cooking from being freshly made.

1. Sieve the flour and salt into a mixing bowl, break in the eggs, then whisk

2. Cream the butter and icing sugar together, beat in lemon and orange rind

3. After beating in the orange juice, add the Cointreau and beat until well mixed

4. *Cook the crêpes until set, then, using a spatula, turn the pancake over*

5. *Melt the orange butter, fold the crêpes into quarters and add to the pan*

6. *After heating the crêpes through, add brandy, remove from heat and ignite*

Ice cream bombe

Rich, luscious home-made strawberry, tutti frutti and chocolate ice cream, all frozen together to make a stunning dessert. It'll take a little longer to prepare than some puddings, but the taste is pure luxury, and it's worth every minute spent.

Calories per portion: 771 | **Serves 8**

1. Lightly wash the strawberries and raspberries then blend to make a purée

2. For tutti frutti ice cream, chop glacé cherries, angelica, apricots and sultanas

3. Fold the strawberry and raspberry purée into the lightly whipped cream

FOR THE STRAWBERRY ICE CREAM:
12 oz/350 g strawberries
4 oz/100 g raspberries
juice of ½ lemon
10 oz/300 g icing sugar, sifted
½ pint/300 ml double cream

FOR THE TUTTI FRUTTI ICE CREAM:
4 oz/100 g sugar
9 fl oz/275 ml milk
1 vanilla pod
2 oz/50 g glacé cherries, washed
1 oz/25 g angelica, washed
2 oz/50 g no-need-to-soak apricots
2 oz/50 g sultanas
¼ pint/150 ml double cream

FOR THE CHOCOLATE ICE CREAM:
1 tbsp cornflour
¼ pint/150 ml milk
4 oz/100 g plain chocolate, melted
2 oz/50 g sugar
¼ pint/150 ml whipping cream
¼ pint/150 ml fromage frais

FOR THE STRAWBERRY SAUCE:
8 oz/225 g strawberries, washed
2 oz/50 g icing sugar
1 tbsp redcurrant jelly
2 tbsp whipped cream

Set freezer to rapid freeze. Have ready three clean, dry, freezable containers.

To make the strawberry ice cream, lightly wash the strawberries and raspberries, then pass through a food processor with the lemon juice to form a purée. Sieve to remove any pips. Stir icing sugar into purée. Whip cream until thick, fold in purée. Pour into container and freeze until just firm.

Dissolve the sugar for the tutti frutti ice cream in 3 tbsp water. Cool, then chill. Heat the milk with the vanilla pod to just below boiling point. Remove from heat, cover and leave to infuse for 15 mins. Discard the vanilla pod. Then chop the cherries, angelica, apricots and sultanas. Whip cream until thick, fold milk, sugar syrup and fruit into cream, pour into container and freeze until just firm.

To make the chocolate ice cream, blend the cornflour with a little of the milk. Heat remainder of the milk then pour on to the cornflour. Cook over a gentle heat, stirring until mixture thickens. Remove from heat, stir in the melted chocolate and sugar. Leave to cool. Lightly whip the cream and fromage frais together, then stir in chocolate mixture. Pour into container. Freeze until firm.

When the strawberry ice cream is lightly frozen, spoon into a 3 pint/1.7 litre pudding basin and with the back of a spoon, mould over the base and up the sides. Return to freezer until firm.

Using the tutti frutti ice cream, mould over the strawberry ice cream, leaving a hollow in the centre for the chocolate. Freeze until firm.

Fill centre with the chocolate ice cream and smooth over to give a flat base. Return to freezer until solid.

To unmould the bombe, carefully run a knife round the inner edge of basin, invert on to serving plate and wrap a hot towel round. Leave a couple of mins, then remove towel and basin. Decorate the bombe with rosettes of cream and a few extra strawberries.

To make the strawberry sauce, place the strawberries, icing sugar and redcurrant jelly in a food processor, purée until smooth and then sieve to remove any pips.

HANDY TIP

Leave bombe in the fridge for 20 mins before serving. Return freezer to normal setting.

4. Smooth the strawberry ice cream up sides of basin using the back of a spoon

5. When the strawberry ice cream has frozen, spoon in the tutti frutti ice cream

6. Fill the remainder of the basin with the chocolate ice cream. Smooth top

Floating Islands

When you want to serve something a little different, try this classic dessert. A smooth creamy custard with the subtle tang of cinnamon, topped with lightly poached meringues then drizzled with caramel syrup.

Calories per portion: 246 | **Serves 4**

¾ pint/450 ml semi-skimmed milk
2 cinnamon sticks
4 egg yolks, size 3
1 egg, size 3
4 oz/100 g caster sugar

Place the milk in a pan. Tap the cinnamon sticks lightly with a rolling pin to bruise them slightly without breaking them completely, add to milk and bring to just below boiling point. Remove from the heat and leave to infuse for at least 30 mins then strain and discard the cinnamon sticks. Place the egg yolks into a bowl. Separate the whole egg and place the yolk with the other egg yolks. Place the white in a clean bowl (reserve for later). Whisk 1 oz/25 g of the sugar into the egg yolks then the strained milk. Pour into a heavy-based saucepan or into a double boiler, cook over a gentle heat, stirring throughout until the custard thickens and coats the back of a spoon. Pour into a serving bowl then chill in the fridge for at least 1 hr.

Whisk the egg white until stiff and standing in peaks, then gradually whisk in 1½ oz/40 g of the remaining sugar. Continue to whisk until the mixture is stiff and glossy and small peaks are made when the whisk is pulled away from the meringue.

Half fill a frying pan with cold water and bring to a gentle boil. Reduce heat so that the surface of the water is just moving. Using two spoons, shape the mixture into ovals then carefully place in the water. Poach for at least 5 mins or until meringues are set. Remove from the pan and drain on absorbent paper before arranging on top of the chilled custard.

Place the remaining 1½ oz/40 g of caster sugar in a heavy-based saucepan with 2 tsp of cold water. Place over a gentle heat and stir until dissolved. Increase the heat and boil steadily until a golden caramel coloured syrup is formed. Carefully drizzle a little caramel syrup over the top of each meringue then serve.

HANDY TIPS

You can vary the flavour of the custard by replacing the cinnamon sticks with a vanilla pod, or use ½ tsp vanilla essence. Try infusing the milk with the finely pared rind of an orange or lemon.

1. Place pan over a very gentle heat and cook, stirring throughout until the custard thickens and coats the back of a spoon

2. Whisk the egg white until stiff and standing in peaks, gradually whisk in the sugar, whisk until stiff

3. Half fill a frying pan with cold water, bring to a gentle boil then spoon in the shaped meringues

4. Remove the meringues from the pan and allow to drain thoroughly on absorbent paper

5. Dissolve remaining sugar in a heavy-based pan, bring to the boil, boil until a golden syrup is formed

6. Arrange drained meringues on top of the custard. Carefully drizzle a little of the syrup over the meringues, then serve

Charlotte Russe

Sugary biscuits, surrounding a delicious home-made custard filling, flavoured with pineapple, create this mouthwatering dessert which looks as good as it tastes. A superb ending to any meal.

Calories per portion: 376 | **Serves 6**

½ pint/300 ml fresh apple juice
2 x ½ oz/15 g sachets gelatine
1 small star fruit
2-3 fresh strawberries
20 sponge finger biscuits
3 eggs, size 3, separated
3 oz/75 g caster sugar
7 fl oz/200 ml milk
7 oz/197g can pineapple chunks in natural juice
½ pint/300 ml whipping cream
frosted grapes to decorate (see handy tips)

Pour the apple juice into a clean pan and bring to boil. Switch off heat and sprinkle in one sachet gelatine. Whisk until completely dissolved. Allow to cool, then pour a thin layer into a 7 in/18 cm round cake tin and leave until the jelly is completely set.

Meanwhile, wash, then slice the star fruit thinly. Wash, dry and halve the strawberries. Dip fruit slices into remaining liquid jelly (if it has started to set, gently warm it through to melt it again). Using a skewer, arrange fruit in a decorative pattern over the set apple jelly. Allow the fruit to set, then pour in another ½ in/1.25 cm layer of liquid jelly on top.

Dip both sides of the sponge finger biscuits into the liquid jelly. Arrange biscuits, sugar-side out, around the edge of the tin. Leave until set.

Place the egg yolks and sugar in a bowl over a pan of gently simmering water. Whisk until pale and creamy. Remove from the heat. Warm the milk to blood heat, then beat into egg mixture. Strain into a clean pan and cook over a gentle heat, stirring throughout, until the mixture thickens and coats the back of a spoon. Strain into a clean bowl and leave to cool, stirring occasionally.

Dissolve the remaining packet of gelatine in 3 tbsp hot water and stir into cooled custard. Drain the pineapple and chop. Whip the cream until thick. Whisk the egg whites until stiff and in peaks. Gently fold the cream, pineapple and egg whites into custard mixture, then spoon over the set apple jelly, ensuring there are no air pockets.

Smooth the top and chill until set. When ready to serve, trim biscuits, if necessary, to the level of the filling. Dip base of tin quickly into hot water. Invert on a serving plate. Decorate with frosted grapes.

Handy Tips

To frost grapes, whisk one egg white until frothy. Wash and dry small bunches of grapes, dip them in egg white or water, then roll in caster sugar. Leave to dry. Other fruits, such as satsuma segments, strawberries and currants can also be frosted in this way. Use within two days. You can also frost edible flowers such as primroses and violets in this way.

1. Add the gelatine to the apple juice and whisk until completely dissolved

2. Using a skewer, arrange the dipped fruit on top of jelly in a decorative pattern

3. Dip the sponge biscuits in the liquid apple jelly and place around tin

4. *Stir custard over a gentle heat until it coats the back of a spoon*

5. *Gently fold cream, pineapple and egg whites into the custard*

6. *Spoon custard and cream mixture over the set jelly. Smooth the top*

Croquembouche

Choux buns, filled with tasty crème pâtissière, sitting on a shortcake base, decorated with a delicate web of fine sugar.

Calories per portion: 611 | **Serves 8**

1. On a lightly floured surface, roll out shortcake dough to an 8 in/20.5 cm circle

2. Add flour to choux mixture, beat to form a ball. Add beaten eggs, beat again

3. Place choux paste in a piping bag. Pipe small rounds on a damp baking sheet

FOR THE SHORTCAKE BASE:
6 oz/175 g plain flour
1½ oz/40 g caster sugar
3 oz/75 g butter or margarine, softened
1 egg, size 3
FOR THE CHOUX BUNS:
4 oz/100 g plain flour
3 oz/75 g butter
3 eggs, size 3, beaten
FOR THE CREME PATISSIERE:
3 eggs, size 3
2 oz/50 g caster sugar
3 tbsp plain flour
3 tbsp cornflour
¾ pint/450 ml milk, warmed
1 teaspoon vanilla essence
1 oz/25 g butter
FOR THE CARAMEL:
8 oz/225 g caster sugar

Preheat the oven to Gas 4, 350°F, 180°C. To make the base, sieve the flour into a bowl, then add the caster sugar. Cut the fat into small pieces and rub into the flour and sugar until the mixture resembles breadcrumbs. Bind together with the egg. Knead dough lightly, then roll out on a lightly floured surface to an 8 in/20.5 cm circle. Place on a baking sheet, prick lightly, then bake for 20-25 mins, or until pale golden. Remove from oven, cool slightly, then transfer to a wire cooling rack.

To make the choux buns, increase the oven temperature to Gas 6, 400°F, 200°C. Sieve the flour. Place the butter in a pan with 7 fl oz/200 ml water and bring to the boil, stirring occasionally. Remove from the heat, then add the flour. Beat vigorously until the mixture forms a ball. Add the beaten eggs, a little at a time, beating well after each addition. Place mixture in a piping bag with a ½ in/1.25 cm plain nozzle, then pipe small rounds on to a damp baking sheet. Bake for 15-20 mins, or until golden. Remove buns from the oven, make a small slit in each one, then return to the oven for 5 mins. Cool and reserve.

To make crème pâtissière, beat eggs and caster sugar together and sieve flours. Beat the flours into the egg mixture until smooth, then gradually beat in the milk. Strain, then place in a pan over a gentle heat and cook, stirring continuously, until thickened and smooth. Remove from the heat and beat in the vanilla essence and butter. Leave covered until cold.

To make caramel, dissolve the caster sugar in ½ pint/300 ml water in a heavy-based saucepan. Bring to boil and boil until a light caramel forms. Place base of pan in cold water.

To assemble, fill buns with crème pâtissière. Dip base and outer side of each bun into the caramel, place around edge of shortcake base, then on top of each other, building up to form a pyramid.

Reheat the caramel slightly, then spin strands by dipping a spoon in the caramel, placing a fork on top, then pulling the two apart. As the caramel cools, strands will form between the spoon and fork. Use to decorate the Croquembouche. Serve with a selection of fresh fruit.

HANDY TIP

Make the base and choux buns earlier, freeze until required. When ready to use, thaw then crisp the choux buns in oven for 5 mins, fill and proceed as above.

4. Dip the filled choux buns into caramel, then arrange on the shortcake base

5. Continue dipping buns into caramel and building them up to form a pyramid

6. Dip a spoon in the caramel, place a fork on top, pull apart to spin strands

CHRISTMAS BOMBE

For something a little lighter than the traditional puddings this Christmas or at any time, try this sensational dessert. Tutti frutti ice cream and Raspberry Crush encased in plain chocolate, served with a creamy white chocolate sauce.

Calories per portion: 576 | **SERVES 8**

1¾ pint/1 litre tub tutti frutti ice cream

FOR THE RASPBERRY CRUSH:

8 oz/225 g frozen raspberries (do not thaw)
8 fl oz/250 ml buttermilk
2-3 tbsp icing sugar
8 oz/225 g plain chocolate

FOR THE SAUCE:

4 oz/100 g white chocolate
½ oz/15 g butter
¼ pint/150 ml double cream
1-2 tbsp brandy
mint leaves to decorate

Set freezer to rapid freeze. Using a metal spoon, press the ice cream into a 2½ pint/1.5 litre bombe mould or pudding basin, forming a well in the centre. Cover and freeze for 30 mins.

Meanwhile, prepare the Raspberry Crush. Reserving 2 oz/50 g of the frozen raspberries for decoration, place remainder in a food processor or blender. Whilst crushing the raspberries pour in the buttermilk and enough icing sugar to taste, until a soft, icy mixture is formed. Pile this mixture into the centre of the ice cream lined mould. Cover and freeze for 15 mins.

Place bombe in a bowl of hot water for 10 secs and invert on to a greaseproof paper lined plate to remove from mould. Re-freeze for 15 mins whilst preparing the plain chocolate casing.

Break the plain chocolate into pieces and place in a heatproof bowl over a pan of simmering water until melted. Beat until glossy and smooth.

Remove bombe from freezer and spoon over the chocolate, ensuring all the ice cream is covered – work quickly to prevent ice cream melting too much. Refreeze for 30 mins whilst making the sauce.

Break white chocolate into pieces and place in a heatproof bowl over a pan of simmering water until melted. Remove from heat and beat in the butter, and gradually beat in the cream. Stir in brandy to taste.

Remove bombe from freezer, allow to thaw slowly in the fridge for 20 mins before serving.

Decorate the bombe with the reserved raspberries and mint leaves. Run the blade of a sharp knife under hot water and slice the bombe to serve, accompanied by the white chocolate sauce.

HANDY TIPS

The raspberry crush freezes very hard if left too long in the freezer, making slicing difficult. Remember to return freezer to normal setting.

1. Using a metal spoon, press the ice cream into a 2½ pint/1.5 litre bombe mould or pudding basin

2. Blend raspberries. While blending, pour in buttermilk and icing sugar until a soft icy mixture is formed

3. Pile Raspberry Crush into the centre of the ice cream mould. Cover and freeze for 15 mins

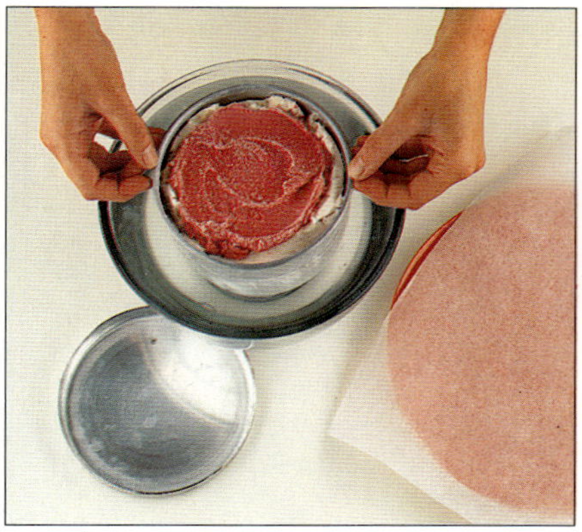

4. *Place mould in hot water for 10 secs and invert on to a greaseproof paper-lined plate*

5. *Working quickly spoon melted plain chocolate over the bombe ensuring all the ice cream is covered*

6. *Melt white chocolate, beat in the fat, then gradually beat in the cream. Stir in the brandy to taste*

CAKES & BAKES

Who can resist the smell of baking wafting from the kitchen? From every-day family cakes and special occasion treats to breads and home-made biscuits, these recipes are guaranteed to tempt everyone. Try the simple, inexpensive Victoria Sponge, the stunning Chocolate Caraque Cake or the tasty Cherry & Date Cake. Sample the Chelsea Buns and Danish Pastries, Doughnuts and Chocolate Brownies or Gâteaux and Gingerbread. There's much more besides...

BATTENBURG CAKE

Deliciously light and fluffy sponge, half flavoured with chocolate, and wrapped in marzipan, makes this cake irresistible. Follow this easy step-by-step guide and bake the family a real tea-time treat.

Calories per portion: 656 | **CUTS INTO 15 SLICES**

12 oz/350 g butter or margarine
12 oz/350 g caster sugar
6 eggs, size 3, beaten
12 oz/350 g self-raising flour, sieved
1 oz/25 g cocoa powder
12 oz/350 g apricot jam
2 tbsp lemon juice
1 lb/450 g white marzipan
little extra caster sugar

Preheat oven to Gas 5, 375°F, 190°C, 10 mins before baking. Line a 10 in x 7½ in/25 cm x 19 cm baking tin with lightly greased greaseproof paper. Make a partition down the centre of the tin with greaseproof paper. Lightly brush with a little cooking oil. Cream the butter or margarine with the sugar until light and fluffy. Add eggs a little at a time, with 1 tbsp of flour after each addition. Beat well. Add the remaining flour and fold in using a metal spoon to form a soft dropping consistency.

Place half the mixture into one side of the prepared tin and smooth the top. Sift the cocoa powder into the remaining mixture and fold in. If necessary, add 1-2 tbsp of cooled boiled water to form a smooth, dropping consistency. Place into the other half of the prepared tin and smooth top. Bake for 45-50 mins or until cooked and the mixture springs back when lightly pressed with fingertip. Remove from oven and leave until cold before discarding the lining paper.

Cut both of the sponges in half lengthways. If necessary, trim the halves so that all four sections are equal. Heat the jam with the lemon juice then rub through a sieve. Brush one side of a white section and one side of a chocolate section with sieved jam. Press firmly together. Brush the base and one side of the other chocolate section with jam and place on top of white sponge. Repeat with remaining white section and place on top of chocolate sponge to give a chequered effect. Press cake firmly together.

Roll marzipan out to an oblong 12 in x 9 in/30 cm x 23 cm on a lightly sugared surface. Trim edges if necessary. Brush base of cake with jam, place in centre of marzipan. Brush cake completely with jam then fold the marzipan up the sides and over the top of the cake. Press the sides firmly. Press the join firmly together and smooth by rolling lightly with a rolling pin. Turn over so join is underneath.

Make a decorative pattern along the top outside edges of the marzipan and mark diagonal lines across the top. Dust the top of the cake lightly with a little caster sugar.

HANDY TIP

If liked, food colouring can be used to colour the different sections of the cake. Allow 2 tsp of food colouring for half the basic mixture. The colour will fade when the cake is cooked.

1. Line the tin with greased greaseproof paper, dividing it in half lengthways

2. Place plain sponge mixture in one half. Add cocoa to the mixture in the bowl

3. Cut cooled sponges in half lengthways to give four equal-sized sections

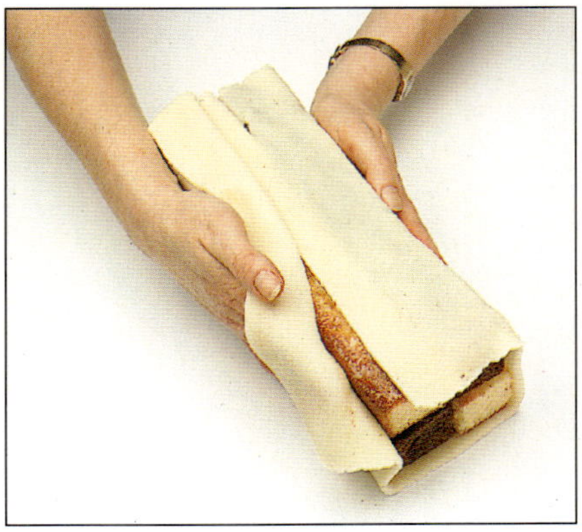

4. Brush sections with jam and press together to give a chequered effect

5. Place cake in centre of the rolled-out marzipan and brush with jam

6. Press marzipan firmly around cake then turn over so join is underneath

CHERRY & DATE CAKE

This delicious cake is guaranteed to be a family favourite. It's crammed full of cherries and dates and sprinkled with flaked almonds. The ground almonds help the cake keep its wonderful moist texture.

Calories per portion: 253	CUTS INTO 12 SLICES

4 oz/100 g glacé cherries
6 oz/175 g fresh dates
4 oz/100 g butter or margarine
4 oz/100 g caster sugar
3 eggs, size 3
6 oz/175 g self-raising flour
2 oz/50 g ground almonds
½ tsp almond essence
1 oz/25 g flaked almonds
2 tsp caster or granulated sugar for dredging

Preheat oven to Gas 4, 350°F, 180°C, 10 mins before baking. Grease and line the base and sides (if not using a non-stick cake tin) of a 7 in/18 cm deep cake tin with lightly oiled greaseproof paper.

Wash the cherries and roughly chop. Wash again to remove all the syrup then dry thoroughly. Wash the dates and pit, then chop roughly. Place the fat and sugar in a mixing bowl then using a wooden spoon, beat the ingredients together until they are pale and creamy. Beat the eggs and sift the flour. Add the egg a little at a time to the creamed mixture together with 1 tbsp of flour. (This will help to prevent the mixture curdling which can result in a heavy, close-textured cake.) Once all the egg has been added stir in half the flour using a metal spoon. Add the chopped cherries and the dates and fold in carefully. Add the remaining flour, the ground almonds and almond essence and gently fold into the mixture. Turn the mixture into the prepared cake tin and sprinkle the top with the flaked almonds and 1 tsp caster sugar or granulated sugar. Bake in the oven for 1 hr or until cooked. To test if the cake is cooked, insert a clean skewer into the centre of the cake, leave for approximately 10 seconds, then remove. If the skewer comes out clean the cake is cooked. Remove from oven and leave to cool in the tin. Just before serving, dredge with the remaining caster or granulated sugar.

HANDY TIP

If you cannot find fresh dates, use dried ones, look for the non sugar-coated chopped dates.

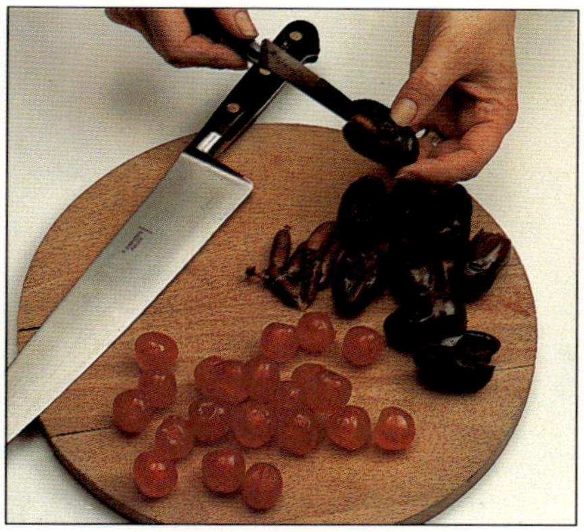

1. Wash and dry the cherries, wash and pit the dates, then chop roughly

2. Cream the fat and sugar until light and fluffy then add the eggs with 1 tbsp flour

3. Fold in cherries and dates, remaining flour, ground almonds and almond essence

4. Turn the prepared cake mixture into the greased and lined cake tin, then smooth over the top with a palette knife

5. Scatter the flaked almonds over the top of the cake and sprinkle with 1 tsp of caster or granulated sugar

6. To test if the cake is cooked, insert a clean skewer into the centre. It is cooked when it comes out clean

Swiss Roll

When friends pop round for tea or the family fancies a home-made cake, try whisking up this easy-to-make Swiss Roll. It's light enough not to worry too much about those inches, but filling enough to keep them all happy.

Calories per portion: 252 | **Serves 6**

3 eggs, size 3
4 oz/100 g caster sugar
4 oz/100 g flour
extra caster sugar for dredging
6 tbsp whole fruit jam

Preheat oven to Gas 7, 425°F, 220°C, 15 mins before baking. Line and lightly grease a Swiss roll tin 13 in x 9 in/ 33 cm x 23 cm with a large sheet of greased greaseproof paper.

Place eggs and sugar in a large mixing bowl, place over a pan of gently simmering water and whisk until really thick and creamy. Remove from the heat and continue to whisk until cool.

Sieve the flour into the mixture then carefully fold it in, in a figure of eight movement. Then mix in 1 tbsp warm water. Pour mixture into tin, covering the whole surface evenly by tilting it gently backwards and forwards. Tap lightly on the work surface. Bake on the shelf above centre of the oven for 8-10 mins or until it's well risen, golden brown and the cake springs back when lightly touched with the fingertip.

Have ready a large sheet of greaseproof paper, liberally sprinkled with caster sugar. Place the greaseproof on a clean tea towel wrung out in hot water (this will make it easier to roll up). Turn the cooked sponge out on to the sugared greaseproof paper and remove the lining paper. Trim off the crusty edges with a sharp knife (if preferred trim when the Swiss roll is cold). Roll up the sponge and greaseproof firmly. Leave to cool.

When cold, carefully unroll. Trim edges if necessary. Gently warm the jam and stir lightly to ensure the jam is smooth. Spread the warmed jam over the Swiss roll, to within ¼ in/6 mm of edges then re-roll the sponge and dredge the top with extra sugar if liked. Place on a serving plate.

Whisked sponges are best eaten on the day they are made; as they contain no fat, they quickly become stale.

HANDY TIP

For a special treat, spread 4 tbsp whipped cream on top of the jam.

1. Whisk mixture until it's thick and creamy and leaves a clear trail

2. Fold in sifted flour. Don't beat it in otherwise the sponge won't rise

3. Pour mixture into tin. Lightly tap on work surface to remove air pockets

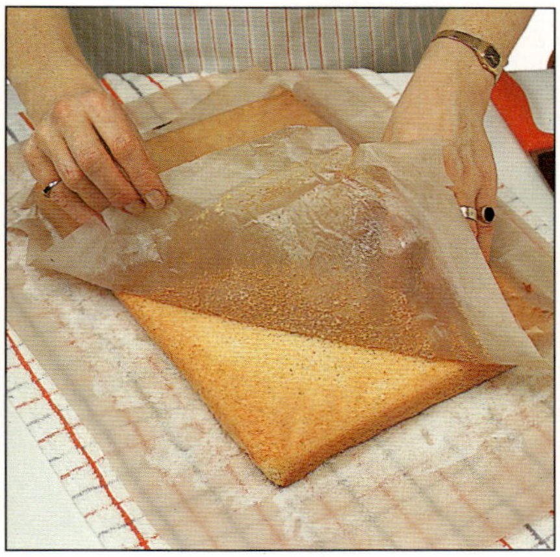

4. Take care when stripping off lining paper that you don't break the sponge

5. Hold tea towel in one hand and lift slightly to make cake easier to roll

6. Spread the Swiss roll with warmed, not hot, jam – using back of a spoon

DUNDEE CAKE

Bake a cut-and-come-again cake your family and friends will all love. Filled with sultanas, currants, raisins and almonds, it's a true Scottish treat, perfect for any tea-time celebrations. It's so easy with this step-by-step recipe.

Calories per portion: 280 | **CUTS INTO 20 SLICES**

8 oz/225 g butter or margarine
8 oz/225 g golden caster sugar
4 eggs, size 3, beaten
11 oz/325 g self-raising flour
3 oz/75 g ground almonds
1 orange, scrubbed and dried
8 oz/225 g sultanas
8 oz/225 g currants
6 oz/175 g raisins
1-2 tbsp sherry or milk
2 oz/50 g whole almonds, unskinned
1 tsp milk

Preheat the oven to Gas 4, 350°F, 180°C, 10 mins before baking. Grease and line sides of a 9 in/23 cm round × 3 in/7.5 cm deep cake tin with a double thickness of greaseproof paper. Cut out two 9 in/23 cm rounds of greaseproof paper to line base. Lightly grease the paper.

Cream the fat and caster sugar together until light and fluffy. Gradually add the eggs to the creamed mixture, beating well after each addition and adding 1 tbsp flour each time, to prevent the mixture curdling. After adding all the egg, fold in half the remaining flour and the ground almonds.

Finely grate rind from the orange and add to the creamed mixture. Squeeze out the juice and reserve. Fold the sultanas, currants and raisins into the mixture, using a metal spoon or spatula. Fold in the remaining flour and the reserved orange juice, then add sufficient sherry or milk to give a soft dropping consistency. Spoon the mixture into the prepared cake tin. Smooth the surface, making a slight hollow in the centre (when the cake rises during cooking, this will help to ensure that the top remains flat).

Put the whole almonds in a small glass bowl, pour boiling water over and leave to stand for 2 mins. Remove blanched almonds individually with a spoon and, using your thumb and forefinger, remove skins. If you find that, as the water cools, the skins are not so easy to remove, drain almonds, cover again with boiling water. Dry skinned almonds on kitchen paper, then arrange in circles on top of the cake mixture.

Brush nuts with milk, then bake cake on a shelf below centre for 1½ -2 hrs, or until cooked. If the top browns too quickly, cover with a round of greaseproof paper or foil. Allow cake to cool in the tin before turning out on to wire rack.

Leave until cold, then discard the greaseproof paper and store the cake in an airtight tin.

HANDY TIP

This cake improves if kept 2-3 days before eating.

1. Grease a 9 in/23 cm cake tin and line the sides with a double thickness of greaseproof paper

2. Cut out two 9 in/23 cm rounds of greaseproof paper to line the base of the tin. Lightly grease the paper

3. Finely grate the rind from the orange and fold into the creamed mixture. Squeeze out the juice and reserve

4. Add dried fruit and remaining flour. Mix to dropping consistency with juice and sherry or milk. Spoon into prepared tin

5. Put whole almonds in a bowl, pour boiling water over, leave to stand for 2 mins, remove skins

6. Dry the skinned almonds, then arrange in circles on top of cake mixture. Brush with milk and bake

Walnut Cake

Light coffee-flavoured sponge, layered with a delicious French butter icing and topped with crunchy walnuts – this cake is mouthwatering. So go on, treat yourself and spoil your family and friends; you'll find one slice just won't be enough.

Calories per portion: 640 **Serves 10**

8 oz/225 g softened butter or margarine
8 oz/225 g caster sugar
4 eggs, size 3, beaten
8 oz/225 g self-raising flour
2 tbsp liquid coffee or very strong black coffee
5 oz/150 g walnut halves
FOR THE ICING:
4 oz/100 g granulated sugar
2 egg yolks, size 3
10 oz/300 g unsalted butter
2 tbsp liquid coffee or very strong black coffee

Preheat oven to Gas 5, 375°F, 190°C, 10 mins before baking. Lightly grease and line the bases of two 8 in/20.5 cm sandwich tins. Cream the fat with the sugar until light and fluffy. Gradually add the eggs with a little of the flour, beating well between each addition. Stir in the coffee and ensure mixture is thoroughly mixed together. Stir in remaining flour with 2 tbsp of water to give a soft dropping consistency.

Reserve a few of the walnuts for decoration, then chop the remainder and fold into the mixture. Divide between the two prepared sandwich tins and smooth the tops.

Bake on the centre shelf for 25-30 mins, or until cooked. The cake is cooked when the top springs back if lightly pressed with the finger. Remove from the oven and leave for 5 mins to cool slightly before turning the cakes out on to a wire cooling rack. Leave until cold. Discard lining paper.

Meanwhile, make the icing. Mix the sugar with 8 fl oz/250 ml of water in a heavy-based pan. Heat gently, stirring occasionally, until sugar has dissolved. Then increase the heat and boil steadily until a sugar syrup is reached to the thread stage, or a sugar thermometer registers 220°F, 105°C. Remove from heat and pour into a glass jug. Place egg yolks in a bowl and whisk lightly, then gradually whisk in the sugar syrup. Continue to whisk until cold.

Cut butter into small pieces then gradually whisk into the mixture, whisk only small amounts in at a time – don't be tempted to add the butter all at once. When all the butter has been used, whisk in the liquid coffee. Use one quarter of the icing to sandwich the cakes together. Cover the cake completely with the remaining icing. Then, with a palette or round-bladed knife, work around the cake in a swirling pattern. Place the reserved walnut halves on top.

Handy Tips

When making the icing, if you don't have a sugar thermometer, you can easily test if the syrup is ready. Dip a spoon into syrup, press another on to the back of it and pull away. If a thread is formed, the syrup is ready. To freeze sponge cakes, cook then wrap separately in clearwrap and then foil. Thaw before decorating.

1. Cream fat and sugar, beat in eggs and a little flour, add liquid coffee

2. Fold in the remaining flour. Chop the walnuts, then fold into the mixture

3. Dissolve sugar in water over a gentle heat. Boil until it's 220°F, 105°C

4. Whisk egg yolks, then whisk in sugar syrup, pouring in a thin stream

5. Whisk until cold. Add the butter, whisking well between each addition

6. Using icing, sandwich cakes together, coat whole cake and swirl with knife

VICTORIA SANDWICH

This simple sandwich cake proves that good cooking doesn't need flashy tricks or expensive ingredients. A deliciously light sponge cake filled with raspberry jam – it will be a favourite with all the family. So give them a treat today!

Calories per portion: 444 | **CUTS INTO 8 SLICES**

6 oz/175 g butter or margarine
6 oz/175 g caster sugar
3 eggs, size 3, beaten
6 oz/175 g self-raising flour
3-4 tbsp raspberry jam
caster sugar for dredging

Preheat oven to Gas 4, 350°F, 180°C, 10 mins before baking. If not using non-stick sponge tins, then line bases with greased greaseproof paper. Or lightly grease the bases and sides of two 7 in/18 cm sponge tins with a little oil.

Cream the butter or margarine and sugar together until soft and fluffy. Gradually beat in the eggs, a little at a time, sifting in a little flour between each addition. This ensures that the mixture does not curdle.

Sift in the remaining flour and fold into the mixture with a metal spoon. Do not mix in vigorously. Use a cutting action to ensure that you do not destroy the air you have beaten in by the original creaming. If the mixture is too dry carefully fold in 1-2 tbsp tepid boiled water. This will keep the mixture light and fluffy. Other liquids tend to be dense and often result in a heavier sponge. The mixture should have a soft dropping consistency (when you pick the spoon up, and lightly tap on the side of the bowl the mixture should gently drop back into the bowl).

Divide the mixture evenly between each tin. A foolproof method is to weigh each tin after you have put the mixture in. Smooth over the top of the mixture and bake in the centre of the oven for 20-25 mins or until the cake is golden brown and when touched lightly with the tip of a finger, it springs back.

Turn out and cool on wire cooling racks. When cold, if necessary, remove lining paper. Sandwich the sponges together with jam and dredge the top with caster sugar.

HANDY TIP

For a change, cream 2 oz/50 g butter with 4 oz/100 g icing sugar and the grated rind of one lemon, and use as a filling.

1. Assemble and weigh the ingredients before you start to make the sponge

2. Beat the eggs, a little at a time, into creamed sugar and butter mixture

3. Sift the remaining flour into the cake mixture and fold in carefully

4. Fold in a little tepid water until the mixture is a soft dropping consistency

5. Divide the mixture between prepared cake tins and smooth the top

6. Sandwich both the cooled cakes together with the raspberry jam

Yule Log

This light and fluffy chocolate sponge, filled with vanilla butter cream and covered in chocolate, is a must for everyone's Christmas! It's so quick and easy to make, and so much nicer to serve a home-made cake for Christmas tea.

Calories per portion: 462 | **Cuts into 8 slices**

3 eggs, size 1
4 oz/100 g caster sugar
3½ oz/90 g self-raising flour
½ oz/15 g cocoa powder
6 oz/175 g softened butter or soft margarine
12 oz/350 g icing sugar, sifted
½ tsp vanilla essence
4 oz/100 g dark chocolate

Preheat oven to Gas 7, 425°F, 220°C, 15 mins before baking. Lightly grease and line a 13 in x 9 in/32.5 cm x 23 cm Swiss roll tin with greased greaseproof paper.

Crack eggs into a large mixing bowl with sugar over a pan of gently simmering water and whisk until thick and doubled in volume. The whisk should leave a trail across top of mixture when lightly pulled across. Remove from the heat and continue to whisk until the mixture is cold.

Sift flour and cocoa powder together and gently fold into mixture in a figure of eight movement. Then fold in 1 tbsp of tepid water. Take care not to over mix or the air you have whisked in will

be knocked out. When all the flour and cocoa powder has been thoroughly incorporated pour into prepared Swiss roll tin, allowing the mixture to find its own level. Tap lightly on the surface to remove any air bubbles.

Bake on the shelf above centre for 8-10 mins or until the sponge is cooked. The top should spring back when touched lightly with the finger. Have ready a large sheet of greaseproof paper lightly sprinkled with a little caster sugar.

When sponge is cooked, remove from oven, turn out on to greaseproof paper and carefully strip away lining paper. Roll the sponge with the greaseproof paper inside. Allow to cool.

Meanwhile prepare butter cream. Cream butter or margarine until soft, then gradually beat in icing sugar, making sure there are no lumps. Beat until soft and fluffy. If necessary add a little warm water. Place 4 tbsp butter cream in a small bowl then beat in the vanilla essence.

Melt chocolate in a small bowl over a pan of gently simmering water, or in a microwave following manufacturer's instructions, stir well, then beat into remaining butter cream.

Unwrap cold Swiss roll, discard greaseproof paper, trim all edges and spread vanilla butter cream to within ¼ in/6 mm of the edge. Carefully roll up with the join underneath. Trim away both ends by ¼ in/6 mm. Cut Swiss roll diagonally in half and arrange in log shape as shown. Cover with chocolate butter cream and use a fork to mark the bark. Place on a serving board. Dust with icing sugar and decorate.

HANDY TIPS

If you have a free standing electric mixer, make Swiss roll by placing eggs and sugar in a bowl, then using the balloon whisk attachment whisk the mixture, without placing the bowl over a pan of simmering water – takes about 8-10 mins. Put 1-2 tsp granulated sugar in the buttercream for an extra crunch.

To make mini Swiss rolls, cook as before, roll up and leave until cold. Cut unrolled cake in half lengthways, then into 4 pieces (making 8 pieces in all). Cover with butter cream, roll up and coat as before.

1. Whisk the eggs and sugar over a pan of gently simmering water until thick and doubled in volume

2. Gently fold in the sifted flour and cocoa powder in a figure of eight movement. Then fold in 1 tbsp of tepid water

3. Turn the cake out on to a sugared piece of greaseproof paper. Discard the lining paper

4. Roll the Swiss roll up with the sheet of greaseproof paper and leave until cold

5. Cut the filled Swiss roll diagonally in half and place together to form the log

6. Spread log with chocolate butter cream, mark with prongs of fork for the bark

Simnel Cake

This cake was originally baked for mothers on Mothering Sunday, in the days when many girls went into service, and that was the one day they were allowed home. Now Easter wouldn't be complete without a slice of this tasty treat.

Calories per portion: 665

Cuts into 10 slices

10 oz/300 g self-raising flour
2 oz/50 g ground almonds
5 oz/150 g butter or margarine
5 oz/150 g caster sugar
1 lb/450 g mixed dried fruit
grated rind and juice of 1 large lemon
5 eggs, size 3
2-3 tbsp milk
1¼ lb/550 g ready-made marzipan
2 tbsp apricot jam, sieved

Preheat oven to Gas 4, 350°F, 180°C, 10 mins before baking. Grease and line an 8 in/20.5 cm cake tin with greaseproof paper. Sift flour into mixing bowl and stir in ground almonds. Rub in fat until mixture resembles fine breadcrumbs. Stir in sugar, dried fruit and lemon rind. Beat the eggs and stir into mixture with lemon juice and sufficient milk to form a soft dropping consistency. Place half the mixture in cake tin and smooth the top.

Divide marzipan into three and on a surface lightly dusted with icing sugar roll out one third to an 8 in/20.5 cm round and place on top of cake mixture. Spoon remaining cake mixture over the marzipan and smooth the top.

Bake in the centre of the oven for 1¼ -1½ hrs or until cooked. To test if the cake is cooked, insert a skewer into the centre of the cake and if clean when removed, the cake is cooked. Allow to cool in tin before turning out.

Shape a further third of the marzipan into small balls. Roll out the final third of the marzipan to an 8 in/20.5 cm round. Remove the greaseproof paper from the cake and brush the top with the apricot jam.

Place the marzipan circle on top of the cake and press down lightly and pinch up the sides with the forefinger and thumb to form a decorative edge. If liked place under a preheated grill for 3-5 mins turning round frequently to lightly brown on the top.

Place the marzipan balls round the edge, fixing with a little of the apricot jam. Decorate the top with Easter chicks and tie a band of ribbon round the outside of the cake to add the perfect finishing touch.

HANDY TIP

Traditionally a Simnel cake has 11 balls of marzipan to represent the Apostles minus Judas. But you can in fact decorate the cake with as many as you like. Alternatively, decorate the top with little Easter eggs.

1. Rub fat into flour and almonds until mixture resembles fine breadcrumbs

2. Stir in fruit, add eggs gradually and beat together well; stir in the lemon juice

3. On lightly sugared surface, roll out one third of marzipan to 8 in/20.5 cm round

4. Place half the prepared mixture in tin, smooth surface. Place marzipan on top

5. Allow the cake to cool, brush top with apricot jam and add marzipan circle

6. Fix the marzipan balls on top of the cake with just a little apricot jam

Angel Food Cake

Simple to make, heavenly to eat, this luscious cake is a perfect tea-time treat, especially for those with a sweet tooth! Coated with a sugary frosting, it's so light, you can even indulge in a second slice.

Calories per portion: 202 **Serves 12**

FOR THE CAKE:
plain flour for dusting
3 oz/75 g plain flour
6 oz/175 g caster sugar
5 egg whites, size 3
1 tsp cream of tartar
pinch of salt
½ tsp vanilla essence
¼ tsp almond essence
FOR THE FROSTING:
12 oz/350 g caster sugar
2 egg whites, size 3
pinch each of cream of tartar and salt
dried rose petals, lemon-scented geranium leaves and grapes, all lightly washed, and dried for decoration

Preheat the oven to Gas 4, 350°F, 180°C, 10 mins before baking. Lightly dust a 2½ pint/1.5 litre ungreased ring mould with a little plain flour.

Sieve the flour and half of the sugar six times. This helps to aerate the ingredients and ensures a light texture. Whisk the egg whites until softly peaking, then whisk in the cream of tartar, salt, vanilla and almond essences, until thoroughly incorporated. Gradually add remaining half of the sugar, whisking well after each addition, until fully incorporated. The mixture should be stiff and standing in peaks by this time.

When all the sugar has been added, sieve in one third of the flour and sugar mixture, and fold in carefully using a spatula or metal spoon – add half the remaining flour and sugar, sieving and folding it in.. Repeat once more. Spoon the mixture into the prepared ring mould, then tap lightly on the surface and smooth the top. Bake in the oven for 30-40 mins or until cooked – the top should spring back when lightly touched with a finger.

Remove from the oven and invert on to a wire cooling rack. Leave until cold then remove mould. (On cooling the mixture retracts slightly and the mould can easily be removed.) If necessary, gently ease the cake away with the tip of a round-bladed knife.

To prepare the frosting, place a large bowl over a pan of gently simmering water and allow to warm. Remove bowl from pan and place caster sugar, egg whites, cream of tartar and salt in the bowl. Add 4 tbsp of water and whisk until well blended. Turn off heat, then replace bowl over pan and whisk until mixture forms soft peaks.

Place the cake the right way up on a serving plate and cover with frosting. Decorate with rose petals, geranium leaves and grapes, or any other decoration of your choice. Carefully wipe round edge of cake to remove any frosting on plate. Leave until set.

Handy tip

Try crystallizing the decoration: brush the leaves and grapes lightly with beaten egg white, coat in caster sugar and leave to dry.

1. Sieve the flour and the sugar six times. This will ensure a light texture

2. Whisk egg whites until peaking, add cream of tartar, salt and essences

3. Whisk in half the sugar, ensuring each addition is thoroughly incorporated

4. *Sieve a third of the flour and sugar mixture into egg whites and fold in*

5. *Spoon into a clean, ungreased ring mould, tap lightly to level top*

6. *After baking leave on wire cooking rack until cold. Carefully remove mould*

PASSION CAKE

Show the one you love that you really care by making this special cake for Valentine's Day. Wonderfully moist, it has a superb light texture and a delicious butter and crème fraîche filling, subtly flavoured with passion fruit juice.

Calories per portion: 502 | **CUTS INTO 12 SLICES**

6 oz/175 g butter or margarine
6 oz/175 g light soft brown sugar
3 eggs, size 3
10 oz/300 g self-raising flour
2 oz/50 g walnut pieces
6 oz/175 g carrots, peeled and grated
FOR THE FROSTING:
2 oz/50 g unsalted butter
2 fl oz/50 ml crème fraîche
12 oz/350 g icing sugar, sifted
2 passion fruit
3 oz/75 g walnut pieces, finely chopped
1 oz/25 g dark chocolate, melted

Preheat oven to Gas 5, 375°F, 190°C, 10 mins before baking. Grease and line with greased greaseproof paper, bases of two 7 in/18 cm sandwich cake tins.

Cream butter or margarine with sugar in a bowl until light and fluffy. Beat eggs, then gradually beat into creamed mixture with 1-2 tbsp of flour to prevent the mixture curdling. Fold in remaining flour using a metal spoon or spatula, with 3-4 tbsp warm water to form a soft dropping consistency. Chop walnuts finely then mix into cake with grated carrot. Divide between cake tins, smoothing over top.

Bake on centre shelf for 30-35 mins or until mixture springs back when lightly touched with a clean finger. Remove from oven, leave to cool for 5 mins. Turn on to wire cooling rack. Leave until cold. Discard the lining paper.

To make the frosting: beat the butter with the crème fraîche then gradually beat in 8 oz/225 g icing sugar.

Cut the passion fruits in half, scoop out the seeds into a fine sieve then press out the juice. Use 1-2 tbsp to flavour frosting. Sandwich the cold cake together with a little of the frosting.

Spread the outside edge with frosting then, holding the cake firmly with both hands, roll in the chopped walnuts until the sides are thoroughly coated. Place on serving plate.

Put remaining frosting in a piping bag fitted with a small star nozzle and pipe small rosettes around the edge of the cake. Mix the remaining icing sugar with the remaining passion fruit juice and a little water if necessary to form a smooth icing, then carefully flood the top of the cake, allowing the icing to find its own level. Allow to set completely before piping the wording of your choice with melted chocolate.

HANDY TIP

Passion fruit are ripe when the skins are soft and wrinkled. You can also use other flavourings in the frosting. Try orange, lemon, vanilla or, for a special treat, brandy.

1. Before starting to make the cake, finely chop the walnuts and grate the carrot

2. Cream butter and light soft brown sugar together until fluffy. Beat in eggs

3. After folding in flour, carefully mix in grated carrot and then chopped walnuts

4. Divide mixture between prepared cake tins; smooth top with palette knife

5. Sandwich cakes together, spread frosting around edges, coat with walnuts

6. Place frosting in piping bag fitted with star nozzle and pipe rosettes on cake

Christmas Cake

Bake a wonderfully rich and moist cake, packed full of luscious fruits, cherries and nuts. Traditionally iced and decorated, all your family and friends will want slice after slice of this Christmas treat – and it's so simple to make.

Calories per portion: 586 | **Makes 9 in/13 cm round cake**

1. Make the cake mixture, spoon into a greased, lined cake tin and smooth top

2. Warm jam and lemon juice, pass through a sieve, then use to glaze cake

3. Roll out almond paste into two strips, place around cake and trim sides

12 oz/350 g butter or margarine
12 oz/350 g light soft brown sugar
5 eggs, size 3, beaten
10 oz/300 g plain flour
4 oz/100 g ground almonds
½ tsp ground cinnamon
½ tsp ground ginger
½ tsp ground cloves
½ tsp freshly grated nutmeg
1 tbsp black treacle, warmed
grated rind and juice of 1 lemon
10 oz/300 g sultanas
10 oz/300 g seedless raisins
6 oz/175 g currants
3 oz/75 g chopped mixed nuts
3 oz/75 g glacé cherries, washed, dried and chopped
approx 1½ tbsp brandy or fruit juice

FOR THE ALMOND PASTE:
12 oz/350 g ground almonds
6 oz/175 g caster sugar
6 oz/175 g icing sugar, sieved
2 eggs, size 5, beaten
½ tsp vanilla essence
½ tsp almond essence

FOR THE APRICOT GLAZE:
1 tbsp apricot jam
2 tsp lemon juice

FOR THE ROYAL ICING:
3 egg whites, size 3
1½ lb/675 g icing sugar, sifted
1 tbsp lemon juice
1-2 tsp glycerine

Preheat the oven to Gas 2, 300°F, 150°C, 15 mins before baking. Grease and line a 9 in/23 cm round cake tin with four layers of greaseproof paper.

Cream the fat and sugar until light and fluffy, then beat in the eggs, adding 1 tbsp of flour after each addition. Add the ground almonds, together with the spices and black treacle. Mix well. Stir in half the remaining flour with the lemon rind and juice, dried fruit, nuts and cherries. Stir thoroughly. Add the remaining flour with the brandy or fruit juice, to give a soft dropping consistency. Turn mixture into prepared cake tin and smooth the top. Make a slight hollow in the centre to ensure a flat cake. Bake towards the bottom of the oven for 2 hrs, then reduce the oven temperature to Gas 1, 275°F, 140°C, and cook the cake for a further 1½-2 hrs, or until a skewer inserted into the centre comes out clean. If the top is browning too quickly, cover with greaseproof paper. When cooked, remove from the oven and leave in the tin until cold. Remove from tin, store wrapped in greaseproof paper, then foil in a cool, dry place. If liked, prick with a skewer and pour 1-2 tbsp brandy over.

When ready to decorate, discard lining paper. If necessary, trim cake.

Mix the ground almonds and sugars in a bowl, stir in sufficient egg to make a soft but not wet consistency, then add the essences and knead until smooth. Wrap in clearwrap.

Heat the jam and lemon juice together, rub through a sieve. Cool, use to glaze surface of cake.

Reserve a third of the almond paste, then divide the remainder into two. On a lightly sugared surface, roll each piece into a strip the depth of the cake and half the circumference. Place around sides of cake, trim and press firmly. Roll out remaining almond paste into a round the same size as the cake. Place on top of cake. Smooth top and sides using a rolling pin, place on a cake board and leave to dry for three days.

Whisk egg whites until lightly stiff, then whisk in the icing sugar a little at a time. If the mixture becomes too stiff, add a little of the lemon juice. Whisk in the glycerine. The mixture should be stiff enough for you to form soft peaks with a knife. Cover cake completely. Then make small swirls with a palette knife over the whole cake. Decorate, then leave to set for at least two days.

HANDY TIP

For a change, decorate the cake with glacé fruit and nuts. Omit the almond paste and royal icing, brush the top of the cake with apricot glaze and decorate with fruit and nuts.

4. Roll remaining almond paste into a round the size of a cake top, position

5. Spoon prepared royal icing on to cake, using palette knife cover completely

6. Ensure the icing is of uniform depth, then make swirls all over the cake

Stollen

This delicious bread is a great German classic, full of moist cherries, sultanas, apricots and nuts, with a hint of spice. Encased is a mouthwatering layer of marzipan, bake it for a tasty change.

Calories per portion: 387 | **Each loaf cuts into 12 slices**

3 oz/75 g glacé cherries
3 oz/75 g dried apricots
4 oz/100 g sultanas
2 oz/50 g mixed peel
¼ pint/150 ml rum, optional
3 oz/75 g flaked almonds
grated rind of 1 lemon
3 eggs, size 3
½ pint/300 ml milk
2 x ½ oz/15 g sachets dried yeast
8 oz/225 g golden caster sugar
8 oz/225 g butter, cut into small pieces
2 lb/900 g strong white flour
2 tsp ground cinnamon
12 oz/350 g white marzipan
2 tbsp icing sugar, sieved

Preheat the oven to Gas 6, 400°F, 200°C, 15 mins before baking. Lightly grease two baking sheets. Wash and dry the cherries. Chop cherries and apricots roughly. Put the chopped fruit in separate small bowls, and the sultanas and mixed peel in another. Heat rum, if using, and add ¼ pint/150 ml tepid water. Pour over fruits and leave to soak for at least 2 hrs. (If not using rum, use ½ pint/300 ml tepid water.)

Drain fruits, then mix together. Add the flaked almonds and grated lemon rind. Reserve. Place eggs in large bowl and beat thoroughly.

Heat milk to blood heat, add dried yeast and a pinch of caster sugar. Leave in a warm place for 15 mins until frothy. Heat remaining sugar with the butter. Stir until sugar has dissolved and butter has melted. Remove from heat, add to yeast mixture, then pour over the eggs, beating well.

Sieve flour into large bowl, then stir half into the egg mixture, together with the cinnamon. Mix well, then cover and leave in a warm place for 1 hr, or until mixture has risen and is spongy. Add remaining flour to mixture, mix well, then turn out on to a lightly floured surface and knead until smooth.

Add prepared fruits and nuts, and knead until fully incorporated.

Halve dough and roll out to form an oblong. Roll out half the marzipan to a thin oblong, about a quarter of the size of the dough, and place in centre. Fold edges of dough over, then roll up, completely encasing marzipan. Shape ends to form a neat oval. Repeat with remaining dough and marzipan.

Place on baking sheets, cover with a tea towel, then leave to rise for about 1 hr. Bake in oven for 15 mins, then reduce temperature to Gas 4, 350°F, 180°C, and bake for a further 1-1¼ hrs, or until cooked. (The loaves should sound hollow when tapped lightly on the base.)

Remove from oven and dust with the icing sugar. Eat within 24 hrs.

Handy tip

If liked freeze until required, warming through gently after thawing.

1. Chop the cherries. Soak the fruit, drain, then add almonds and lemon rind

2. Beat the eggs in a large bowl, then pour in the yeast and butter mixture

3. Sieve the flour into a large bowl. Gradually stir half into the egg mixture

4. Knead the dough, then add the prepared fruit and nuts and knead well

5. Place marzipan on top of the rolled dough. Fold edges over and roll up

6. Shape dough into an oval loaf. Repeat with remaining dough and marzipan

Cream Gateau

This feather-light sponge is sandwiched together with Cointreau-flavoured cream, then rolled in toasted nuts and topped with ripe strawberries. Serve this delicious gâteau as a special tea-time treat or as a stunning finish to a dinner party.

Calories per portion: 429 **Cuts into 12 slices**

8 oz/225 g butter or margarine
8 oz/225 g caster sugar
4 eggs, size 3
8 oz/225 g self-raising flour, sieved
¾ pint/450 ml whipping cream
2 tbsp Cointreau, optional
4 oz/100 g chopped mixed nuts, lightly toasted
8 oz/225 g fresh fruit, such as strawberries, hulled
1 tbsp redcurrant jelly
1 tbsp lemon juice

Preheat the oven to Gas 4, 350°F, 180°C, 10 mins before baking. Grease and line base of a deep 8 in/20.5 cm cake tin with greased greaseproof paper. Cream fat with caster sugar until light and fluffy, add the eggs, one at a time, beating well after each addition. (It is always a good idea to add a little flour with the egg, as this helps to prevent the mixture from curdling. If the mixture does curdle, it can result in a close-textured, heavy cake.)

Once the eggs have been added, carefully stir in the flour, using a metal spoon or spatula, in a figure of eight movement. Gently fold in approx 2 tbsp tepid boiled water to give a soft dropping consistency.

Spoon the mixture into prepared tin, smooth the top and bake in the centre of the oven for 55 mins-1 hr or until the cake is cooked – it should feel firm when it's lightly touched with the finger. Remove from the oven, allow to cool for 5-10 mins, then turn out on to a wire cooling rack and leave until cold.

When cold, discard lining paper and, using a serrated knife, carefully cut cake into three layers. Whip the cream until thick and standing in peaks, then fold in the Cointreau if using. Reserving a third of the cream for decoration, spread some of the remaining cream over two layers, then sandwich cake together. Spread the nuts out on a sheet of greaseproof paper. Coat sides of cake with more cream, then roll in the nuts until the sides of the cake are completely covered. Transfer to a serving plate. Place reserved cream in a piping bag fitted with a large star nozzle and pipe rosettes around top of cake.

Wash and dry fruit, if necessary, then arrange on top of the cake. Heat the redcurrant jelly and lemon juice in a small pan, stirring throughout, until smooth. Cool slightly, then use carefully to glaze the fruit. Serve with cream.

Handy tip

If liked, make the sponge in advance and freeze until required. Thaw, then proceed as above. Once filled, store in fridge.

1. Cream fat with sugar until light and fluffy, then add eggs, one at a time, with 1 tbsp of flour

2. Discard lining paper from cake tins, then using a sharp serrated knife, carefully cut cooled cake into three layers

3. Whip cream until thick and standing in peaks, fold in Cointreau and use to sandwich cake together

4. Coat the sides of the cake with whipped cream, then roll in the toasted mixed nuts

5. Transfer cake to a serving plate, then pipe rosettes of cream around the top of the cake

6. Arrange the fruit on top of the cake, then glaze with the cooled redcurrant jelly. Serve with cream

DEVIL'S FOOD CAKE

Bake a truly wicked treat with this really mouthwatering classic American recipe. A rich, moist chocolate sponge, covered in a tasty fudge icing, this cake is sure to become an all-time favourite.

Calories per portion: 473 | **CUTS INTO 12 SLICES**

1. Break the chocolate into pieces, place in heavy-based pan with yogurt and 3 oz/75 g brown sugar

2. Cream fat with remaining sugar until light and fluffy. Beat in eggs with a little flour and cocoa powder

3. Stir cooled chocolate mixture into creamed ingredients, stir lightly together. Add sifted flour and cocoa

3 oz/75 g plain chocolate
¼ pint/150 ml low-fat natural yogurt
7 oz/200 g light soft brown sugar
4 oz/100 g butter or margarine
4 eggs, size 3
8 oz/225 g self-raising flour, sifted
2 tbsp cocoa powder, sifted
FOR THE FUDGE ICING:
12 oz/350 g icing sugar
2 tbsp cocoa powder
4-6 tbsp semi-skimmed milk
2 oz/50 g plain chocolate
2½ oz/65 g white vegetable fat

Preheat the oven to Gas 4, 350°F, 180°C, 10 mins before cooking. Grease two 7 in/18 cm sandwich tins, line bases with greaseproof paper.

Break the chocolate into small pieces, place in a heavy-based pan with the yogurt and 3 oz/75 g of the brown sugar. Place over a gentle heat and warm the mixture through, stirring occasionally, until chocolate has melted. Remove from heat, allow to cool. Cream remaining sugar and fat together until light and fluffy, then beat in the eggs one at a time, adding a little of the sifted flour and cocoa powder after each egg.

Once the chocolate mixture has cooled, add to the creamed ingredients and stir lightly together. Then add the remaining flour and cocoa powder. Mix lightly together until blended, then divide between the lined sandwich tins, smooth tops with a palette knife and bake in the oven for 25-35 mins, or until cooked. When ready, the top of each cake will spring back if touched lightly with the finger. Remove both cakes from oven and leave for 5 mins before turning out on to wire cooling racks. Leave until both the cakes are cold before beginning the icing.

To make the icing, sift the icing sugar and the cocoa powder together. Place 4 tbsp of the milk, the chocolate broken into small pieces and the white vegetable fat into a small pan. Place the pan over a gentle heat and stir the ingredients until they have melted and blended together. Remove from the heat, then stir into the sifted icing sugar and cocoa powder. Beat the mixture thoroughly with a wooden spoon, until the icing is smooth, thick and of a spreadable consistency, adding extra milk if required.

Discard the lining paper from the cold sponges, sandwich them together with a third of the prepared icing. Use remaining icing to cover the top and sides of the cake, swirling with a palette knife to create a decorative effect. Allow at least 2 hrs for icing to set before cutting.

HANDY TIP

For a change try a mocha icing: simply add 2 tbsp strong black coffee to the chocolate and white vegetable fat. Use only 2-4 tbsp of milk, when making the icing.

4. For the icing, mix the melted chocolate mixture into the sifted icing sugar and cocoa. Beat until thick and smooth

5. Discard lining paper from cakes. Spread prepared icing over one of the cooled cakes, place the other on top

6. Place the remaining icing on top of the cake, then swirl over the top and sides with a palette knife to decorate

Chocolate Caraque Cake

A Sachertorte is the ultimate chocolate cake. The original recipe, created in Vienna is a closely guarded secret, but this recipe is equally delicious.

Calories per portion: 539 | **Serves 12**

1. Cream the butter and sugar together until light and fluffy, beat in the egg yolks then the cooled chocolate

2. Discard lining paper, place on cooling rack. Brush the sides and top of the cake, once cold, with the sieved apricot jam

3. Make the chocolate icing and leave for 20 mins until cold or until thickened slightly, then pour over the cake

FOR THE CAKE:
8 oz/225 g plain dark chocolate
6 oz/175 g unsalted butter
6 oz/175 g caster sugar
6 eggs, size 3
1 oz/25 g ground almonds
5 oz/150 g self-raising flour
FOR THE ICING:
2 tbsp apricot jam
6 oz/175 g plain dark chocolate
3 oz/75 g unsalted butter
2 tsp golden syrup
FOR THE CARAQUE CURLS:
4 oz/100 g plain dark chocolate

Preheat the oven to Gas 4, 350°F, 180°C, 10 mins before baking the cake. Grease and line the base of an 8 in/20.5 cm loose-bottomed spring-form tin with greaseproof paper. (If not using a non-stick cake tin, grease and line the sides as well.) Break the chocolate into small pieces, place in a small bowl and stand over a pan of gently simmering water, stirring occasionally and allow the chocolate to melt. Remove the bowl from the pan and leave to cool.

Cream the butter and sugar together until light and fluffy. Separate the eggs then beat in the egg yolks one at a time, then beat in the cooled chocolate. Add the ground almonds then sieve the flour and stir into the mixture with 3 tbsp tepid boiled water.

Whisk the egg whites until stiff then gradually stir into the cake mixture. When all the egg whites have been thoroughly incorporated, turn the mixture into the prepared tin. Tap the tin lightly on the work surface to remove any air bubbles.

Bake in the oven for 40-45 mins or until a skewer inserted into the centre comes out clean. Remove from the tin and allow to become cold before removing from the tin.

Warm the apricot jam then sieve. Discard the lining paper from the cake then place on a wire cooling rack placed over a large plate. Brush the top and sides with the sieved apricot jam.

Make the icing by breaking the chocolate into small pieces and placing in a heavy-based saucepan with the butter and golden syrup. Place over a gentle heat and cook, stirring throughout until the chocolate melts and the icing is smooth and glossy. Remove from the heat and leave to cool for about 20 mins or until the icing has thickened slightly.

Pour over the cake covering it completely and smooth with a palette knife. Make a few swirls if liked around the sides and on the top to give a decorative effect. Leave until set before transferring to a serving plate.

Meanwhile make the chocolate caraque curls. Melt the chocolate in a small bowl over a pan of gently simmering water. Stir until completely smooth then pour on to a marble slab, laminated board or a baking sheet. Using a palette knife spread the chocolate evenly over the surface. Place in the fridge for 10 mins or until firm but not set hard.

Using a large kitchen or palette knife push the blade across the chocolate to form thin scrolls. (If using a laminated board or baking sheet, place on a damp tea towel.) Use cocktail sticks to pick up the scrolls and place them on top of the cake.

HANDY TIP

Make extra scrolls and store covered in a dry place and use as decorations for desserts, other cakes and as toppings for ice cream.

4. Using a palette knife smooth the icing over the top and sides of the cake. Make a few swirls to give a decorative finish

5. Melt the chocolate in a small bowl, stir until smooth, pour on to a marble slab. Place in fridge until firm

6. Using a large kitchen or palette knife push the blade across the chocolate to form scrolls

GINGERBREAD HOUSE

Delight the children with this charming cake made from spicy, soft gingerbread, decorated with all sorts of sweets and goodies. It'll make their day.

Calories per portion: 536 | **SERVES 12**

1. Measure halfway across the top of shorter side and trim down both sides to form a long triangle

2. Spread some icing around the circles and stick the cellophane over. Cover round the outside of window with sweets

3. Spread two of the larger pieces with icing, arrange chocolate buttons over to form roof tiles, leave space for chimney

FOR THE GINGERBREAD:
12 oz/350 g clear honey
4 oz/100 g caster sugar
4 oz/100 g butter or margarine
1 egg, size 3, beaten
½ tsp each of ground mixed spice, ground cinnamon, ground coriander
1 tsp ground ginger
1 tsp baking powder
1 tsp bicarbonate of soda
1 lb 2 oz/500 g plain flour
FOR THE DECORATION:
2 sweets in cellophane wrappers
12 oz/350 g royal icing
8 oz/225 g chocolate buttons
assorted sweets and cake decorations
1 chocolate wafer biscuit
icing sugar to dust

Preheat oven to Gas 4, 350°F, 180°C, 10 mins before baking. Lightly grease and flour three 13 in x 9 in/33 cm x 23 cm baking tins.

Place honey, sugar and fat in a pan and melt slowly – do not boil. Stir in egg, all spices, baking powder and bicarbonate of soda, and mix well. Sieve in the flour and mix to form a smooth dough. Cover and leave for 2-3 hrs. Divide dough into three and roll each portion out on a lightly floured surface to fit each tin. Bake for 20-25 mins until risen and golden. Cool slightly before turning on to wire racks.

Whilst still warm, trim the crusts from the edges of the gingerbread and discard. Cut the gingerbread, using a sharp knife and ruler, into pieces as follows: three pieces: 10 in x 7 in/ 25.5 cm x 18 cm, and three pieces: 6½ in x 5 in/16.5 cm x 12.5 cm.

Taking two of the smaller pieces, measure halfway across the top of shorter side and trim down both sides to form a long triangle. Repeat with other piece. Using a small round cutter stamp out a circle from each piece to form a window, and a small rectangle from one side to form a door. Using the cellophane wrapping from 2 boiled sweets, trim them down to fit the circles, with a bit over. Spread some icing around the insides of the circles and stick the cellophane over. Cover round the outside of the window with sweets and decorations as liked. Set aside to dry.

Spread two of the larger pieces with icing and arrange chocolate buttons over to form roof tiles, leaving a small square on one piece to attach the chimney. Leave to dry for 30 mins.

Place remaining small piece on a cake board or serving plate and spread icing on each narrow end. Stand the two triangle pieces on the base at either end and secure in place using cocktail sticks. Leave to dry for 30 mins.

Spread icing all around the inside edge of the roof portions and gently press on to the triangular end pieces and the base. Carefully trim any pieces that overhang and tile up the middle of the roof section with more chocolate buttons and icing.

Trim the chocolate wafer at an angle so it will sit straight on the roof and secure in position with icing. Leave to set for 30 mins.

With remaining piece of gingerbread stamp out figures and Christmas trees to stand on board. Decorate as desired.

Spread icing over roof top and chimney to resemble snow and attach a small piece of cotton wool to the chimney to resemble smoke. Attach figures and tree to the board and the door to the door frame using icing, and dust with icing sugar to serve.

HANDY TIP

This is best eaten within two days. To store longer, wrap closely with tin foil, taking care not to damage the decoration and keep in a cool, dry place for up to one week.

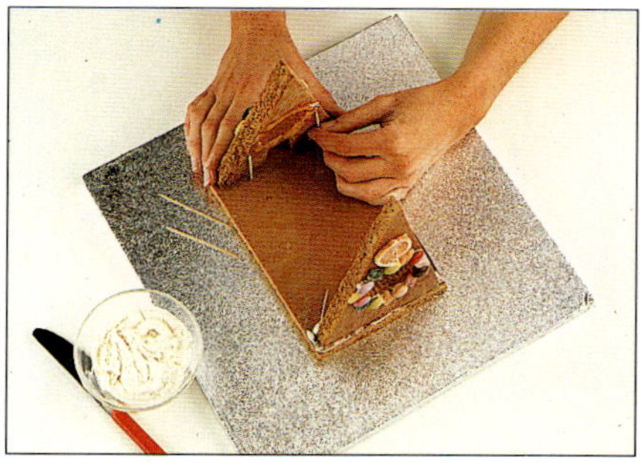

4. Stand the two triangle pieces on the base at either end and secure in place using cocktail sticks

5. Carefully trim any pieces that overhang, tile the middle section of the roof with more chocolate buttons and icing

6. Trim the chocolate wafer at an angle and secure on the roof with icing. Leave to set for 30 mins

STRAWBERRY TARTS

Crisp, melt-in-the-mouth pastry, filled with smooth chocolate and velvety-rich custard, topped with luscious strawberries, make these delicious tarts a really wicked treat for the whole family to enjoy!

Calories per portion: 393 | **MAKES 6**

FOR THE PASTRY:
6 oz/175 g plain white flour
4 oz/100 g butter or margarine
1 egg yolk, size 5
FOR THE FILLING:
½ pint/300 ml semi-skimmed milk
1 tbsp plain white flour
1 egg, size 5
1 tbsp caster sugar
1 tsp butter
2-3 drops vanilla essence
3 oz/75 g plain chocolate
FOR THE TOPPING:
8 oz/225 g strawberries, hulled, washed and lightly dried
3 tbsp redcurrant jelly
1 tbsp lemon juice

Preheat the oven to Gas 6, 400°F, 200°C, 15 mins before baking the pastry cases.

Sieve the flour into a bowl. Cut the fat into cubes and add to the flour with the egg yolk and 1 tsp cold water. Using your hands, work the mixture together to form a pliable, but not sticky, dough. Wrap, then chill for at least 1 hr. Roll the dough out on a lightly floured surface. Use to line six 3 in/7.5 cm individual fluted flan or patty tins.

Prick the bases lightly with a fork, then place a small sheet of greaseproof paper and some baking beans in each one. Bake blind for 12-15 mins, or until the pastry is cooked. Remove from the oven, discard the paper and baking beans and leave until cold.

To make the filling, warm the milk to blood heat. Place the flour in a small bowl, add the egg, then beat until smooth. Gradually beat the warmed milk into the flour and egg mixture, then strain into a clean pan. Return to heat and cook gently, stirring throughout, until mixture thickens and coats the back of a wooden spoon. Remove from the heat and beat in the sugar, butter and vanilla essence. Pour the custard into a small bowl, then cover with damp greaseproof paper and leave to one side until cold.

When the pastry cases are cold, melt the plain chocolate in a small bowl, over a pan of simmering water. Carefully brush insides of cases with chocolate, then leave until the chocolate has set. Beat the cooled custard to ensure there are no lumps, then spoon into pastry cases. Arrange strawberries attractively over the custard filling.

Heat the redcurrant jelly and lemon juice together and stir until smooth. Leave to cool slightly, then use to coat the strawberries. Leave for at least 15 mins to allow the glaze to set before serving.

HANDY TIP

Replace the strawberries with any prepared ripe soft fruit – alternatively use well-drained canned fruit such as apricots, then use apricot jam and lemon juice for glazing.

1. Line tins with pastry. Prick bases, place greaseproof and baking beans in each tin

2. Heat milk, beat into flour and egg. Strain into clean pan, cook until thickened

3. Once the pastry cases have cooled, brush the insides with melted chocolate

4. *Leave the chocolate to set, then fill the tarts with the cooled, prepared custard*

5. *Arrange the washed and hulled strawberries attractively over the custard*

6. *Allow redcurrant jelly and lemon juice to cool slightly, brush over strawberries*

ECCLES CAKES

Delicious rounds of feather-light flaky pastry, filled with a lightly spiced currant mixture, these classic cakes from Lancashire just melt in the mouth! Serve them warm for a super-tasty mid-morning snack or as a winning tea-time treat.

Calories per portion: 303 | **MAKES 8 CAKES**

1. Rub one quarter of fat into flour. Mix to a dough with water and lemon juice

2. Roll chilled dough into an oblong. Dot a quarter of the fat over top two thirds

3. Fold bottom third of pastry up over centre third. Cover this with top third

FOR THE FLAKY PASTRY:
8 oz/225 g plain flour
¼ tsp salt
4 oz/100 g butter or margarine
1 oz/25 g white vegetable fat
1 tbsp lemon juice
FOR THE FILLING:
6 oz/175 g currants
2 oz/50 g chopped mixed peel
grated rind of 1 orange
1 oz/25 g caster sugar
1 tsp mixed spice
2 oz/50 g butter, melted
FOR THE GLAZE:
1 egg white, size 3, lightly beaten
1 oz/25 g caster sugar

Preheat oven to Gas 7, 425°F, 220°C, 15 mins before baking.

To make the pastry, sieve flour and salt into a mixing bowl. Blend the fats together with a fork, then divide into four equal portions. Rub one portion of the fat into the flour until the mixture resembles fine breadcrumbs. Make a well in the centre, add approx 4 fl oz/120 ml water and the lemon juice, and mix to form a soft, but not sticky dough. Knead lightly on a floured surface until smooth. Wrap in clearwrap and chill in fridge for 20 mins. Roll the chilled dough out on a floured surface to an oblong about 12 in x 6 in/30 cm x 15 cm.

Dot the second portion of fat, in small pats, evenly over the top two thirds of the pastry. Fold the bottom third of the pastry up to the centre, then fold the top third down to cover. Press the edges together firmly with a rolling pin to seal.

Re-wrap the pastry, place on a plate and chill for 20 mins. Repeat the rolling and folding process twice more, using the remaining portions of fat. (After each rolling and folding, give the pastry oblong a half turn, before rolling again.)

When the last portion has been added, roll the pastry out again immediately, then fold into three as before. Wrap and chill for at least 1 hr, or overnight, before going on to the next stage.

Put all the ingredients for the filling into a bowl and mix well. Thinly roll out the chilled flaky pastry then cut out eight 6 in/15 cm rounds. Divide the filling equally between the rounds, placing it in the centre of each one. Taking one pastry round at a time, brush the edges with egg white, then gather the edges together in the centre to enclose the filling. Pinch well to seal.

Turn the cakes over and roll them to a neat round, rolling until the currants just start to show through the pastry. Place cakes on a baking tray and chill for 20 mins before baking.

Brush the chilled Eccles cakes with egg white and make three deep slashes across the top of each one. Bake for 15 mins, then remove from the oven, brush once again with egg white and sprinkle lightly with caster sugar. Return to the oven for a further 5 mins, or until golden brown. Transfer the cakes to a wire rack with a palette knife to cool. They're best eaten slightly warm.

HANDY TIP

If wished, the pastry may be made using a combination of polyunsaturated margarine and polyunsaturated white vegetable fat, for a lower cholesterol level. The flavour will be the same, but the pastry will be a little less flaky. As the fat is much softer to work with, chill the pastry for 30 mins between each rolling and folding.

4. Seal the edges with a rolling pin. Chill for 20 mins, then repeat twice more

5. Divide filling between rounds. Brush edges with egg white, then gather and seal

6. Turn the cakes over and roll flat until currants just begin to show through

GINGERBREAD

Rich, stick, gooey gingerbread, topped with smooth, tangy lemon glacé icing. A slice or two is a tasty treat that's just perfect for when the kids come home from school – or for Sunday tea.

Calories per portion: 375 | **CUTS INTO 12 SLICES**

8 oz/225 g plain flour
8 oz/225 g self-raising wholemeal flour
1½ tsp mixed spice
3 tsp ground ginger
3 oz/75 g demerara sugar
3 oz/75 g sultanas
3 oz/75 g mixed peel
8 oz/225 g butter or margarine
8 oz/225 g golden syrup
8 oz/225 g black treacle
2 eggs, size 3, beaten
1 pint/600 ml milk
2 tsp bicarbonate of soda
FOR THE GLACÉ ICING:
12 oz/350 g icing sugar
juice 2 large lemons, strained
stem ginger to decorate

Preheat oven to Gas 4, 350°F, 180°C, 10 mins before baking. Grease and line base of a 10 in x 8 in/26 cm x 20.5 cm oblong cake tin with greased greaseproof paper.

Place flours and spices in a large bowl and mix together. Stir in sugar, sultanas and mixed peel. Place fat, syrup and black treacle in a bowl and heat over a pan of gently simmering water until melted. Stir occasionally, then beat into the flour and fruit. Then gradually beat in the eggs, ensuring they are thoroughly blended in.

Heat the milk to blood heat, then add the bicarbonate of soda and stir until dissolved. Beat milk into the mixture to form a smooth batter with no lumps. Pour into prepared tin.

Bake on centre shelf for 50-60 mins, or until cooked. To test if cooked, insert a skewer into the centre and if it comes out clean, the gingerbread is cooked. Remove from oven and leave to cool for 5 mins, then turn out on to a wire cooling rack and discard lining paper. Leave until cold before coating with icing.

Sieve icing sugar into a mixing bowl, then gradually beat in the lemon juice and sufficient hot water to make a smooth icing. It should be thick enough to coat the back of a wooden spoon. Pour over top of gingerbread and spread evenly with a palette knife.

Decorate with small pieces of stem ginger. Cut into squares when cold.

HANDY TIP

Keep the gingerbread in an airtight tin, not a plastic container.

1. Add the mixed peel and sultanas to the flour, spices and demerara sugar

2. Melt the fat, syrup and treacle in a bowl over a pan of simmering water

3. Beat melted ingredients into flour, fruit and spices, mixing together well

4. Add beaten eggs to gingerbread mixture. Beat until completely blended in

5. Pour mixture into a greased and lined tin, allow mixture to find its own level

6. Pour icing on to cooled gingerbread and spread over top with a palette knife

Doughnuts

You'll be in everyone's good books if you make these delicious doughnuts! Try them ring or jam-filled and tossed in lemon-flavoured caster sugar. Serve them while they're still warm.

Calories per portion: 217 — **Makes 9**

8 oz/225 g strong plain white flour
½ tsp salt
1 x 6 g sachet easy-blend yeast
4 oz/100 g caster sugar
1 oz/25 g butter
3-4 fl oz/75-120 ml milk
1 egg, size 3, beaten
1½ tbsp seedless raspberry jam
oil for deep-fat frying
grated rind 1 lemon

Sift flour and salt into a large mixing bowl and stir in easy-blend yeast and ½ oz/15 g of the caster sugar. Cut butter into small pieces then rub into the flour until mixture resembles fine breadcrumbs. Then warm the milk to blood heat. Make a well in the centre of dry ingredients and stir in beaten egg. Mix to a smooth, not sticky, dough with the warmed milk. Knead on a lightly floured surface until smooth and pliable.

Lightly grease the cleaned mixing bowl with a little oil then return the dough to the bowl and cover, either with a clean tea towel or clearwrap, or place inside a large polythene bag. Leave in a warm place away from draughts or direct heat for 1-2 hrs or until doubled in size.

Turn out on to a lightly floured surface and knead again until smooth. Divide dough in half, roll out one half and cut into 3 in/7.5 cm rounds. Cut out centres using a 1 in/2.5 cm plain cutter. Put the trimmings together and roll out again until all the dough has been used.

Cut the remaining dough into 4-5 balls and pat or roll them into 3 in/7.5 cm rounds. Place 1 tsp raspberry jam in the centre then form into a ball and pinch together firmly to encase the jam. Place on a lightly greased baking sheet. Cover with a piece of muslin or lightly oiled clearwrap and leave the doughnuts in a warm place until doubled in size – about 30-45 mins.

Bring the oil in a deep-fat fryer to 375°F, 190°C. If you don't have a thermometer, the oil has reached the correct temperature when a cube of bread turns golden after 30 seconds. Fry the doughnuts a few at a time for 2-3 mins on each side. Turn with a spatula to cook the other side.

Mix the remaining sugar with the lemon rind, place either on a sheet of greaseproof paper or in a polythene bag. When the doughnuts are golden brown and cooked through, drain well on absorbent kitchen paper, then toss in the sugar and lemon rind until thoroughly coated. The doughnuts are best eaten while still warm.

Handy tip

Vary the flavour by adding grated lemon rind or ground cinnamon to the basic mixture.

1. Sift the flour and salt into a large mixing bowl, then rub in the butter

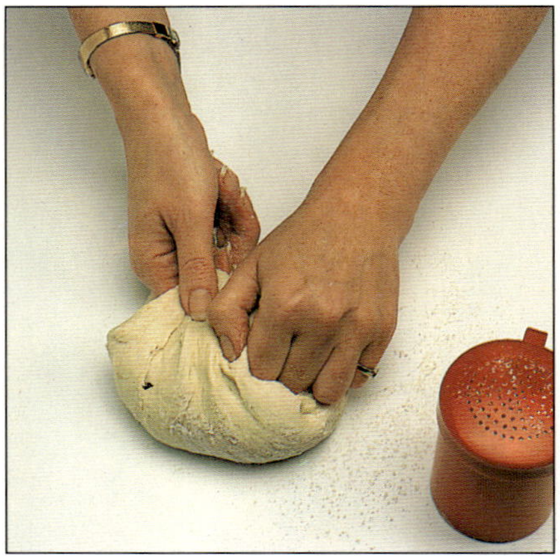

2. Using the knuckles, knead the dough well until it is smooth and pliable

3. After proving, the dough should have doubled in size. Knead again until smooth

4. Use one half of dough for ring doughnuts and other half for jam ones

5. Roll or pat dough to a 3 in/7.5 cm round, place a spoonful of jam in centre

6. Fry a few of the doughnuts at a time in hot oil for 2-3 mins on each side

CHELSEA BUNS

Bake the best-ever Chelsea Buns! Filled with plump raisins, sultanas and currants, and just a hint of cinnamon, they're delicious, especially when eaten warm. Follow this easy step-by-step recipe and give the family a tasty tea-time treat.

Calories per portion: 491 | **MAKES 12**

1 lb/450 g strong white plain flour
½ level tsp salt
3 tsp dried yeast
8 fl oz/250 ml milk, tepid
2 tsp caster sugar
3 oz/75 g butter
1 egg, size 1, beaten
8 oz/225 g mixed dried fruit
4 oz/100 g light soft brown sugar
2 tsp ground cinnamon
1-2 tbsp clear honey

Preheat oven to Gas 5, 375°F, 190°C, 10 mins before baking. Lightly grease a 12 in x 10 in/30 cm x 25 cm baking tin. Sieve the flour and salt into a mixing bowl. Sprinkle yeast over ¼ pint/150 ml milk, add a pinch of caster sugar, stir. Leave for 15 mins or until frothy.

Meanwhile cut the butter into small cubes, then rub into the flour until the mixture resembles fine breadcrumbs. Make a well in the centre, then pour in the yeast and milk mixture, remaining milk and beaten egg. Bring ingredients together to form a soft, but not sticky, dough, which doesn't cling to the bowl. Turn on to a lightly floured surface and knead until smooth and elastic. Place in a lightly oiled bowl, cover with oiled clearwrap or a clean tea towel and prove in a warm place for 1 hr or until doubled in size.

Turn out dough on to a lightly floured surface, knead again then roll out to a 12 in x 9 in/30 cm x 22.5 cm oblong. Mix together the dried fruit, sugar and cinnamon and spoon over the dough to within ½ in/1.25 cm of the edge. Roll up the dough tightly lengthways, as you would for a Swiss roll. Press edges together firmly to seal. Cut the roll into 1½ in/4 cm rounds. Lay each round flat in greased baking tin. Cover with oiled clearwrap or a clean tea towel and leave for 30 mins or until doubled in size.

Bake in oven for 30 mins or until well risen. Warm honey then brush over cooked buns, sprinkle with remaining caster sugar. Cool slightly before turning out.

HANDY TIPS

Add 1 tsp ground cinnamon to the basic dough and sprinkle the cooked buns with demerara sugar for a crunchy topping.

1. Sieve flour into mixing bowl. Sprinkle dried yeast over ¼ pint/150 ml milk

2. Bring all the ingredients together to form a soft, but not sticky, dough

3. Knead the dough on a lightly floured surface until smooth and elastic

4. Roll out to a 12 in x 9 in/30 cm x 22.5 cm oblong. Spoon over dry ingredients

5. Roll up the dough tightly lengthways, as you would for a Swiss roll

6. Cut dough into 1½ in/4 cm rounds, place close together in a greased tin

CRUMPETS

Cook a tasty tea-time treat and serve these delicious wholemeal crumpets. Toasted and then spread lightly with butter, you'll enjoy every golden mouthful. They're very easy to make and so much nicer than the shop bought ones.

Calories per portion: 118 | **MAKES 10**

6 oz/175 g plain flour
2oz/50 g wholemeal flour
½ tsp salt
½ oz/15 g fresh yeast or 1½ tsp dried yeast, or 1 x 6 g sachet easy-blend dried yeast
2 tsp clear honey
12 fl oz/350 ml milk, warmed
1-2 tbsp vegetable oil

Sift flours and salt into a large bowl and leave in a warm place while creaming fresh yeast. Blend yeast with the honey then pour on the warmed milk. Stir and leave in a warm place for approx 15 mins or until liquid is frothy.

If using dried yeast, dissolve honey in the warmed milk, sprinkle the dried yeast on top, stir lightly, then leave in a warm place away from any draughts for 10-15 mins until frothy.

Pour frothy liquid into warmed flour in a steady stream, beating as you go to form a smooth batter. Beat well then cover with either clearwrap or a clean tea towel. Leave in a warm place away from draughts for 40-50 mins until batter is frothy.

If making crumpets with easy-blend dried yeast, place flours and salt in bowl and leave in a warm place for 15 mins. Dissolve honey in milk, then stir into flours and add yeast, mix to a batter, then cover and leave for 45 mins or until frothy. Before cooking the crumpets, transfer the batter to a measuring jug for easy pouring.

Lightly grease a heavy-based frying pan or griddle and either some crumpet rings or 4 in/10 cm plain cutters with the oil. When hot pour in ½ in/1.25 cm of the batter into each ring and cook over a moderate heat for 5-8 mins or until bubbles burst. Remove rings, turn crumpets and cook for 1 min.

The crumpets can now be removed from the pan, stored in an airtight tin and toasted later the same day. Otherwise remove rings or cutters and turn crumpets over and cook on the other side for 1 min. Drain on absorbent kitchen paper and serve immediately spread with butter.

HANDY TIPS

If you prefer white crumpets simply replace the wholemeal flour with plain white flour and proceed with the recipe. The crumpets are best eaten on the same day or may be frozen and used within two months.

1. Cream yeast with honey until smooth, beat in warm milk, leave until frothy

2. Add the frothy yeast and milk mixture to the flours then beat in well

3. Beat to a smooth batter ensuring there are no lumps left in the mixture

4. *Cover batter with clearwrap and leave in a warm place for 40-50 mins*

5. *Grease frying pan or griddle and crumpet rings, then pour in batter*

6. *When bubbles have burst, remove rings, turn crumpets and cook for 1 min*

Mince Pies

Christmas just wouldn't be the same without mince pies! So why not give everyone a real treat by making your own mincemeat with this deliciously rich but healthy recipe, which is also suitable for vegetarians.

Calories per 1 lb/450 g: 1,225; per 1 oz/25 g:77 **Makes 7 lb/3 kg**

1 lb/450 g carrots
8 oz/225 g parsnips
1 lb/450 g cooking apples
1 lb/450 g currants
1 lb/450 g sultanas
1 lb/450 g seedless raisins
4 oz/100 g mixed chopped peel
4 oz/100 g whole almonds, blanched
1 lb/450 g muscovado sugar
8 oz/225 g vegetable suet
1 tsp grated nutmeg
1 tsp ground cinnamon
½ tsp ground mace
½ tsp ground cloves
2 lemons
1 large or 2 small oranges
4-6 tbsp brandy
FOR 18 MINCE PIES:
1 lb/450 g prepared shortcrust pastry
8 oz/225 g prepared mincemeat

Preheat oven to Gas 6, 400°F, 200°C, 15 mins before baking pies. Peel carrots, parsnips and cooking apples. Discard apple core. Grate carrots, parsnips and apples coarsely and place in a large mixing bowl. Stir in the currants, sultanas, raisins and mixed peel. Chop almonds fairly small and add to mixture with the sugar, suet and spices. Stir well.

Scrub the lemons and orange well and dry thoroughly. Then grate the rind finely and squeeze out the juice. Add to the mixture with sufficient brandy to give a moist consistency. The exact amount of brandy will vary slightly as this will depend on the amount of juice obtained from the lemons and orange.

Stir well, then pot in clean dry jars, packing the mixture down with the back of a spoon. Cover with a waxed disc and cellophane covers. Label clearly. Leave in a cool dry place for two weeks to mature.

When ready, make your mince pies. Roll out the pastry on a lightly floured surface and cut into 18 x 3 in/7.5 cm rounds with a fluted pastry cutter. Use to line 18 bun or patty tins. Roll out the remaining pastry and cut out the same number of 2½ in/6.5 cm fluted rounds and reserve for lids.

Place a heaped tsp of mature mincemeat in the centre of each of the pastry-lined tins. Dampen edges with a little water then place lids in position and press edges together. Brush tops with a little water and sprinkle them with a little caster sugar. Make a small slit in the centre of each mince pie to allow steam to escape. Bake for 15-20 mins or until cooked.

Dredge with a little extra sugar before serving. This mincemeat should be used within eight weeks of maturing.

Handy Tip

To press edges of pies together, turn an egg cup upside down, dust the opening with flour then place on top of mince pies and press down lightly.

1. Prepare ingredients before. Weigh fruit and grate parsnips, carrot and apple

2. Mix all the ingredients in a large mixing bowl, stirring with a wooden spoon

3. Finely grate nutmeg into mixture. Add remaining spices, rind and juice of fruit

4. Pack mincemeat into 1 lb/450 g jars. Press down with back of a spoon

5. When ready to use, line tins with pastry and place 1 heaped tsp in centre

6. Dampen edges of pastry and place lids in position. Press edges together

DANISH PASTRIES

Flaky golden pastries, filled with a selection of scrumptious fillings and glazed with apricot jam, make a delicious treat for any time of the day. Crescents, Windmills, Cockscombs, Pinwheels... every shape is so simple to make.

Calories per portion: 235 | **MAKES 28**

1. Rub fat into flour, stir in sugar, beat egg into milk, add to flour with yeast

2. Roll out dough, place rolled butter on top. Fold pastry to encase butter

3. Roll dough into two strips, place marzipan in centre, fold, seal, cut out combs

FOR THE DOUGH:
1 lb/450 g plain white flour
2 oz/50 g lard or white vegetable fat
2 level tbsp sugar
2 eggs, size 3
7 fl oz/200 ml milk, warmed
½ oz/15 g easy-blend dried yeast
8 oz/225 g butter
FOR THE COCKSCOMBS:
6 oz/175 g white marzipan
FOR THE WINDMILLS:
4 canned apricot halves, drained
½ oz/15 g flaked almonds
FOR THE PINWHEELS:
4 oz/100 g mixed dried fruit
2 oz/50 g soft brown sugar
1 tsp ground mixed spice
FOR THE CRESCENTS:
2 oz/50 g butter
2 oz/50 g soft brown sugar
½ tsp ground cinnamon
FOR THE GLAZE AND DECORATION:
6 tbsp apricot jam
juice of ½ lemon, strained
2 oz/50 g icing sugar, sieved

Preheat the oven to Gas 7, 425°F, 220°C, 15 mins before baking the pastries. Sieve flour into a bowl, rub in fat until mixture resembles bread-crumbs. Add sugar. Beat 1 egg into milk, then add to flour mixture with yeast and mix to a soft pliable dough. Knead for 5 mins or until dough is shiny and smooth. Wrap and allow to rest for 10 mins.

Place butter between two sheets of greaseproof and roll out to an oblong. On a lightly floured surface, roll pastry out to an oblong three times longer than the butter. Place butter in centre of dough, fold over and seal, encasing the butter completely. Wrap and chill for 10 mins. Repeat rolling and folding twice more. Divide pastry in four.

To make the Cockscombs, roll pastry into two long strips, approx 4 in x 12 in/10 cm x 30 cm each. Divide the marzipan in half and shape each piece into a long thin roll. Place the marzipan rolls in centre of pastry strips, brush pastry edges with the remaining egg, beaten, and fold the pastry over, sealing the edges well. Cut into 3 in/7.5 cm lengths, then make 3-4 small cuts in pastry edges, towards marzipan. Bend slightly into a curve.

For the Windmills, roll pastry out and cut into four 4 in/10 cm squares. Place 1 apricot in centre of each. Cut the four corners towards the centre, then bring corners into centre to form a windmill. Secure pastry with the beaten egg, then brush all over with egg and sprinkle with the flaked almonds.

For Pinwheels, roll pastry out to an oblong, 12 in x 8 in/30 cm x 20.5 cm. Sprinkle with the fruit, sugar and mixed spice, brush the edges with beaten egg and roll up. Cut into eight 1 in/2.5 cm pieces. Place on baking sheet.

For the Crescents, roll pastry into two 8 in/20.5 cm circles and cut each into quarters. Cream butter, sugar and cinnamon together, then place at pointed end of each quarter. Brush with egg, roll up and bend to form a crescent. Seal edges.

Leave pastries on a greased baking sheet to prove for 20 mins, brush again with egg, then bake for 12-15 mins.

Meanwhile, heat jam and lemon juice. Sieve. When pastries are cooked, brush with glaze. When cold, mix icing sugar with 1 tsp hot water. Place in a piping bag with a plain icing nozzle, pipe thin lines across or over the Pinwheels and Crescents to decorate.

HANDY TIP

Once cold, freeze. When required, thaw, then warm through before serving.

4. Cut dough into squares, place an apricot in the centre, cut corners and fold

5. Roll dough out to a rectangle, sprinkle with fruit, sugar and spice, roll up and cut

6. Roll dough into two circles, quarter. Roll up into crescents, encasing filling

Tea Cakes

Originating from Yorkshire, these fruity buns are just the thing for a tea-time treat. They're simply delicious served warm with butter – or, for an extra indulgence, split them in half, lightly toast then spread with butter and strawberry jam.

Calories per portion: 340 | **Serves 8**

1 lb/450 g strong plain white flour
pinch of salt
2 oz/50 g butter or margarine
2 tsp easy-blend dried yeast
1 oz/25 g caster sugar
2 oz/50 g chopped mixed peel
4 oz/100 g currants
½ pint/300 ml semi-skimmed milk
1 tbsp milk to glaze

Preheat the oven to Gas 6, 400°F, 200°C, 15 mins before baking tea cakes. Lightly oil two baking sheets. Sieve the flour and pinch of salt into a large mixing bowl, then add the butter or margarine and rub into the flour until mixture resembles fine breadcrumbs. Sprinkle in the easy-blend dried yeast, then add the caster sugar, chopped mixed peel and currants.

Warm the semi-skimmed milk, pour into the mixing bowl and mix to a soft, but not sticky, dough. Turn out on to a lightly floured surface and knead for about 5-10 mins, or until smooth. Transfer the dough to a clean, lightly oiled bowl, cover, then leave in a warm place for 1 hr, or until doubled in size. (Do not leave the dough in a draught, or it won't rise.)

When the dough has risen, turn out on a lightly floured surface. Using your knuckles, knock the dough down, then, using one hand, pull the dough out (taking care not to tear it), then push it back to the centre, kneading until smooth and elastic. (The more you knead the dough, the lighter your tea cakes will be.)

Shape the dough into a 16 in/41 cm long roll, then carefully cut into eight equal-sized pieces. Using your hands, lightly dusted with flour, revolve each piece between your hands to form a perfect round. Place four rounds on to each oiled baking sheet, then flatten lightly with the palm of your hand. Cover, then leave again in a warm place for 20-30 mins, or until doubled in size. (The dough should spring back when lightly touched with a clean finger.)

Brush the tops of the tea cakes with a little milk, then bake in the oven for 20 mins, or until golden brown and cooked. To test if the tea cakes are cooked, lightly tap the base of each – it should sound hollow. Leave the tea cakes to cool on a wire rack.

To serve, split the cooled tea cakes in half, toast lightly, then spread them with butter. Serve with home-made strawberry jam. The tea cakes are best eaten the same day.

Handy tip

For a change, add to the sieved flour, either 1 tsp ground cinnamon, 1 tsp mixed spice, or the grated rind of 1 lemon.

1. Sieve flour and salt into a large mixing bowl, then add fat and rub into flour. Sprinkle in yeast

2. Add the caster sugar, chopped mixed peel and currants to the mixture in the bowl

3. Warm the milk, then pour into the mixing bowl and mix to a soft, but not sticky, dough

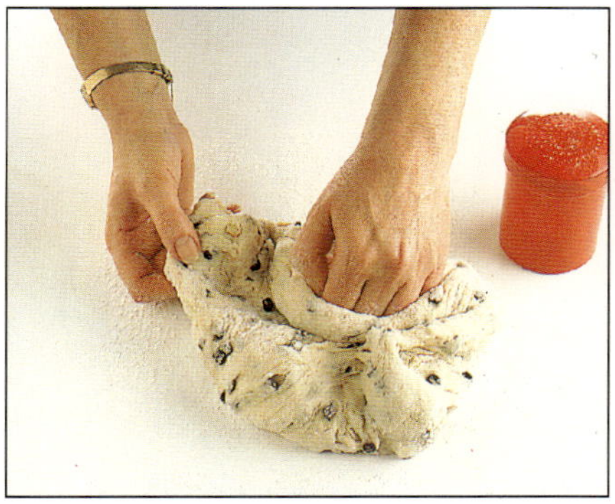

4. Turn the dough out on a lightly floured surface. Using your knuckles, knead well until the dough is smooth and elastic

5. Shape the dough into a 16 in/41 cm long roll, then carefully cut into eight equal-sized portions

6. Lightly dust hands with flour, shape dough into rounds, then place on baking sheets

CHOCOLATE BROWNIES

The secret of this American classic is the pecan nut taste. Add to that a truly delicious chocolate sponge and a dreamy fudge-icing topping and you have a taste of heaven that the family will love!

Calories per portion: 351 | **CUTS INTO 20**

8 oz/225 g butter or margarine
4 oz/100 g plain chocolate
14 oz/400 g granulated sugar
4 eggs, size 3
6 oz/175 g plain flour
1 tsp vanilla essence
½ tsp salt
3 oz/75 g milk chocolate
3 oz/75 g pecan nuts
FOR THE TOPPING:
2 oz/50 g plain chocolate
1 oz/25 g butter or margarine
3½ oz/90 g icing sugar
2-3 tbsp milk
2 oz/50 g white chocolate

Preheat the oven to Gas 4, 350°F, 180°C, 10 mins before baking. Grease and base-line a 13 in x 9 in/33 cm x 23 cm baking tin with a piece of lightly oiled grease-proof paper.

Place fat in a heatproof bowl. Break plain chocolate into pieces, add to bowl and place over a pan of gently simmering water.

Heat gently, stirring occasionally until melted. Remove the bowl from the pan and stir in the granulated sugar. Allow the mixture to cool for 10 mins and then add the eggs, one at a time and whisk in, ensuring they are thoroughly incorporated.

Sieve flour into the mixture and fold in using a metal spoon. Add the vanilla essence and salt. Chop milk chocolate into small pieces and roughly chop pecans. Add chocolate and nuts to cake mixture, then stir thoroughly. Spoon into prepared tin, smooth top and bake for 40 mins, or until cooked.

To test if the cake is cooked, insert a clean skewer into the centre – it should come out clean. Place tin on a wire rack and allow the cake to cool completely before making topping.

To make topping, melt the plain chocolate and fat in a bowl over a pan of gently simmering water, stirring occasionally. Remove the bowl from the heat, then sieve in the icing sugar and whisk until smooth. Add sufficient milk to give a spreading consistency, and then spread over the top of the cake. Leave to set for 30 mins. Cut into 20 portions, then transfer brownies individually to a wire rack.

Melt the white chocolate in a bowl over a pan of gently simmering water and stir until smooth. Remove from the heat, then, using a small spoon or fork, drizzle the white chocolate over the brownies. Leave them to set completely before serving.

HANDY TIP

Substitute 3 oz/75 g chopped almonds for the pecan nuts and add 3 oz/75 g chopped dates to the basic mixture.

1. Melt plain chocolate and fat over hot water, remove from heat and stir in sugar

2. When the chocolate mixture has cooled slightly, whisk in the eggs, one at a time

3. Sieve flour into mixture and fold in. Add vanilla essence, salt, chocolate and nuts

4. To ensure that the cake is thoroughly cooked, insert a clean skewer into centre

5. For the topping, melt the chocolate and fat together, then whisk in the icing sugar

6. Decorate the iced brownies by drizzling the melted white chocolate over the top

Croissants

France is famous for its cuisine and one of the best things to come across the channel must be their croissants. Delicious flakes of buttery pastry that just melt in the mouth as you eat them.

Calories per portion: 233 | **Makes 16**

1 lb/450 g strong white flour
pinch of salt
1 oz/25 g sugar
1 oz/25 g milk powder
1 oz/25 g lard
1 x 6 g sachet easy-blend yeast
1 egg, size 3
8 oz/225 g unsalted butter
beaten egg to glaze

Preheat oven to Gas 7, 425°F, 220°C, 15 mins before baking the croissants.

Sift the flour into the bowl and stir in the salt, sugar and milk powder. Cut the lard into small pieces then rub into the flour until the mixture resembles fine breadcrumbs. Sprinkle in the easy-blend yeast then mix to a soft and pliable dough with the egg and approx 8 fl oz/250 ml of tepid water.

Turn out on a lightly floured surface and knead until the dough is smooth and free from cracks. Place in a clean and lightly oiled bowl, cover and leave in a warm place for approx 30 mins or until doubled in size. Turn out on to a lightly floured surface and knock the dough down. Knead very lightly then return to the bowl, cover and leave to relax in the fridge for 1 hr.

Roll the dough out to an oblong 20 in x 8 in/51 cm x 20.5 cm and divide the butter into three. Dot the top with two thirds of the dough with small pats of butter then fold the bottom portion up to the centre and the top third down to the centre. Gently seal the edges with the rolling pin then half turn the dough so that the seal is on the side. Wrap in greaseproof and chill in the fridge for 30 mins.

Repeat the rolling, folding and chilling twice more until the butter is used. Wrap again and chill for a further 30 mins. Roll and fold the dough three more times (this is after you have added all the butter) then leave to rest in the fridge for 1 hr.

Roll the dough out on a lightly floured surface to an oblong 12 in x 24 in/30 cm x 61 cm and trim the edges. Cut the dough lengthways in half then into squares and finally into triangles. Brush the triangles very lightly with the beaten egg then starting from the long end, roll up to form crescents.

Place on baking sheets, cover and leave for 30 mins. Brush with egg, bake for 10-15 mins or until cooked. Serve.

HANDY TIP

After brushing the top of the croissants with the beaten egg, try sprinkling with grated cheese, poppy or sesame seeds.

1. Sift the flour into the bowl, stir in salt, sugar and milk powder. Rub in lard, add the yeast, mix to a soft dough with water

2. Roll the dough out on a lightly floured surface then dot top two thirds of the dough with the butter

3. Lightly seal the edges of the dough with the rolling pin, half turn dough, wrap and leave to rest in the fridge for 30 mins

4. Roll out the rested dough on a lightly floured surface, to an oblong, trim edges, cut in half then in squares

5. Cut the squares into triangles, brush very lightly with beaten egg, roll up starting from the long end

6. Place the croissants on to a baking sheet, cover and allow to relax for 30 mins. Brush with egg then bake

Herb & Cheese Loaf

Packed full of flavour, this delicious bread with cheeses, herbs and garlic, makes a tasty and satisfying snack or accompaniment. It is best served warm with butter.

Calories per portion: 306 | **Serves 8**

¾ oz/20 g fresh yeast
1 tsp caster sugar
¼ pint/150 ml milk
1 lb/450 g wholemeal flour
4 tbsp freshly grated Parmesan cheese
6 oz/175 g Cheddar cheese, grated
1 garlic clove, peeled and crushed
1 tbsp each of freshly chopped basil, parsley and thyme
1 tsp salt
freshly ground black pepper
1 egg, size 5, beaten
1 tbsp poppy seeds
1 tbsp sesame seeds

Preheat oven to Gas 7, 425°F, 220°C, 15 mins before baking bread. Grease and line an 8 in/20.5 cm round cake tin. Place the yeast in a small bowl or jug with the sugar and cream together until smooth. Heat the milk to blood heat and gradually add to the yeast, mixing well, leave to one side until frothy (this will take approx 10-15 mins).

Place the flour in a bowl and mix in the Parmesan cheese, 4 oz/100 g of the Cheddar cheese, the crushed garlic, the herbs and seasoning. Stir in the frothy yeast mixture and approx ¼ pint/150 ml tepid water and mix together until the mixture forms a soft and pliable dough.

Turn out on to a lightly floured surface and knead for approx 5 mins until smooth and free from cracks. Place in a lightly oiled bowl. Cover with a clean, plain tea towel and leave to prove in a warm place for 30-40 mins or until the dough has doubled in size.

Re-knead the dough, knock the dough with your knuckles until smooth and pliable, then divide into eight portions. Form each portion into a smooth round and arrange in the tin, placing seven round the edge with one in the middle. Cover with a tea towel and leave to rise in a warm place for 20-30 mins.

Brush with beaten egg, sprinkle with remaining cheese and the poppy and sesame seeds. Bake for 35-40 mins until risen and golden. When cooked the loaf will sound hollow if tapped on the base. Break into portions to serve. Best served warm.

Handy Tips

Use a medium flavoured Cheddar cheese for best results. Try serving the bread as part of a Ploughman's snack at lunch or supper-time.

1. Place the yeast in a small bowl or jug with the sugar, and cream together until smooth

2. Mix in Parmesan cheese, 4 oz/100 g of the Cheddar cheese, crushed garlic, herbs and seasoning

3. Turn dough on to a lightly floured surface and knead for approx 5 mins until smooth and free from cracks

4. *Re-knead dough, knock it with knuckles until pliable. Divide into eight portions. Form each portion into a smooth round*

5. *Arrange the rounds in the tin – seven round the edge and one in the middle. Cover with tea towel and leave to rise*

6. *Brush with beaten egg, sprinkle over remaining cheese, poppy and sesame seeds. Bake for 35-40 mins*

Cottage Loaf

There's nothing quite like the aroma of freshly baked bread to welcome the family home after a busy day. The flavour and texture of home baked bread is unique, once tasted you're hooked. Make a double batch and freeze a loaf for another day.

Calories per portion: 212 | **Serves 8**

1lb/450 g strong white flour
pinch of salt
2 tsp caster sugar
1 x ¼ oz/6 g sachet easy-blend yeast
½ oz/15 g butter or margarine
1 tbsp milk
butter to serve

Preheat the oven to Gas 8, 450°F, 230°C, 15 mins before baking the loaf. Sieve the flour into a large mixing bowl, stir in the salt, sugar and easy-blend yeast. Using your fingertips rub the fat into the flour until the mixture resembles fine breadcrumbs. Make a well in the centre of the dry ingredients then add approx ½ pint/300 ml tepid boiled water. Mix together using a fork or wooden spoon and then with your hands work to form a firm dough. Turn out on lightly floured surface and knead thoroughly for about 10 mins until the dough feels smooth and elastic.

Lightly oil a clean bowl then place the dough in the bowl, cover with a clean tea towel or piece of clearwrap and leave to rise in a warm place away from draughts for approx 1 hr or until the dough has doubled in size and springs back when pressed lightly with a floured finger.

Turn dough out on to a lightly floured surface and knock down. Knead again with the knuckles, flattening and stretching without tearing the dough to remove as many of the air bubbles as possible.

Once the dough feels really smooth and elastic cut off approx one third. Shape the larger piece into a smooth round then place on a lightly greased baking sheet. Take the other piece of dough and shape into a smaller round. Brush the top of the large round lightly with water then place the smaller round on top. Press down firmly. Dust your forefinger with flour then make an indent in the centre of the smaller round.

Cover the loaf with a clean tea towel then leave again to rise in a warm place away from draughts for approx 30 mins or until the dough springs back when pressed lightly with the finger.

Brush the loaf with a little milk then bake in the preheated oven for 20-25 mins or until cooked. To test if cooked, turn the loaf upside down and tap lightly on the base, it should sound hollow. Cool on a wire rack. Serve spread with butter.

Handy Tip

If liked replace 6 oz/175 g of the white flour with strong wholemeal flour. Also try sprinkling the loaf with sesame or poppy seeds after brushing with the milk and before baking.

1. Sieve the flour into a mixing bowl, stir in the salt, sugar and easy-blend yeast, rub in the fat

2. Mix to a firm dough with tepid boiled water then knead on a lightly floured surface for approx 10 mins

3. After the dough has risen and doubled in size, turn out on to a lightly floured surface and knock down

4. Knead the dough until it feels smooth and elastic, knocking out as many of the air bubbles as possible

5. Cut off approx one third of the dough and then shape the larger piece into a round. Place on greased baking sheet

6. Shape the smaller piece of dough, brush the base of the loaf with water, place smaller round on top

Florentines

Chopped glacé cherries, angelica, almonds, peel and sultanas in a wonderful toffee biscuit coated with rich dark chocolate... wicked? Yes, but spoil your family and friends with these delicious chewy treats.

Calories per portion: 97 — **MAKES 12**

- **1½ oz/40 g glacé cherries, chopped**
- **1 oz/25 g angelica, chopped**
- **2 oz/50 g butter or margarine**
- **2 oz/50 g demerara sugar**
- **1 tbsp golden syrup**
- **1 oz/25 g mixed peel, chopped**
- **2 oz/50 g sultanas, chopped**
- **1½ oz/40 g flaked almonds, chopped**
- **2 oz/50 g plain white flour, sifted**
- **2 tbsp cream**
- **6 oz/175 g plain chocolate**

Preheat oven to Gas 4, 350°F, 180°C, 10 mins before baking. Lightly grease three baking sheets with oil. Wash and dry the glacé cherries and angelica and finely chop.

Heat butter or margarine with sugar and syrup, stirring occasionally until sugar has melted. Remove from heat, stir in the glacé cherries, angelica, chopped peel, sultanas and nuts. Stir flour into the mixture with the cream. Mix until blended.

Place small teaspoons of the mixture on to the greased baking sheets, allowing for the mixture to expand during cooking. Place on the centre shelf of the oven and cook for 8-10 mins or until the florentines are golden in colour. Remove from the oven and allow to cool for 1-2 mins. (It's quite all right if you bake one batch at a time – the mixture won't spoil if it's kept waiting a while.)

Then, with a round-bladed knife, carefully push the outside edges of each florentine towards the centre to make them as round as possible. Leave for a further 2-3 mins, or until they're just beginning to harden, then with a palette knife carefully transfer to a wire cooling rack. Leave until completely cold before decorating the bases with the melted chocolate.

Break the chocolate into small pieces and place in a small glass bowl over a pan of gently simmering water. Stir until melted and free from lumps. Coat the flat side of each florentine with a little melted chocolate. With the prongs of a fork, mark wavy lines across the chocolate and leave to set.

Store in an airtight tin layered with sheets of greaseproof paper. Florentines will keep for at least a week. They do not freeze well.

HANDY TIP

Make tiny florentines, by putting very small amounts on to baking sheets. Cook for 4-6 mins. Use as petit fours.

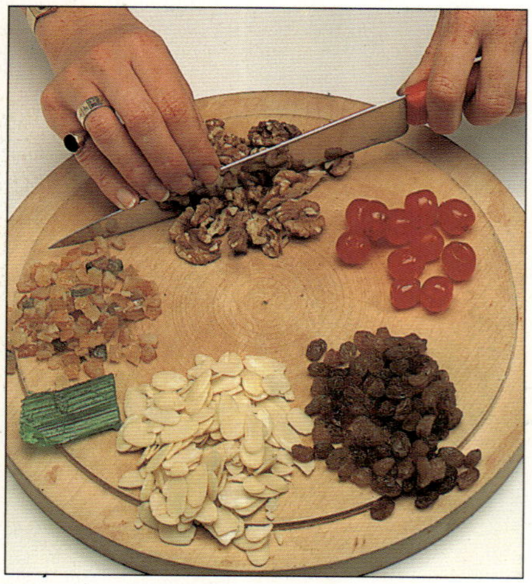

1. Wash and dry cherries and angelica. Chop with sultanas, almonds and peel

2. Melt fat, demerara sugar and syrup in a small pan and stir until dissolved

3. Put teaspoonfuls on to a greased baking sheet, allowing room to spread

4. Allow florentines to stand for 1-2 mins then transfer to a wire cooling rack

5. When cold, coat the flat side of each florentine with the melted chocolate

6. Finally, using the prongs of a fork, make a decorative pattern on the base

Home-made Biscuits

Welcome the kids home with a tray of home-made biscuits. It's really easy to do with this recipe. Make the dough in advance and leave it chilling in the fridge then just shape and bake the biscuits as and when you need them.

Calories per portion: 97 | **Makes approx 60**

1. Cream the fat and sugar in two bowls until pale and fluffy, add egg, then the flour and cocoa or vanilla

2. For pinwheels, roll the chocolate and vanilla doughs together, as for a Swiss roll. Cut thin slices, place on baking sheet

3. For chequerboards, arrange equal lengths of chocolate and white doughs to give a chequered effect

10 oz/300 g butter or margarine
10 oz/300 g caster sugar
2 eggs, size 3
15 oz/425 g plain white flour, sieved
1 oz/25 g cocoa powder, sieved
½ tsp vanilla essence
few glacé cherries, sliced
2 oz/50 g vanilla-flavoured butter cream
extra caster sugar and icing sugar for dredging
1 oz/25 g plain chocolate, melted

Preheat oven to Gas 5, 375°F, 190°C, 10 mins before baking the biscuits. Lightly oil three baking sheets. (You will find it easier to make the dough in two separate bowls so that the proportions are correct.)

In each bowl cream together 5 oz/150 g of fat and sugar until pale and fluffy. Lightly whisk the eggs and gradually beat into each mixture. Into one bowl stir in 7 oz/200 g of the plain flour and the 1 oz/25 g of cocoa powder. Mix well until the mixture forms a soft dough. Wrap in baking parchment and chill for 30 mins. Add the remaining flour and vanilla essence to the other bowl, mix ingredients together to form a soft dough, wrap then chill for at least 30 mins.

After shaping, chill the biscuits for 30 mins before baking for 8-10 mins. Remove from the oven and cool for 1 min before transferring to a wire cooling rack.

To make pinwheels, roll out an equal amount of both doughs on a lightly floured surface and cut out two oblongs, ensuring they are the same thickness and size. Place the chocolate dough on top of the vanilla dough and roll up as for a Swiss roll. Cut out thin slices and place on baking sheet. Chill before baking.

To make chequerboards, roll out equal amounts of both doughs to form two oblongs, cut each in half length-ways. Place one white and chocolate length side by side then place the remaining chocolate oblong on top of the white oblong and the remaining white oblong on the chocolate. Press lightly together. Cut into thin slices and place on baking sheets. Chill then bake.

To make garlands, with the white dough, use your hands to form eight small balls about the size of a pea. Place together on a baking sheet forming a circle. Cut very thin slices from a glacé cherry and place in between the joins. Dredge lightly with caster sugar, chill then bake.

To make chocolate dodgers, roll the chocolate dough out on a lightly floured surface to approx ¼ in/6 mm thickness. Cut out equal amounts of 2 in/5 cm rounds with a plain cutter. Using a ½ in/1.25 cm plain cutter, cut out the centres of half the rounds. Place on baking sheet and chill then bake. Once cold sandwich together, with the butter cream, one plain biscuit and one with the hole. Dredge lightly with icing sugar.

To make chocolate twists, roll out the white dough to an oblong ¼ in/6 mm thick. Cut out thin slices approx ¼ in/6 mm wide. Twist two strips together then place on a baking sheet. Dredge lightly with caster sugar and chill. When cooked and cold dip both ends in the melted chocolate and leave until set.

HANDY TIP

The dough can be made and left in the fridge then small batches can be baked as required.

4. For garlands, roll out eight small balls, place on baking sheet in a circle with sliced cherries in joins

5. For chocolate dodgers, roll out chocolate dough and cut an even number of rounds with a plain cutter

6. To make chocolate twists, roll out vanilla-flavoured dough, cut into thin strips and twist two strips together

VIENNESE FINGERS

Tempt the whole family with these delicious biscuits. Filled with a vanilla buttercream and dipped in plain chocolate, they just melt in the mouth. They taste so good you'll have to hide them away if you want any left for tea-time.

Calories per portion: 438 | MAKES 10 BISCUITS

7 oz/200 g unsalted butter or margarine
2 oz/50 g icing sugar, sifted
½ oz/15 g cornflour
4 oz/100 g self-raising flour
4 oz/100 g plain flour
1 tsp vanilla essence
FOR THE BUTTERCREAM FILLING:
3 oz/75 g butter or margarine
6 oz/175 g icing sugar, sifted
½ tsp vanilla essence
5 oz/150 g plain chocolate

Preheat oven to Gas 4, 350°F, 180°C, 10 mins before baking. Lightly grease two baking sheets. Cream the fat with the sifted icing sugar until soft and fluffy, then beat in the cornflour. Sift both flours together then gradually beat into the creamed mixture until thoroughly blended. Beat in the vanilla essence. The mixture should be stiff, but smooth, and free from lumps.

Spoon into a medium-sized piping bag fitted with a large star nozzle. Pipe 3 in/7.5 cm lengths on to the greased baking sheets, allowing room for expansion. You may find it easier to pipe the mixture if the piping bag is only half filled as this will enable you to put more pressure on to the bag as you pipe.

Bake on the centre shelf of the oven for 15-20 mins or until the biscuits are cooked and light golden brown. If necessary turn the baking sheet halfway round during cooking time for even baking. Remove from the oven and allow to cool for a few minutes before carefully transferring to a wire cooling rack. Leave until completely cold.

To make buttercream, cream the butter or margarine with the sifted icing sugar until soft and fluffy. Beat in the vanilla essence. Place to one side.

Break the chocolate into pieces and put into a small bowl over a pan of gently simmering water and allow to melt, stirring occasionally. Dip each end of the biscuit into the melted chocolate, then leave to set on sheets of greaseproof paper.

When the chocolate has completely set, spoon the buttercream into the piping bag. Using a large star nozzle, pipe the buttercream down the centre of one biscuit. Place another biscuit on top and press lightly together. Continue until all the biscuits have been sandwiched together in pairs.

HANDY TIPS

Take care when handling the biscuits. They are so 'short' they do tend to break very easily. Vary the flavour by using a chocolate buttercream, or by adding lemon or orange rind to the biscuit mixture with rind and juice to the buttercream.

1. Cream the butter or margarine with the sifted icing sugar until fluffy

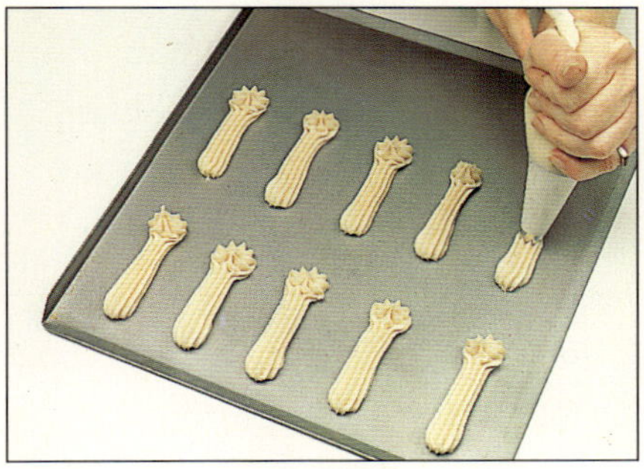

2. Pipe 3 in/7.5 cm lengths of mixture on to lightly greased baking sheets

3. When biscuits are cooked, cool slightly, then place on a wire cooling rack

4. Dip biscuits into the melted chocolate, leave to set on greaseproof paper

5. Fold the piping bag down over your hand, spoon in prepared buttercream

6. Pipe the buttercream on to the biscuits and carefully sandwich together

GINGERBREAD PEOPLE

Treat the kids with these delicious crunchy biscuits. Rich with honey and syrup, they're easy to make and ready in minutes. And why not pop one into a lunch box for a tasty surprise.

Calories per portion: 286 **MAKES 14**

1-2 tsp vegetable oil
12 oz/350 g plain flour
1 level tsp bicarbonate of soda
2 level tsp ground ginger
4 oz/100 g block margarine
4 oz/100 g light soft brown sugar
2 level tsp clear honey
2 tbsp golden syrup
1 egg, size 3
few currants
3 oz/75 g icing sugar

Preheat the oven to Gas 5, 375°F, 190°C, 10 mins before baking. Lightly grease three baking sheets with the oil. Sieve the flour, bicarbonate of soda and ground ginger into a mixing bowl. Add the margarine, then rub into the flour until the mixture resembles fine breadcrumbs. Stir in the soft brown sugar and mix well.

Place the honey and syrup in a small pan and heat through gently, stirring until it is thoroughly blended. Take care not to allow the mixture to boil. Remove from the heat. Beat the egg, then beat into the warmed syrup mixture until thoroughly incorporated. Stir into the flour mixture and mix to form a soft dough. Knead lightly until smooth.

Place on a lightly floured surface (don't use too much flour as this will affect the proportions and the finished result). Roll out the dough to ¼ in/6 mm thickness then, using cutters, cut out the gingerbread people. Place on the greased baking sheets and arrange two currants on each to represent the eyes. Bake in the oven for 10-12 mins or until cooked. Cool slightly. Then transfer to wire cooling racks until cold.

Sieve icing sugar then mix with about 1½ tbsp tepid boiled water until a smooth piping consistency is formed. Place in a piping bag fitted with a small plain piping nozzle. Carefully pipe along the outline of the gingerbread men and pipe a tie or buttons, too. Pipe an apron on the gingerbread women. Store in an airtight tin.

HANDY TIPS

Gingerbread people cutters can be bought from some supermarkets, kitchen shops and department stores.
If preferred, draw shapes on a clean piece of card and cut round shapes.
These biscuits are really easy to make, and if you keep an eye on your kids while they're handling the warmed honey and syrup, they make a super, fun piece of cooking for them to do!

1. Sieve flour, bicarbonate of soda and ground ginger into a large mixing bowl

2. Add margarine to flour, then rub in until mixture resembles fine breadcrumbs

3. Add the warmed ingredients to the flour, then mix to form a soft dough

4. Knead, then roll out the dough on a floured surface to ¼ in/6 mm thickness

5. Using gingerbread cutters, cut out the dough and place on baking sheets

6. Arrange the currants on the gingerbread people to represent their eyes

Cookie Biscuits

Quick and easy to bake, you can't beat home-made biscuits! The varieties you can make are endless – the choice is yours. And they taste so delicious, with a melt-in-the-mouth texture, you'll have to hide them to save any for tea.

Calories per portion: 160 | **Makes 35**

10 oz/300 g butter or margarine
1 lb/450 g plain flour
9 oz/250 g caster sugar
1 egg, size 3, beaten
2 oz/50 g chocolate cooking chips
2 tbsp raspberry jam
½ tsp almond essence
2 oz/50 g chopped almonds
2 oz/50 g glacé cherries
grated rind of ½ orange
1 tsp ground cinnamon
2 tbsp porridge oats

Preheat oven to Gas 5, 375°F, 190°C, 10 mins before baking. Lightly grease five baking sheets. Rub the butter or margarine into the sieved flour and sugar with your fingers, until the fat has been thoroughly incorporated. Bind together with sufficient beaten egg to give a stiff but pliable dough. On a clean surface, knead the dough until smooth then divide into five equal portions.

Into one portion add chocolate chips and knead until the chocolate chips are thoroughly distributed throughout the dough. Form into small balls about the size of a walnut and place well apart on lightly greased baking sheet.

With another portion of dough, again form into small balls the size of a walnut. Roll round in the hands until smooth then place well apart on a baking sheet. Make a small hole in the centre, ensuring you don't go right through to the base. Spoon a small amount of raspberry jam in the centre.

Into a further portion of dough knead ½ tsp of almond essence. Place chopped almonds in a small bowl then form dough into small balls about the size of a walnut and roll in the almonds. Place on to greased baking sheet.

Wash and dry the glacé cherries then chop finely. Knead the cherries into another portion of dough. Form this dough into balls and place on to greased baking sheet.

Into the last remaining portion of the dough, add the grated orange rind and cinnamon. Knead well. Form into balls and roll in the porridge oats. Place on to greased baking sheet and sprinkle tops with a few more porridge oats.

Bake in the oven for 15-20 mins or until the biscuits are lightly golden brown. Remove from the oven, leave to cool for 3 mins before transferring to a wire cooling rack. When cold, store in an airtight tin.

Handy tip

You can vary the biscuits according to taste. Try using lemon curd instead of jam, raisins or currants instead of the chocolate chips, chopped walnuts in place of the cherries. Or use a different spice such as ginger, mixed spice, nutmeg or ground mace. All are delicious!

1. Mix fat into sieved flour and sugar. Bind together with beaten egg

2. Place on to a clean surface then knead the dough gently until smooth

3. Divide dough into equal portions. Knead the chocolate chips into one portion

4. Form another portion into balls, place on baking sheet. Make hole, add jam

5. After flavouring a portion with almond essence, roll the balls in nuts

6. Chop cherries finely, add to dough portion. Knead then roll into balls

Gateau St. Honore

This choux pastry gâteau, called the 'masterpiece of pâtisserie' is named after St. Honorius, patron saint of bakers. It is filled with delicious custard, then topped with caramel and chocolate curls.

Calories per portion: 356 | **Serves 10**

1. For the pâte sucrée, work the sugar, butter and egg yolks into the flour

2. Beat the eggs, a little at a time, into the cooled choux pastry mixture

3. Pipe choux pastry into small mounds on a lightly greased baking sheet

FOR THE PATE SUCREE:
4 oz/100 g plain flour
pinch of salt
2 oz/50 g caster sugar
2 oz/50 g butter, cut into cubes
2 egg yolks, size 3
FOR THE CHOUX PASTRY:
4 oz/100 g butter
5 oz/150 g plain flour, sieved
4 eggs, size 3
FOR THE CREME PATISSIERE:
2 eggs, size 3
2 oz/50 g caster sugar
2 tbsp flour
2 tbsp cornflour
½ pint/300 ml milk
few drops vanilla essence
FOR THE CARAMEL:
6 tbsp granulated sugar
chocolate curls and icing sugar to decorate

Preheat the oven to Gas 6, 400°F, 200°C, 15 mins before baking. Sieve the flour for the pâte sucrée on to a clean work surface with the salt. Make a well in the centre and add the sugar, butter and egg yolks. Work into the flour with the fingertips to form a smooth pastry. Cover in clearwrap and chill for 1 hr. On a floured surface, roll out the pâte sucrée into a 9 in/23 cm circle. Place on a greased baking sheet and prick the base with a fork.

To make the choux pastry, melt butter in a saucepan with ½ pint/300 ml water. Bring to boil. Remove from heat and add sieved flour to pan. Beat well until mixture becomes glossy and forms a ball. Don't overbeat mixture. Cool for 5 mins. Beat in eggs, a little at a time, bringing the mixture back to its original consistency after each addition. Place the choux pastry in a piping bag fitted with a large plain nozzle. Pipe a circle around the edge of the pastry about 2 in/5 cm in width. Lightly grease another baking sheet and using the remaining choux pastry, pipe 14-18 walnut-sized mounds. Place both baking sheets in oven for 15-20 mins, or until the choux pastry is risen and golden. Remove from the oven and leave until cold.

To make the crème pâtissière, whisk eggs and sugar together until pale and thick. Place flour and cornflour in a bowl and blend to a smooth paste with a little milk. Heat remaining milk in a pan until almost boiling. Pour over egg mixture, stirring constantly. Return custard to pan and stir in the cornflour mixture. Stir over a low heat until the mixture coats the back of a wooden spoon, then add the vanilla essence. Cover with a damp sheet of greaseproof paper and cool. When cooled, place in a piping bag fitted with a plain potato nozzle. Make a hole in the base of each choux bun and pipe in a little crème pâtissière.

To make the caramel, place sugar in a pan with 6 tbsp water. Heat, stirring occasionally, until the sugar dissolves. Increase heat and boil until mixture turns golden. Remove from the heat and place base of pan in a bowl of cold water. Dip base and top of each choux bun into the liquid caramel.

Arrange the buns around choux ring. Fill gâteau with remaining crème pâtissière. Decorate with chocolate curls, dust with icing sugar and serve.

HANDY TIPS

Assemble the gâteau no more than ½ hr before serving. For accurate measuring always use measuring spoons, available from all kitchen ware shops and departmental stores.

4. Heat crème pâtissière until it coats the back of a wooden spoon

5. Dip base and top of buns into the caramel and arrange around choux ring

6. Fill the centre of the gâteau with the remaining crème pâtissière

INDEX

Almonds:
- Pear and almond tart 186

Angel food cake 248
Apples:
- Apple dumplings 200
- Apple pie 168
- Apple strudel 192
- Blackberry Charlotte 188
- Fruit crumble 198
- Tarte Tatin 184

Apricots:
- Fruit crumble 198
- Mount Vesuvius 208

Bacon:
- Bacon pie 80
- Pea and ham soup 28

Battenburg cake 232
Beef:
- Beef carbonnade 106
- Beef tournedos 110
- Beef Wellingtons 104
- Beefburgers 60
- Cannelloni 150
- Chilli con carne 112
- Lasagne 154
- Meatloaf 76
- Pasties 70
- Roast beef 100
- Spaghetti Bolognese 152
- Steak and stout pie 102
- Steak puddings 108

Beer:
- Beef carbonnade 106
- Steak and stout pie 102

Biscuits:
- Cookie biscuits 298
- Florentines 290
- Gingerbread people 296
- Home-made biscuits 292
- Viennese fingers 294

Blackberry Charlotte 188
Blackcurrants:
- Sultana cheesecake 160

Bouillabaisse 24
Bread:
- Cottage loaf 288
- Herb and cheese loaf 286

Bread puddings:
- Blackberry Charlotte 188
- Bread and butter pudding 162
- Summer pudding 202

Brownies, chocolate 282
Buns:
- Chelsea 272
- Tea cakes 280

Cakes:
- Angel food cake 248
- Battenburg cake 232
- Cherry and date cake 234
- Chocolate brownies 282
- Chocolate caraque cake 260
- Christmas cake 252
- Devil's food cake 258
- Dundee cake 238
- Eccles cakes 266
- Gingerbread 268
- Gingerbread house 262
- Passion cake 250
- Simnel cake 246
- Swiss roll 236
- Victoria sandwich 242
- Walnut cake 240
- Yule log 244

Calamari, fried 44
Cannelloni 150
Caramel:
- Crème brûlée 206
- Crème caramel 158
- Croquembouche 226
- Floating islands 222
- Gâteau St. Honoré 300

Carrots:
- Carrot soup 14
- Passion cake 250

Cassoulet 122
Charlottes:
- Blackberry charlotte 188
- Charlotte Russe 224

Cheese:
- Cannelloni 150
- Cheese soufflé 56
- Chicken Cordon Bleu 92
- Herb and cheese loaf 286
- Pizza Margherita 74
- Tortelloni 64

Cheesecakes:
- Chocolate cheesecake 180
- Sultana cheesecake 160

Chelsea buns 272
Cherry and date cake 234
Chicken:
- Chicken and leek pie 88
- Chicken chasseur 96
- Chicken chowder 22
- Chicken Cordon Bleu 92
- Chicken gumbo 58
- Chicken korma 86
- Chicken Marengo 94
- Chicken satay 38
- Coronation chicken 84
- Roast chicken 90

Chilli con carne 112
Chocolate:
- Chocolate brownies 282
- Chocolate caraque cake 260
- Chocolate cheesecake 180
- Chocolate roulade 176
- Chocolate soufflé 178
- Chocolate toffee pud 182
- Christmas bombe 228
- Devil's food cake 258
- Florentines 290
- Profiteroles 174
- Viennese fingers 294
- Yule log 244

Choux pastry:
- Croquembouche 226
- Gâteau St. Honoré 300
- Profiteroles 174

Chowder, chicken 22
Christmas bombe 228
Christmas cake 252
Christmas pudding 214
Cod:
- Golden fish pie 140

Cod's roe, smoked:
- Taramasalata 32

Coffee:
- Tiramisu 212
- Walnut cake 240

Cookie biscuits 298
Coquilles Saint-Jacques 34
Coronation chicken 84
Cottage loaf 288
Crab, dressed 54
Cream gâteau 256
Crème brûlée 206
Crème caramel 158
Crêpes Suzette 218
Croissants 284
Croquembouche 226
Crumble, fruit 198
Crumpets 274
Cucumber:
- Cream of cucumber soup 26

Cullen skink 20
Curries:
  Coronation chicken 84
  Roghan josh 120
Custard:
  Floating islands 222

Danish pastries 278
Dates:
  Cherry and date cake 234
Devil's food cake 258
Doughnuts 270
Dried fruit:
  Christmas cake 252
  Christmas pudding 214
  Dundee cake 238
  Simnel cake 246
  Tea cakes 280
Duck, Peking 98
Dumplings, apple 200
Dundee cake 238

Eccles cakes 266
Eggs:
  Spanish omelette 68

Fish:
  Bouillabaisse 24
  Fish casserole 138
  Fish mousse 48
  Fishcakes 72
  Smoked fish pâté 36
  see also under individual types of fish
Floating islands 222
Florentines 290
Fruit:
  Summer pudding 202
Fruit cakes:
  Christmas cake 252
  Dundee cake 238
  Simnel cake 246
Fruit crumble 198

Gammon, baked 130
Gâteaux:
  Cream gâteau 256
  Gâteau St. Honoré 300
Gazpacho 30
Gingerbread 268
Gingerbread house 262
Gingerbread people 296
Golden fish pie 140

Haddock:
  Cullen skink 20
  Golden fish pie 140
Ham:
  Chicken Cordon Bleu 92
Haricot beans:
  Cassoulet 122
Hazelnut vacherin 204
Herb and cheese loaf 286
Huss:
  Fish casserole 138

Ice cream:
  Christmas bombe 228
  Ice cream bombe 220
  Mount Vesuvius 208
Iced orange bowl 216
Icing, royal 252

Jam roly poly pudding 164

Kebabs:
  Chicken satay 38
  Lamb kebabs 50
Kedgeree 66

Lamb:
  Cassoulet 122
  Lamb en croûte 124
  Lamb kebabs 50
  Meatloaf 76
  Noisettes of lamb 118
  Roast lamb 116
  Roghan josh 120
  Shepherd's pie 108
Lasagne 154
Leeks:
  Chicken and leek pie 88
  Potato and leek soup 18
Lemon:
  Lemon meringue pie 166
  Lemon syllabub 196
  Sussex pond pudding 172
Lentils:
  Pea and ham soup 28
  Winter lentil soup 10

Marzipan:
  Battenburg cake 232
  Simnel cake 246
  Stollen 254
Meatloaf 76

Melba toast 32, 37
Meringue:
  Floating islands 222
  Hazelnut vacherin 204
  Lemon meringue pie 166
  Mount Vesuvius 208
Mince pies 276
Minestrone soup 12
Monkfish:
  Paella 148
Moules à la marinière 52
Mount Vesuvius 208
Mousse, fish 48
Mussels:
  Moules à la marinière 52
  Paella 148

Omelette, Spanish 68
Onion tart 62
Oranges:
  Crêpes Suzette 218
  Iced orange bowl 216
  Orange soufflé 190
Oriental pork 136

Paella 148
Passion cake 250
Pasties 70
Pastries, Danish 278
Pâté, smoked fish 36
Pea and ham soup 28
Pears:
  Pear and almond tart 186
  Pears in red wine 194
Peking duck 98
Peppers:
  Spanish omelette 68
Pies:
  Apple pie 168
  Bacon pie 80
  Beef Wellingtons 104
  Chicken and leek pie 88
  Golden fish pie 140
  Lamb en croûte 124
  Mince pies 276
  Pork pie 78
  Salmon en croûte 142
  Steak and stout pie 102
Pizza Margherita 74
Plaice:
  Plaice Florentine 146
  Plaice goujons 40
Pork:
  Oriental pork 136
  Pork chasseur 132

Pork chops in cider 128
Pork escalopes 126
Pork pie 78
Roast stuffed pork 134
Potatoes:
Cullen skink 20
Potato and leek soup 18
Shepherd's pie 108
Spanish omelette 68
Prawns, sweet and sour 42
Profiteroles 174

Raspberries:
Christmas bombe 228
Red kidney beans:
Chilli con carne 112
Rice:
Kedgeree 66
Paella 148
Roghan josh 120
Roly poly pudding, jam 164
Roulade, chocolate 176
Royal icing 252

Salad Niçoise 46
Salmon:
Kedgeree 66
Salmon en croûte 142
Scallops:
Coquilles Saint-Jacques 34
Shepherd's pie 108
Sherry trifle 210
Simnel cake 246
Smoked fish pâté 36
Sole, paupiettes of 144
Soufflés:
Cheese 56
Chocolate 178
Orange 190
Soups 10-30
Spaghetti Bolognese 152
Spanish omelette 68
Spinach:
Plaice Florentine 146
Tortelloni 64
Squid:
Fried calamari 44
Steak and stout pie 102
Steak puddings 108
Stollen 254
Strawberries:
Cream gâteau 256
Strawberry tarts 264
Strudel, apple 192
Sultana cheesecake 160
Summer pudding 202
Sussex pond pudding 172
Sweet and sour prawns 42
Sweetcorn:
Chicken chowder 22
Swiss roll 236
Syllabub, lemon 196

Taramasalata 32
Tarts:
Lemon meringue pie 166
Onion tart 62
Pear and almond tart 186
Strawberry tarts 264
Tarte Tatin 184
Tea cakes 280
Teabreads:
Stollen 254
Tiramisu 212
Toast, Melba 32, 37
Toffee pud, chocolate 182
Tomatoes:
Cream of tomato soup 16
Gazpacho 30
Tortelloni 64
Treacle pudding 170
Trifle, sherry 210
Tuna:
Salad Niçoise 46

Victoria sandwich 242
Viennese fingers 294

Walnut cake 240
Wine, pears in red 194
Winter lentil soup 10

Yule log 244

ACKNOWLEDGEMENTS

All photography by John Elliott

Except for:

Winter Lentil Soup, Onion Tart, Roast Stuffed Pork, Fish Casserole, Sultana Cheesecake, Tarte Tatin, Orange Soufflé, Pears in Red Wine, Chocolate Caraque Cake, Tea Cakes, Croissants, Cottage Loaf and Home-made Biscuits by Karl Adamson

Chicken Satay, Plaice Goujons, Chicken Gumbo, Chicken Marengo, Cassoulet, Crème Caramel, Mount Vesuvius, Stollen, Cream Gâteau, Chelsea Buns and Danish Pastries by David Armstrong

Smoked Fish Pâté, Blackberry Charlotte, Christmas Bombe, Gingerbread House and Herb and Cheese Loaf by Ken Field

Bacon Pie and Tiramisu by Ferguson Hill

Pear and Almond Tart and Iced Orange Bowl by Ian 'O' Leary

Pork Chops in Cider by Bill Richmond

Chocolate Brownies by Clive Streeter

Gina Steer would like to thank Kathryn Hawkins and Jenny Brightman for their help in assisting in some of the photography, styling and recipe testing.